State Sovereignty

STATE
SOVEREIGNTY

Change and Persistence
in
International Relations

Edited by

Sohail H. Hashmi

Foreword by
Stanley Hoffmann

The Pennsylvania State University Press
University Park, Pennsylvania

Work on this volume was supported by the MacArthur Foundation and the
Social Science Research Council's Committee on International Peace and Security

Library of Congress Cataloging-in-Publication Data

State sovereignty: change and persistence in international relations / edited by
    Sohail H. Hashmi; foreword by Stanley Hoffmann.
        p.   cm.
    Includes bibliographical references and index.
    ISBN 0-271-01696-5 (cloth: alk. paper).
    ISBN 0-271-01697-3 (paper: alk. paper)
    1. Sovereignty.   2. International relations.   I. Hashmi, Sohail H., 1962–   .
JX4041.S74   1997
320.1'5—dc 21   96-50181
                                                                                 CIP

Contents

Foreword   vii
   Stanley Hoffmann

Acknowledgments   xi

Introduction   1
   Sohail H. Hashmi

1 Ideas and the Evolution of Sovereignty   15
   Daniel Philpott

2 Pan-Islamism, State Sovereignty, and
   International Organization   49
   Sohail H. Hashmi

3 Sovereignty, Self-Determination, and Security:
   New World Orders in the Twentieth Century   81
   Beatrice Heuser

4   New Approaches to International Human Rights:
    The Sovereign State Revisited   105
        Gregory H. Fox

5   Clash of Principles: Self-Determination,
    State Sovereignty, and Ethnic Conflict   131
        Kamal S. Shehadi

6   Shared Sovereignty, Enhanced Security:
    Lessons from the Yugoslav War   151
        James Gow

7   Conservation, Development, and State Sovereignty:
    Japan and the Tropical Forests of Southeast Asia   181
        Miranda A. Schreurs

Contributors   205

Index   209

Foreword

Stanley Hoffmann

This fine collection of essays grapples with the slippery notion of state sovereignty and the fate of the so-called Westphalian state. It does not arrive at any incontestable conclusions. It shows how state sovereignty (defined, in Daniel Philpott's careful analysis, as "supreme legitimate authority") is put in question both by internal fragmentation and by economic and ecological interdependence, which not only deprives states of much of their power but also seems to transfer portions of "legitimate authority" to public and private international organizations, and to the free and largely rogue market. It shows that the evolution of sovereignty in recent centuries results from material, technological developments, from the ever-changing realities of power, and from the influence of ideas such as self-determination, human rights, and pan-Islamism.

The paradox of state sovereignty today is one that these essays point out starkly. On the one hand, we witness both an erosion of what Robert Keohane has called operational sovereignty—the power needed to exert supreme legitimate authority—and a curtailment of the latter in areas as important as the protection of human rights, the right to resort to war, and a broad variety of trade practices. To be sure, states exert their sovereignty in signing agreements that curtail it—but they do indeed curtail it in the process.

On the other hand, state sovereignty remains the organizing principle of world order. In the public sphere, the institutions that have acquired some fragments of legitimate supreme authority at the expense of the states are interstate institutions, manifestations of "pooled sovereignty." There is no world state or world federation. Moreover, these collective public institutions lack autonomous power (financial, military, etc.). Power still resides primarily in the states, however great may be the losses of power that they have experienced.

This is not, theoretically, true in the realm of chapter VII of the UN charter, insofar as members of the Security Council not endowed with a right of veto, and nonmembers of that Council, have transferred the authority to wage war to it. But the power to wage it against troublemakers belongs, in fact, to "coalitions of the willing." And while, in the European Union, supreme legitimate authority in a vast number of areas has been transferred to Brussels, the Union's institutions remain very largely inter-governmental—the only "supranational" one with real authority and power being the European Court of Justice.

Hence the predicament of world order. This is a world of sovereign states that is not too stable, because of the factors of internal disintegration fueled by demands for self-determination and for other forms of human-rights protection. And these states no longer have either the power or the full authority they used to enjoy. And yet the institutions that could per-form the functions that states no longer monopolize are either predomi-nantly private (the mighty and mysterious market) or public, but limited in authority and weak in power.

There is another paradox behind this one. The kind of world order we have represents a triumph of the liberal ideology. Liberalism both advo-cated and predicted a world of sovereign states that would curtail war and practice cooperation, states whose power would be much reduced because of the increasing scope of transnational economic forces and because of the increasing power of global public opinion. But the world of today is not a world of liberal, democratic states. Many of them are either states with authoritarian regimes that trample human rights and engage in buildups of weapons of mass destruction, or else states that are too weak to be effective. Hence the multitude of actual and potential conflicts, the nonobservance of the principle of nonintervention, the key corollary of sovereignty, the challenge of pan-Islamism analyzed by Sohail Hashmi.

On the other hand, international liberalism itself is in crisis. Its expectations of interstate and transnational harmony were excessive. It has had trouble integrating nationalism into its philosophy and thus reconciling sovereignty and self-determination. It assumed too readily that world public opinion would be genuine and effective and that the market would be a force for good. Consequently, it never gave as much attention to the nature, authority, and powers of institutions for international cooperation (and for supervision of this market) as it devoted to the splintering of internal sovereignty, i.e., to checks and balances and intermediate bodies within.[1]

Thus, what threatens us today is neither the end of ideology, insofar as liberalism's triumph remains fragile, nor the clash of civilizations, insofar as culture and religion are only two of many determinants of state behavior. What threatens us is, rather, an imbalance between the supreme legitimate authority that still resides, as Gregory Fox and Miranda Schreurs assert, in the sovereign state, and the incipient but fragmentary and feeble authority of collective institutions dealing with problems that transcend the states, or exceed their capacities, or require the reduction of their authority. Beatrice Heuser pleads for strengthening these institutions, particularly in the realm of security. But we see every day how difficult this is. Internationalism, so far, has been too superficial, or hollow, to serve as the ideal that could bring about a new revolution in sovereignty, away from the state. What kind of "moral disaster," to use Philpott's expression, would be needed to provoke it?

1. See my essay, "The Crisis of Liberal Internationalism," *Foreign Policy* (Spring 1995): 159–78.

Acknowledgments

This book began to evolve in May 1992 at the Social Science Research Council–MacArthur Foundation Fellows' Conference held in Kuala Lumpur, Malaysia, and attended by four of the contributors. The SSRC–MacArthur Foundation Program in International Peace and Security subsequently funded two conferences, the first held at the Center for International Affairs, Harvard University, in April 1993, the second at the Department of War Studies, King's College London, in December 1993. We thank both the SSRC Committee on International Peace and Security and the John D. and Catherine T. MacArthur Foundation for their generous support. We are also grateful for the interest, assistance, and encouragement of the SSRC staff, in particular Dan Chiplock, Cary Fraser, Lori Gronich, and Steve Heydemann.

The papers that comprise this volume have benefited from review and criticism from a number of individuals who participated in the two conferences. We gratefully acknowledge their contributions: Maha Azzam, Andrew Barlow, Jarat Chopra, David Chuter, Beth DeSombre, Aleksa

Djilas, Malcolm Evans, Maria Green, Malik Mufti, Vicki Norberg-Bohm, Emma Rothschild, Jane Sharp, and Richard Smith. We also thank Michael Fowler and an anonymous reviewer who provided valuable suggestions in the final stages of preparation.

Our gratitude is also extended to Sanford Thatcher, director of Penn State Press, for his support and counsel during the publication process. Cherene Holland, Anne Rehill, and the staff of Penn State Press guided the book from manuscript to publication with remarkable skill and grace. Linda Chesky Fernandes and her capable staff at the International Relations Program of Mount Holyoke College provided indispensable support at every step of production.

Finally, we would like to thank Stanley Hoffmann, who has graciously supported this project from its inception and opened our discussions of sovereignty at the Harvard conference. It is only fitting that the first words of this book be his.

Introduction

Sohail H. Hashmi

For at least the past fifty years, students and practitioners of international politics have been proclaiming and analyzing the changing nature of state sovereignty. Traditional conceptions of the unitary, absolute, and legitimate state—the Westphalian model of sovereign statehood—were to some being "eroded," while to others were already "obsolete." As states became increasingly enmeshed in a variety of interdependencies, as new non-state actors emerged on the international stage, and as challenges to the quality of human life—indeed to human existence—became global in nature, the relevance of state sovereignty was increasingly questioned at both the normative and practical levels.

Yet reports of the demise of the sovereign state have thus far proven to be greatly exaggerated. For at the same time that the erosion of the Westphalian model was occurring on the continent that gave birth to it, the principle of state sovereignty was being enshrined universally as the organizing principle of international society. The Third World states that emerged from the retreat of Western colonialism in the 1950s and 1960s did not challenge the essential structure of the international system; instead they embraced it wholeheartedly and have sought not an overhaul, but internal reform. The notion of state sovereignty has, in fact, been the badge of international legitimacy for states and regimes enjoying at best dubious internal legitimacy.

These simultaneous and apparently contradictory developments provided enough grist for the intellectual mill of two generations of scholars. But from today's perspective, that period appears relatively placid. Today, the problem of state sovereignty has emerged squarely at the center of a maelstrom of international issues unleashed by at least three developments.

The first is the collapse of the Soviet Union and the movement toward a postcommunist order in the Soviet bloc and in Yugoslavia. The immediate consequence was for the Soviet empire and Yugoslavia to fragment along "national" lines, as "self-determination" prevailed over decades of centralization. The disintegration of the Soviet Union appears on the one hand to confirm the triumph of the sovereign nation-state, to vindicate the primacy of nationalism over regionalism or universalism in contemporary international politics.

But on the other hand, the emergence of independent postcommunist states begs the old questions that have been advanced against state sovereignty in the Third World: In what sense are many of the new states in the international system truly sovereign? They may manifest the symbols of "procedural" sovereignty (i.e., they mint their own currencies, send embassies abroad, sit in the UN General Assembly), but can they lay claim to "substantive" sovereignty (i.e., can they provide for external defense, maintain a monopoly on the means of coercion, engage in effective economic planning)? Most important, the explosion of ethnic enmities and irredentist nationalism raise all too familiar questions of the link between sovereignty and self-determination. Does every ethnic group possess the right of sovereign statehood? How is an ethnic community to be defined, and how small would the minimal viable unit be? Moreover, what meaning does the sovereign state have in a context where there is no match between the state and the people, or where the state is the object of competing nationalities?

These questions are closely linked to the second reason why the concept of sovereignty is today more problematic than ever before, namely the global diffusion of democratic values and the development in the last few decades of a truly universal convention of fundamental human rights.

States today rarely reject democracy and international human-rights norms; they are more likely to focus their responses to charges of human-rights violations on allegedly hypocritical standards of enforcement and application of these norms. The universalization of human-rights standards and the growth of nongovernmental human-rights monitoring agencies have seriously undermined the old idea of essentially "domestic" affairs of a state that are beyond the purview of the international community. There is today a growing consensus that claims of state sovereignty should not be an impediment to international intervention in the face of humanitarian crises. The fundamental problem that remains—as vividly demonstrated by ongoing humanitarian disasters throughout the world—is that the threshold beyond which a civil dispute becomes an international humanitarian crisis has yet to be adequately defined, and the mechanism for effective international intervention has yet to be created.

The third reason for the increased importance of reevaluating traditional concepts of sovereignty is the proliferation of transnational and the embryonic formation of supranational institutions founded on an explicit diminution of sovereign prerogatives formerly reserved to the state. The European Union after Maastricht is, of course, the most prominent and advanced example. Yet the evolution of regionalism is by no means confined to this case. Similar developments at various stages of evolution are evident in all regions of the world. Important expansion of traditional UN operations has also occurred in recent interventions in Iraq, Cambodia, and Bosnia. Clearly, a new understanding of the UN charter's proscription against international intervention in "matters which are essentially within the domestic jurisdiction of any state" (article 2[7]) is gradually (and painfully) emerging.

Thus, whether it is human-rights enforcement, economic planning, environmental protection, or conflict management and prevention, competing interpretations or claims of sovereignty repeatedly emerge as the central problem in contemporary international relations. Accordingly, analysts have strained over the past five or six years to find the appropriate metaphor or adjective to describe changes in state sovereignty. State sovereignty today is "diffusing," "shifting," "diminishing," "maturing," "pooling," "leaking," "evaporating"—and all this is happening, it would seem, at once. Clearly we are in the midst of some profound changes in traditional conceptions of state sovereignty and its role in international politics. But such a statement immediately raises some familiar questions: In what, exactly, is the change occurring? In the ideas on how international relations ought to operate? In the institutions that regulate and structure international behavior? What is the relationship between the two?

Much of the difficulty in answering these questions stems from the conceptual confusion surrounding the concepts of "state" and "sovereignty" themselves. Neither is understood in exactly the same way within a particular academic discipline, let alone across various disciplines. James Rosenau writes: "The vast literature on the subject contains a wide array of definitions and formulations, many of which are ambiguous and convey the impression that the state is to politics what the hidden hand is (à la Adam Smith) to economics: its activities are often obscure and unobservable, but nonetheless it somehow manages to regulate the course of events in such a way as to produce specifiable outcomes."[1]

Sovereignty, to extend the analogy, would then be the texture, color, or strength of this "hand." To attempt an analysis of changes in state sovereignty is, therefore, to speculate about a quality of an abstraction.

Still, changes in state sovereignty demand our attention because this quality affects the very substance of international life. State sovereignty is more than an abstraction because it is arguably the determinative principle or norm that shapes the attitudes and governs the behavior of states, and of statesmen and women. As Stephen Krasner has written: "In international relations, the most important diffuse principle is sovereignty. . . . If the constitutive principle of sovereignty were altered, it is difficult to imagine any other international regime would remain unchanged."[2]

Where is this change leading us—toward further international integration or toward greater subnational disintegration? The answers to these questions have never been so confused as at present, for both trends are simultaneously apparent. The post–World War II liberal and cosmopolitan faith in the steady advance of transnational values and institutions seems rather naive today, against the backdrop of resurgent ethno-nationalism on every continent. "The world state," that Walter Lippmann declared in 1946 to be "inherent in the United Nations as an oak tree is in an acorn," has proven to have a rather long gestation period—if indeed it is viable at all.[3]

---

1. James N. Rosenau, "The State in an Era of Cascading Politics: Wavering Concept, Widening Competence, Withering Colossus, or Weathering Change?" in *The Elusive State: International and Comparative Perspectives,* ed. James A. Caporaso (Newbury Park, Calif.: Sage Publications, 1989), 18.

2. Stephen D. Krasner, *International Regimes* (Ithaca: Cornell University Press, 1983), 17–18.

3. Walter Lippmann, "International Control of Atomic Energy," in *One World or None,* ed. Dexter Masters and Katharine Way (Freeport, N.Y.: Books for Libraries Press, 1972), 74.

Finally, what will be the implications of this change for international security, peace, and justice? Will the proliferation of new sovereign states for old ethnic groups move the world toward greater order, stability, and justice, or rather toward greater anarchy, violence, and repression? Will the resurgence of religious politics promote the evolution of a more just and universal international society, or, as Samuel Huntington, among others, has suggested, will it exacerbate societal cleavages and conflicts in a "clash of civilizations" more dangerous than any interstate war?[4]

These questions are the subject of this volume. The essays contained within it address changes in state sovereignty from a variety of scholarly perspectives: historical, political, legal, ethical, sociological. Moreover, they deal with the question of sovereignty as applied to different cultural and geographical contexts: Western European, postcommunist, Islamic, and East Asian. Just as economic, military, and technological developments have increased the permeability of state borders, so must the intellectual and cultural boundaries in the study of world politics become more permeable to incorporate diverse cultural, ideological, and political factors.

Daniel Philpott's essay begins by tackling the definitional challenge. Sovereignty, he argues, is the supreme legitimate authority within a given territory. The legitimate authority is not necessarily the most powerful or effective agent; instead, sovereignty is the condition arising from acknowledgment by the domestic and international community. It is fundamentally an idea of who ought to wield power that is accepted by a community. How, then, do such ideas come to be widely accepted? How are norms of sovereignty shaped and altered? These are the basic theoretical issues that Philpott addresses. His answer is that norms of sovereignty change in response to changes in ideas of legitimate authority. This "theory of ideas" is opposed to realist accounts of international change, which give primacy to shifts in material power. Norms of sovereignty follow changes in the actual structures of international society; philosophers later legitimize these norms by theoretically justifying the structural changes.

By studying three watersheds in the evolution of conceptions of sovereignty, Philpott argues that a strictly realist account is unsatisfactory. First, the Westphalian model emerged as a result of the cataclysmic changes unleashed in Europe by the Reformation. The Reformation laid finally to rest the medieval contests between church and crowns. It provided the

---

4. Samuel P. Huntington, "The Clash of Civilizations," *Foreign Affairs* 72 (Summer 1993): 22–49.

moral and ideological legitimacy for the territorial, unitary, and absolute state—the essence of modern notions of sovereignty.

Second, Philpott considers the impact of liberal thought in the nineteenth-century development of minority-protection treaties and the right of national self-determination. The championing of self-determination by Woodrow Wilson and other Allied leaders can only be understood in the context of late-nineteenth-century conventions aimed primarily at the Ottoman Empire, but that would in the Versailles settlement redound to the European powers themselves. As Philpott acknowledges, the theory of ideas is inconclusive in developments at Versailles, for self-determination was not embraced as a universal norm of the postwar system. Nevertheless, it was applied (sometimes with disastrous consequences in Europe), and it did spell the beginning of the end of European colonial empires, as well as the beginning of the global diffusion of Western norms of sovereign statehood.

By the time of the third turning point that Philpott considers, the creation of the United Nations, liberal thought had gained sufficient ground, both among the colonizers and the colonized, to produce the rapid wave of decolonization. In the wake of World War II, the colonial powers had lost not only their economic predominance but also whatever moral claims they could make to "civilizational preeminence." The triumph of liberal principles was reflected in the terms of the UN charter and in all subsequent international statements on colonization, self-determination, and human rights.

Each of these events, Philpott concludes, demonstrates the realist fallacy of overly emphasizing material over ideational considerations in the evolution of sovereignty. Westphalia, Versailles, and San Francisco show how ideas over time change societies' notions of legitimacy, become sources of power, gradually lead states to reenvision their interests, and, propelled by a systemic war among the great powers, bring about new norms of sovereignty.

My essay considers the impact of essentially Western norms of sovereign statehood upon the Muslim world. With the retreat of European colonialism during the past fifty years, some fifty sovereign states have emerged in which Muslims constitute the overwhelming or significant majority of the total population. Each of these states, without exception, has acceded to the principles and conditions of the contemporary interstate system. Each state, aside from the charter members, filed for UN membership within the first two years of independence. Moreover, each has been swift to claim for itself the full conditions and prerogatives of sovereignty. Thus the Muslim peoples have by no means departed from the traditional pattern of postcolonial states. Instead of rejecting the imposed territorial divisions of the colonial powers, they appear to have embraced them as the organizing principles of modern political life.

Yet, I argue, the sovereign national state has yet to be fully assimilated into Islamic political thought. In fact, challenges to the sovereignty and legitimacy of the Muslim states began to be issued even before they were born and continue unabated to this day. The status of the sovereign state frequently emerges—explicitly and implicitly—at the core of Muslim discourse on international politics.

My essay explores the impact of pan-Islamism and its manifestation in international organizations upon the Muslim state system. From a realist perspective, Islamic ideologies have been and are currently being used by Muslim states to serve a number of instrumental ends in international relations: First, they are used to foster military and economic cooperation by states, such as Pakistan, that face a hostile regional environment. Second, they are used to legitimate conservative regimes, such as that of Saudi Arabia, against domestic and foreign challenges. Since the mid-1960s, the Saudis have generously funded a host of international Islamic organizations, the most universal and politically important being the Organization of the Islamic Conference (OIC). Third, they are used to propagate revolutionary ideology beyond state borders, the most prominent example being the Islamic Republic of Iran's support for Islamic opposition groups throughout the Muslim world.

Like Philpott, I contend, however, that an account focusing on state security and power considerations is inadequate to explain Muslim challenges to state sovereignty. Such explanations cannot adequately account for the ideational motivations underlying many of the pan-Islamist schemes pursued by Muslim leaders, nor more fundamental and direct challenges to the legitimacy of the sovereign state. The reason, I suggest, is that state sovereignty is viewed by many Muslim theorists and activists as incompatible with Islamic ethics, which give primacy to the Muslim community (*umma*). The Islamic state's legitimacy derives from its ability to safeguard and enhance the life of the umma. When it fails to do so, as many modern Muslims contend with regard to the territorial state, its legitimacy will necessarily be undermined. Whereas the Reformation remade the universal community of Christendom into a community of sovereign states, the Islamic resurgence (or perhaps "reformation"?) intends in the minds of many of its leaders to remake the fractious community of sovereign Muslim states into some modern form of the ideal umma.

I argue that the area in which Islamic ethics are most obviously at odds with state sovereignty and intergovernmental organizations like the OIC, which operate upon this principle, is conflict management and resolution. Beatrice Heuser argues in chapter 3 along similar lines at the level of the United Nations. The United Nations as presently constituted labors, she suggests, under the contradiction between its structure as a collectivity of sovereign members and its mandate to preserve international peace and security. Given this dilemma, the United Nations has proven during the past fifty years to be as ineffective as previous world-order schemes.

The post–World War I League of Nations system proved an abject failure in maintaining international peace and security. With its faith in collective security, chances for concerted international action on behalf of victims of aggression were slim and opportunities for defection great. The mechanism indeed proved to be stillborn, as the United States chose isolationism rather than engagement. Britain and France without the United States proved reluctant to shoulder the burdens of enforcement. Britain waffled between an awareness of the need to resist aggressive regimes and that of her inability to police the world without the United States, choosing in the end appeasement.

The post–World War II United Nations system was created supposedly with an awareness of the flaws that had plagued the previous one. The Security Council was supposed to remedy the maladies of collective security by injecting a dose of great-power realism. Yet it too soon became paralyzed under great-power squabbling, as the Cold War overwhelmed the new order. The Security Council, after all, was not intended nor did it have the powers to be more than the sum of its parts.

Following the spectacular demise of communism during the past decade, we have a third opportunity in this century, writes Heuser, to fashion a new and improved world order. This new order must unequivocally give primacy to the promotion of democracy and human rights as essential to the promotion of international security. Traditional conceptions of sovereignty, though intended to promote the rights and political autonomy of particular communities, have in fact become a shield to cover repressive and aggressive regimes. The lessons of failed previous world orders, Heuser argues, lead inexorably to one conclusion: some degree of sovereignty must be universally transferred by the states to the United Nations, which must evolve into a supranational judicial body empowered to enforce international treaty obligations through its own police force.

Heuser's arguments on the need for a UN army to counter cross-border aggression as well as to undertake humanitarian intervention echo similar calls by prominent voices in the wake of the Gulf War.[5] To date, however, they have not gained widespread support. The reason may be, as Gregory Fox argues in chapter 4, that recent humanitarian interventions have in fact bolstered, not undermined, the principles of state sovereignty. Underlying the increased resort to humanitarian interventions and the rapid recent expansion of a body of human-rights norms, Fox argues, is an attempt by states to affirm rather than reshape the sovereign state as the essential political unit of the international system.

More active enforcement of human-rights law seeks to end destabilizing violence within states and replace authoritarian regimes with governments organized along liberal democratic principles. It does not attempt to redraw national boundaries nor to undermine the prerogatives of the state. On the contrary, the goal is to produce stronger states, with a more inclusive political culture, with tolerance as the basis of strengthened legitimacy, and with internal disintegration less likely. The more prominent UN role in humanitarian intervention, Fox argues, is not in reality a "transfer" of increased powers or sovereignty to international organizations, but a pragmatic desire to avoid perceptions of Western imperialism or hegemony. Once the interventions have succeeded in recreating states, the international system grants these states broad discretion in their domestic policies and regards them as fully sovereign in the traditional sense.

The following two chapters examine not international, but internal pressures upon state sovereignty. They consider the phenomenon of ethno-nationalist assaults upon states and their actual or potential disintegration into subnational entities.

Kamal Shehadi begins by surveying the wave of violent "neo-tribalism" that wracks societies as disparate as the former Yugoslavia and India, Sudan and Nagorno-Karabakh, Rwanda and Chechnya. This latest round of ethnic conflict gives urgency to a reconsideration of traditional conceptions of state sovereignty, Shehadi argues, and its reconciliation with the equally troubled notion of self-determination.

The Westphalian model of state sovereignty, universally embraced in the

5. See Brian Urquhart, "For a UN Volunteer Military Force," *New York Review of Books,* 10 June 1993, 3–5; and Bernard Kouchner, "Humanitarian Army Ready to March," *New Perspectives Quarterly* 9 (Spring 1992): 62.

twentieth century, has proven difficult to implant successfully in cultural and geographical contexts different from those of its origins. Realization of state sovereignty has frequently meant a centralization of state authority, more often than not in favor of a particular ethnic group. Through repression or forced assimilation of other communities within their territory, these states have exacerbated demands for autonomy and even secession among minority communities. Shehadi considers the various threats to international peace and security posed by such demands: conflict in a strategically important state, such as a nuclear power; escalation of internal wars to regional conflicts; spreading of ethnic warfare to involve members of the same ethnic groups living in neighboring states.

James Gow's essay focuses upon the clash of sovereignty and self-determination in the dissolution of Yugoslavia. He begins by analyzing the historical roots of Serbian nationalism and its manifestation within the Yugoslav federation. Contrary to the "Yugoslav idea" championed by a mixture of South Slav intellectuals, who envisioned a multiethnic state bound by a common language, Serbian nationalists viewed Yugoslavia as a state unifying all Serbs, with non-Serbian minorities as actual or potential traitors. The experience of World War II, in which large numbers of Croats and Bosnian Muslims joined the Nazis in fighting the Serbs, confirmed the nationalist paranoia. When the momentum for dissolution of the Yugoslav federation developed in the late 1980s, Serbian minorities in Croatia and Bosnia-Herzegovina claimed the same right to self-determination in the form of sovereign statehood that non-Serbian communities in Yugoslavia claimed. The Badinter Commission's attempt to disentangle the ideas of self-determination and human rights from sovereign statehood proved unacceptable to the Serbs, who set about realizing sovereignty in the oldest fashion—through military force.

The lessons of the Balkan wars and the many other conflicts waged in the name of self-determination, argue both Shehadi and Gow, is that the traditional concept of the absolute and unitary state must give way to some form of "shared sovereignty." Shehadi emphasizes that international discussions of sovereignty must give increasing weight to ethnic communities as a unit of analysis rather than focusing, as has been traditionally done, on either the state (or suprastate actors) or the individual. Such an emphasis should not be seen, he argues, as legitimating the claim of sovereign statehood to each "nation" claiming self-determination, but it should require a downward delegation of certain communal rights from the level of the state to minority groups.

Similarly, Gow suggests that minority rights and representation must be formalized within the constitutional structure of deeply divided states. In order for these legal requirements to be meaningful, they must be guaranteed by external powers prepared to intervene in their enforcement. Thus, while interventions may have the goal of reinforcing state sovereignty, as Fox argues, the recreation of stable states or the creation of more stable states from the fragmentation of multiethnic states may be accomplished only through prolonged or indefinite international stewardship that will inevitably weaken state sovereignty.

In the final chapter, Miranda Schreurs analyzes the consequences of recent developments in international environmental planning and protection for state sovereignty. Protection of the earth's ecosystem has emerged as the issue area most graphically demonstrating the inadequacies of purely national planning. Yet, as Schreurs argues, even in this area, the erosion of state sovereignty is not readily apparent. States have strongly resisted the expansion of the idea of "global commons" beyond the atmosphere and the oceans to include land resources that, environmentalists argue, require global management.

Schreurs focuses on one of the most controversial of these resources, the tropical forests of Southeast Asia. Tropical deforestation has been associated with numerous regional and global environmental problems, including air pollution, soil degradation, loss of biodiversity, and global climate change. As such, it has increasingly become a contentious issue involving a number of parties: indigenous peoples and the environmental groups that represent them; lumber companies and agricultural developers; international associations like the International Tropical Timber Organization (ITTO); exporting states, including Malaysia and Indonesia; and importing states, such as Japan and the European Community. Different conceptions of sovereignty abound in this debate, pitting the interests of the North against those of the South, Southeast Asian governments and lumber interests against indigenous peoples.

Schreurs looks specifically at the way sovereignty has been invoked in the policies of Japan and Malaysia. Due to its position as the world's largest importer of tropical hardwoods, Japan has found itself at the center of this sensitive international political and environmental issue. Reacting to pressures from international agencies, foreign media, and conservationists, Japan in recent years has had to reassess its approach toward tropical deforestation. A shift in Japanese consumption patterns inevitably influenced the attitudes of producing states, such as Malaysia. Thus, as a result of both domestic and international pressures, the issue of tropical-forest conservation has slowly gained widespread recognition as a global concern. Yet, to date, no international rain-forest convention has been adopted. Environmental protection, like all the issue areas considered in this book, evinces simultaneously the profound changes and the undeniable persistence of state sovereignty in international relations.

What answers do the separate chapters, taken as a whole, provide to the broad questions underlying this volume? First, with regard to the process of change in conceptions of sovereignty, several of the essays highlight the prominent role of ideas over purely material or functional explanations. Philpott and I stress most explicitly the thesis that challenges and eventual changes in norms of sovereignty often precede and determine institutional behavior or even the creation of new institutions. Neither of us posits an antithetical relationship between material interests and ideals of political community or behavior; rather, we both emphasize the close linkage between the two. Political ideals, we suggest, are not epiphenomenal to or contingent upon changing conceptions of material interests. Instead, ideals derived from religious or ethical criteria provide normative visions of international organization and behavior that are often incompatible with prevailing norms that legitimate the pursuit of material interests. The visions are rarely fully realized, but the struggle for realization produces alterations in both international norms and in conceptions of material interests. The end result of the transformation is a new marriage of ideals and interests.

The same point is made, with varying degrees of emphasis, by all the other contributors. Heuser, for example, outlines a normative argument for the direction in which international institutions must evolve in order to enhance international justice and security. Her essay is indicative of the trailblazing role that Philpott ascribes to ideas; she is outlining yet another watershed in the evolutionary pattern that Philpott charts, in which ideas outpace institutional developments. A revolution in ideas of sovereignty must precede the radical institutional changes that she advocates.

Though several of the essays highlight the point that ideational challenges to the sovereign state are present today, all of them acknowledge the resilience of the sovereign-state ideal and its likely place at the heart of international relations theory and practice for the foreseeable future. The strong sovereign state is the normative goal of the international community, according to Fox, because it—and not international institutions— is seen as the most capable guarantor of human rights and international security. In other words, the goal of the international community is to bring all states to relatively the same point in the evolutionary trajectory of the sovereign state before any major further evolution can be contemplated. New and relatively weak states that have recently emerged from colonization are likely to assert and demand full sovereign prerogatives in the international arena before they contemplate transferring some of their sovereignty to international institutions. As Schreurs's essay indicates, even an issue with such clear-cut, objectively international concern as the earth's ecosystem elicits strong assertions of noninterference in the "domestic" affairs of sovereign states. International institutions thus find themselves assuaging fears of erosion of sovereignty harbored by threatened states before any real progress is possible in resolving vital issues.

Second, with regard to the direction in which changes in sovereignty are leading us, the essays again generally emphasize the staying power of the nation-state model. Whether this ideal is compatible with various non-Western conceptions of political community, and how far it has sunk into the consciousness of peoples other than the tiny fraction of national elites cultivated by colonial powers, remain open questions. To date, very little scholarly attention has been devoted to empirical testing of cultural assimilation of the essentially Western norms underlying international society.[6] Nevertheless, the dominance of the nation-state model over competing world-order models can scarcely be challenged, regardless of cultural context. Heuser and I acknowledge the many obstacles to the creation of the trans- and supranational institutions that we discuss. Shehadi and Gow, who address subnational challenges to the state, argue that self-determination claims should and probably will lead in the future not to successful secessionist movements, but to various degrees of autonomy for ethnic minorities asserting claims to political power.

At the same time, all of the contributors note the incremental transferral of state prerogatives to regional or international organizations such as the United Nations, the European Union, the Organization of the Islamic Conference, and the International Tropical Timber Organization. The transferral of limited authority may be calculated to thwart more extensive erosion of sovereignty, but, as Schreurs argues with regard to environmental protection, states ineluctably narrow "their scope of permissible activities." Authority once transferred is only with great difficulty reclaimed.

6. The most important contribution in this area still remains the quite exploratory work published more than a decade ago by Hedley Bull and Adam Watson, eds., *The Expansion of International Society* (Oxford: Clarendon Press, 1984).

The very creation of intergovernmental organizations sets in motion a dynamic that is sustained in part by functional factors and unforeseen exigencies—what may be termed "mandate creep." But the dynamic is also sustained in part by public opinion and expectations beyond elite control that progressively expand the authority of intergovernmental organizations into areas previously not contemplated by the elites who created them.

Finally, with regard to the implications of changes in state sovereignty for international peace and security, these essays provide the basis for both pessimism and optimism. Philpott's historical survey of the evolution of state sovereignty indicates how even the most sublime ideals of human cooperation, freedom, and justice are accompanied by the most horrifying bloodshed and destruction. The world order of the twenty-first century is emerging with a similar mixture of high aspirations and terrible devastation. But in this third opportunity of the twentieth century to fashion a new world order, perhaps we have learned, as Heuser suggests, the bitter lessons of previous failures. For along with the all-too-familiar pattern of war for political and economic ends, or conflicts driven by religious, sectarian, or ethnic hatreds, the birth of this world order has also known unprecedented degrees of nonviolent political change, the restraint of great powers in the exercise of military force, the implementation of collective action to maintain international peace and security, the prosecution of war criminals, and the strengthening of a universal human-rights regime.

1

Ideas and the Evolution of Sovereignty

Daniel Philpott

Sovereignty is again the issue. Against the spirit of the "end of history," new political entities are claiming new forms of authority: secessionist republics in the former Yugoslavia assert independence; the UN sanctions intervention on the grounds of humanitarianism and democracy in Somalia, Bosnia, Iraq, Rwanda, and Haiti, all without the consent of local parties; and legal scholars have noted an "emerging right to democratic governance" that makes domestic government a matter of international concern.[1] International institutions—the United Nations and the European Union— have recognized and supported the new authority, eroding the sanctity of sovereignty upon which they have vigorously insisted since World War II.[2] Admittedly, it is not yet certain whether these new practices will

1. See Thomas Franck, "The Emerging Right to Democratic Governance," *American Journal of International Law* 86 (1992): 46–91.

2. Since World War II, the only substate claims considered legitimate have been the claims of colonies to independence. The one significant exception is Bangladesh, which seceded from Pakistan in 1971 and was recognized by the international community. For examples of other secessionist movements that failed to elicit support, see Lee C. Buchheit, *Secession: The Legitimacy of Self-Determination* (New Haven: Yale University Press, 1978).

become durable fixtures in the new world order. But if they do, it will represent one of the rare turning points—revolutions in sovereignty—since medieval times that new orders of international authority have come about.

Revolutions in sovereignty are both rare and noteworthy, for they overhaul what I will call the constitution of international relations: internationally agreed-upon rules that define whether the world is one of empires or states, whether intervention is legitimate, and that address other matters of sovereignty, or of fundamental authority. But if the constitution of international relations defines sovereignty, how do the constitutions themselves come about? What causes a revolution in sovereignty? This is my central question. I seek to answer it by looking at three key revolutions in sovereignty since medieval times: first, the rise of sovereign statehood, consolidated at the 1648 Peace of Westphalia; second, international agreements on minority rights in Eastern Europe found in late-nineteenth-century treaties and in the settlement of World War I; and third, decolonization in 1960.

These emergences of international novelty, I argue, are products of prior revolutions in ideas about justice and legitimate authority. The Protestant Reformation led to Westphalia; liberalism led to minority protection; colonial nationalism and metropolitan liberalism led to decolonization. That ideas cause revolutions in sovereignty, or for that matter in any big event in international politics, is not, however, obvious. It could be that armies and navies, territory, technology, populations, and wealth, bureaucracies that raise taxes and troops, and the classes who dominate politics are the real phenomena behind the revolutions, while ideas are illusory projections, deceptive surface reflections. Such would be the claim of skeptical "structural" theories, of which realism is the most prominent in international relations. Indeed, structural historians, sociologists, and political scientists have proffered explanations for history's revolutions in sovereignty in which ideas are not to be found. Ideas' influence, then, must be established. The role of class, technology, and the like I do not deny, but without blizzards of new ideas, blowing across societies, leaving their accumulated remains, leading states to reimagine their interests, fresh constitutions of international relations would never arise.

I begin with a discussion of sovereignty, the constitution of international relations, and the constitution's historical development. I then outline an account of ideas' influence. Finally, I show how ideas have been a central cause of revolutions in sovereignty.

Sovereignty: A Definition and Brief History

Because the idea of sovereignty has evolved profoundly over history, it is surely quixotic to search for a definition that captures every usage since the thirteenth century.[3] Believers speak of the sovereignty of God; philosophers and politicians refer to the sovereignty of monarchs, popular sovereignty, divided sovereignty, the sovereignty of the state, and so on. One can best understand sovereignty in its historical parts, divided into its rich, overlapping, bewildering layers.

There is still a broad concept—not a definition, but a wide category—that unites most of sovereignty's tradition, and with which we can begin: legitimate authority. Authority is "the right to command, and correlatively, the right to be obeyed," and it is legitimate when it is seen as right by those living under it.[4] Legitimate authority must not be confused with simple power—raw, pure, physical, direct. To borrow R. P. Wolff's example, if I am forced at gunpoint to hand over my money, I am subject to power; if I pay my taxes, even though I think I can cheat, I am recognizing legitimate authority.[5] Sovereignty, even at its most monarchical or dictatorial, is never a matter of mere power. Even Hobbes's Leviathan only has total power because the people have completely relinquished to him their natural but vulnerable rights, legitimizing his legislative capacity. Legitimacy confers power but is not itself power. It also, incidentally, works in reverse: power can help establish legitimacy. If early modern states had never developed means of coercion—bureaucracies, the power to tax and raise armies—the legitimate authority of Hobbes's sovereign would never have been possible.

Legitimate authority and power, then, are related but not the same. One can imagine Jean Bodin's monarch, whose sovereign prerogatives give him supreme, incontestable authority, finding that he cannot collect taxes or send an army into battle without making concessions—perhaps illegitimate

---

3. The oldest citation of *sovereignty* in the *Oxford English Dictionary* is dated 1290. See the 2d ed., prepared by J. A. Simpson and E. S. C. Weiner, vol. 16 (Oxford: Clarendon Press, 1989), 77–79.

4. R. P. Wolff, "The Conflict Between Authority and Autonomy," in *Authority*, ed. Joseph Raz (Oxford: Basil Blackwell, 1990), 20. Here, I use *legitimate* in its descriptive sense, meaning not "justified" or "morally defensible," but as Max Weber meant it, that which is assented to, or at least regarded as part of the normal, proper, state of affairs. See Max Weber, *The Theory of Social and Economic Organization,* ed. Talcott Parsons (New York: Free Press, 1947), 124.

5. Wolff, "Conflict Between Authority and Autonomy," 20–21.

concessions—to nobles and legislatures. Or, one can imagine the same monarch controlling them with ease. Both have the same authority but different degrees of power. In the modern state system, one can envision both a small state that is constantly invaded and has little control over its economy, and a small state that is a "holder of the balance," using its strategic position to play off great powers against one another. Both are sovereign states, but they vary in their power.

If legitimate authority is not power, perhaps we can equate it with law. From our modern perspective, this is surely valid: since the eighteenth century, sovereign prerogatives have in fact usually been codified. But it was not always so. To Bodin and Hobbes, the sovereign is above human law, and is in fact the source of it. This does not make him illegitimate, though; he holds his position by some right, some ideal. Bodin, for instance, insists that the sovereign has a divine ordination, the basis of his prerogative to give the human law.[6] Since the eighteenth century, at first in the constitutionally advanced Western states, now virtually everywhere, this has changed. Sovereignty is a wholly legally defined concept; domestic constitutions and international agreements define the scope of all rulers' and citizens' legitimate authority.

Sovereignty, then, is a type of legitimate authority; it is not power, and today it is prescribed by law. But this is still too broad: a police chief, a priest, or a corporate executive could all qualify as sovereigns. Are there other traits that will narrow the concept, yet allow us to capture sovereignty's many colors? In fact, sovereignty has always comprised a certain other ingredient: supremacy. In the chain of authority by which I look up to higher authority, who looks up to yet a higher one, and so on, the holder of sovereignty is highest; this person or institution has final authority. A police chief may have authority over me, but he is not sovereign. This is not to say that the sovereign need be an individual. Supreme authority might lie in a triumvirate, a committee, a constitution, or, in Rousseau's version, in the united will of the people. In all cases, nobody may question the sovereign; nobody may legitimately oppose it.

A final important ingredient in sovereignty's definition is territoriality: the people over whom the holder of sovereignty rules are defined by virtue of their location within borders, not by some other principle such

---

6. Bodin also insists that the sovereign is bound by natural law and by God's law. He writes: "Sovereign princes . . . have been established by Him as His lieutenants for commanding other men." Jean Bodin, *On Sovereignty,* ed. Julian H. Franklin (Cambridge: Cambridge University Press, 1992), 46.

as kinship or religious belief.[7] In the high Middle Ages, when sovereignty did not exist, neither supremacy nor territoriality characterized political authorities, in precise contrast to modern international relations, whose sovereign states have been compared by scholars to private property, in which one person or body of law is supreme within a demarcated piece of turf.[8]

We now have our most specific definition of sovereignty: supreme authority within a territory. All particular uses of sovereignty have been one or another form of supreme authority within a territory, reflecting one or another philosophy in one or another epoch; sovereignty is never without an adjective. The first modern form of sovereignty was absolute sovereignty, the sort that Bodin, Hobbes, and Grotius had in mind. At first, the quality of absoluteness may seem redundant: if sovereign authority is already supreme, how can it be less than absolute? Absoluteness, though, does not refer to the quality or magnitude of sovereignty, for if sovereignty were less than supreme in any particular matter, it would not be sovereignty at all. But a holder of sovereignty need not be sovereign over all matters. Absoluteness refers to the scope of affairs over which a sovereign body governs within a particular territory. Is it supreme over all matters, or merely over some?

In those matters to which a sovereign's authority does not extend, it is typically the international law or institution that prescribes how authority is to be shared that is sovereign. The government of France is supreme in defense policy but not in trade, which it governs jointly with the other European Union members as prescribed by EU law. The French constitution's sovereignty is nonabsolute. For Bodin and Hobbes, by contrast, sovereignty meant authority over all matters; it was absolute, unconditionally.[9] The absolute sovereignty of one particular holder of sovereignty—the state—is archetypal modern sovereignty; it is the norm to

7. On territoriality, see John Gerard Ruggie, "Territoriality and Beyond: Problematizing Modernity in International Relations," *International Organization* 47 (1993): 139–74.

8. See John Gerard Ruggie, "Continuity and Transformation in the World Polity: Toward a Neorealist Synthesis," in *Neorealism and Its Critics,* ed. Robert O. Keohane (New York: Columbia University Press, 1986), 131–57, 142–43.

9. I must somewhat qualify this conclusion in the case of Bodin, whose sovereign is bound by natural law, obliged to respect the liberties and property of subjects as they are entitled to them, and obliged to abide by his contracts with private citizens. There is no right of popular resistance, however, corresponding to these duties. See Bodin, *On Sovereignty,* and J. H. Franklin, *Jean Bodin and the Rise of Absolutist Theory* (Cambridge: Cambridge University Press, 1973).

which the EU and the emerging UN norm of humanitarian intervention are two exceptions. It renders international relations anarchical, for it makes states wholly autonomous; no outside authority requires them to yield or to genuflect.

Absolute and *nonabsolute* are useful distinguishing terms. Helpful too are *internal* and *external*, which do not denote distinct types of sovereignty, but rather complementary, always coexistent, aspects of sovereignty.[10] Supreme authority within a territory means not only sovereignty within borders, but also implies immunity from external interference. Such interference, were it legitimate, would make the sovereign less than supreme. Since the Peace of Westphalia of 1648, the state has been the chief holder of external sovereignty; then it became illegitimate to interfere in other states to influence their governance of religion or of anything else. The external sovereignty of the state is what international lawyers have in mind when they speak of sovereignty, and it is what the UN charter means by "political independence and territorial integrity."[11] If the state is private property, its external sovereignty is a no-trespassing law.

The external sovereignty of the state is also what lawyers and political scientists mean when they speak of international relations as anarchy, a notion that means not necessarily chaos, riot, and violence, but simply the lack of a government, the absence of a higher authority that has claims upon those who live under it. The external sovereignty of the state is also compatible with a variety of holders of internal sovereignty—a monarch, the people, and a constitution can each represent the state within borders and be immune from external intervention. Compared with internal sovereignty, external sovereignty has remained relatively constant—not unrevised (otherwise international revolutions in sovereignty would make little sense), but steady like a suit of armor whose plates and hinges are only occasionally updated and restructured, while the personality inside changes often, from reform to reform, from revolution to revolution.

Who holds sovereignty? What are this holder's prerogatives? During any particular historical period, there are rules that specify these matters.

---

10. It is possible, though, to have one without the other. For instance, a state that is in the midst of civil war, but whose authority is unchallenged from the outside, might have external sovereignty but not internal sovereignty. But when sovereignty is realized, both aspects must be present.

11. See UN charter, art. 2(4); Ian Brownlie, *Principles of Public International Law*, 3d ed. (Oxford: Oxford University Press, 1979); Michael Akehurst, *A Modern Introduction to International Law*, 5th ed. (London: George Allen and Unwin, 1984).

These rules comprise the constitution of international relations, for they define fundamental matters of authority. The constitution defines authority in three specific senses, which I term the three faces of sovereignty, each of which constitutes an answer to a particular question. First, who are the legitimate polities? States? The Holy Roman Empire? The European Union? Second, who is entitled to become one of these legitimate polities? If states are the legitimate polity, who may become a state? Nations that have no state? Colonies? Third, what essential prerogatives in making, enforcing, and judging law do the legitimate polities enjoy? Are states free from all intervention, or are there some matters in which they are legitimately subject to interference? Together, these faces constitute international relations, determining on what terms the world is divided.

Unlike sovereignty, an academic concept, the constitution of international relations is historically realized. States (or other polities) have explicitly agreed to it—we can find the provisions of the constitution in actual agreements. The provisions are also practiced, meaning not that they are never violated, but that they are generally adhered to, regarded as expected behavior. In the generation following Westphalia, states no longer forcibly interfered in the religious affairs of other states. In the twentieth century, the norm of decolonization was accompanied by the freeing of colonies. To say that the constitution's provisions are practiced means also that no revisionist state exists that both rejects a provision and has the power to overturn and constantly violate it. When and where a revisionist state lumbers, we must say that a provision is not practiced, but is contested. Although the 1555 Treaty of Augsburg provided states virtual sovereignty in religious affairs, neither Catholic imperial authority nor Protestant German princes accepted its terms; they continued literally to invade other states' religious privacy, making the norm of state sovereignty contested. After Augsburg was reconstituted in Westphalia in 1648, by contrast, all potentially disruptive powers chose instead to accept it.[12]

The constitution of international relations, then, is agreed upon, practiced, and unopposed. A revolution in sovereignty is simply a major change in the constitution of international relations. More precisely, I define it as a transformation in at least one of the three faces of sovereignty—in the

---

12. Another example of contestation is Napoleon's challenge to state sovereignty, which involved regular intervention to change the character of other states' domestic governments.

legitimate polities, in the rules for becoming one, in the prerogatives that the polities enjoy. Revolutions often follow periods of contestation, but they are not consolidated until the largest powers agree upon the new constitutions. The rise of state sovereignty at Westphalia, the emergence of minority treaties in the late nineteenth and early twentieth centuries, and decolonization are three examples of such revolutions; the founding of the European Coal and Steel Community (later the European Community, then the European Union) and the contemporary rise of humanitarian intervention are also revolutions. Each involved an important transformation in authority; for each we must ask: How did it occur?

Sovereignty, Power, and Ideas

If revolutions in sovereignty create new international constitutions, orders that empower or diminish princes, empires, colonies, nations, minorities, and intervening authorities, if they legitimate fresh ideologies and novel notions of justice, this hardly means that ideas or philosophies themselves bring the revolutions about. Ideas' presence does not alone prove their influence, for it could be true that princes earn their sovereignty only by marshaling enough troops and revenue to defeat a resistant emperor, or that colonies become free only when they become too costly, too restive, in the eyes of their metropoles. This is the view of structural theories, which privilege the role of the international distribution of military and economic power, technology, the array of social classes, the character of political institutions, or any factor that supplants, overrides, or operates without the assistance of ideas, discourse, or reflection. Political realism is one of these theories; for revolutions in sovereignty, it is our principal skeptic.

A theory that ideas are behind revolutions in sovereignty is a theory about contradictions. Iconoclastic ideas declare existing orders invalid, they win converts, and the converts challenge the old order, creating a crisis, bringing a revolution in international authority. But ideas are not the only source of contradiction, and just as Marx stood Hegel on his head, structural theories offer alternatives to ideas' two dynamics. Structural factors—the international balance of power, technology, class—are indeed indispensable for explaining revolutions in sovereignty, but their sufficiency is questionable. Neither are ideas the sole source of change, but they are an inestimably crucial partner to other forms of power—and this, in intricate ways.[13]

Because it is polities who overthrow old orders and agree upon new ones, any theory of revolutions in sovereignty must account for how these polities come to have an "interest" in new constitutions.[14] To explain interests, a theory must in turn offer an account of power: what sort of power shapes interests, pressuring and enabling polities to pursue them against opponents? Structural theories would claim relevance only for the international distribution of power or the structure of political or economic power within the state. In an ideas account, ideas themselves may be a form of power.[15]

There are two dynamics that constitute the mechanism by which ideas exert power, the power that creates the contradiction between the old order and the new. First, ideas shape the identities of people, creating converts at any or all levels of society. Second, ideas translate into forms of social power, power that pressures or enables heads of state to pursue new constitutions of international relations. In the first dynamic, ideas perform their transforming function by shaping identities; people come to want what the ideas prescribe. By identity, I mean simply what a person values according to his chosen role: is he a Protestant, a nationalist, a liberal? An ideas account holds that people shape their identities through reasoned reflection upon ideas' intrinsic propositions, and insists, against a structural account, that changes in identities are not reducible to material or psychological factors. More directly, we may think of ideas as causes of identities.

13. In developing my account of the influence of ideas, I have benefited from a nascent literature on ideas in international relations, of which the most prominent works are Judith Goldstein and Robert O. Keohane, eds., *Ideas and Foreign Policy: Beliefs, Institutions, and Political Change* (Ithaca: Cornell University Press, 1993); and Alexander Wendt's writings from a "constructivist" point of view. See his "Collective Identity Formation and the International State," *American Political Science Review* 88 (1994): 384–96; and "Anarchy Is What States Make of It: The Social Construction of Power Politics," *International Organization* 46 (1992): 395–421.

14. By *interest*, I mean a general long-term goal that the polity actively pursues: maximizing military security or wealth, spreading democracy, realizing a new norm of sovereignty.

15. In contrast to much of the political-science literature, my concepts of interests and power are open-ended. Ideas are not opposed to something else called interests, but instead are one force that may shape interests—or may not, if one is a structural skeptic. Interests themselves may have any content. Similarly, power may include economic, military, and political power, but may also include ideas themselves.

But shaping identities is not enough. Popular conversion alone does not account for how ideas bring leaders of states or empires to campaign or move troops on behalf of new international constitutions, or how ideas hamper or overthrow obstructing leaders. The second dynamic of ideas—ideas as social power—explains how converts apply carrots and sticks upon their prince, parliament, president, or anyone who is in a position to deliver or hinder the new constitution. The social power of ideas results in a transformation of the polity's interest, and eventually in a revolution in sovereignty. The carrots and sticks come in the form of traditional political tools—votes, taxes, bureaucratic power, the threat to rebel—that alter the costs and benefits of promoting policies that the ideas demand. What is distinctive is that those who wield these tools are converts to new identities.

Ideas are not choosy about who sponsors them into politics; a whole variety of "couriers" of ideas may change their identities and exert the social power of ideas. These include publics, networks of intellectuals and activists, party heads, government officials, international organizations, even heads of state. It is not necessary, however, that heads of states themselves convert, but only that they be pressured or enabled by the social power of other converts.

These couriers play no role for structural skeptics, who claim to explain revolutions in sovereignty without appealing to either of ideas' two dynamics. The most sweeping of structural theories, like Marxism or Durkheim's theory of the division of labor, challenge ideas on the deepest level, claiming that identities themselves are products of material forces. Other structural theories—realism, for example—leave identities alone, allowing that ideas may shape them, but claiming that ideas play no further role in exerting social power. It is, rather, material power that shapes the interests of polities. An ideas account must meet both types of criticism, but I want to look particularly at the claims of realism, both because of realism's pedigree (it has developed over millennia) and because realism has a particularly strong claim on explanations of international events.

States are single entities with indivisible interests. These interests are to preserve and rationally expand power. These interests are inescapably pursued, or at least ignored at great cost, because of an anarchical international milieu in which the lack of a common superior makes attack a perpetual threat. These interests cannot include ideals of justice, which the same milieu will bring to defeat. Such are realism's tenets. In modern times, they were first expounded by Machiavelli, and, with some variation, they are generally shared by all realists, extending back to Thucydides and forward to modern realists Hans Morgenthau and E. H. Carr, on up to contemporary realists Kenneth Waltz and Robert Gilpin.

From the realists' belief that anarchy is so pronounced, its effects so overriding, that war-fighting power is polities' inescapable end, it is not hard to infer the realists' view of ideas about justice and legitimate authority: such ideas are manifestly not what states aim to realize. E. H. Carr argues this most vociferously in *The Twenty Years' Crisis*, a scathing commentary on the failure of Anglo-American internationalist ideals to overcome war through international law, free trade, and public opinion.[16] The same idea is found in Thucydides, Machiavelli, Morgenthau, and elsewhere.

This is realism in its most brusque mood, and although it is not a bad general characterization, at times the realists' dismissal of ideas can be less gruff. Even Carr wants to avoid an overly consistent, determinist realism, admitting that freedom of action for states still exists, and other realists allow a limited influence for moral ideas and notions of legitimacy. Realists' ideas about ideas, though, are in the end quite fuzzy. No realist makes ideas a systematic part of his theory, and it is often unclear how ideas exert influence or what kind of effect they may have.[17] What all realists do make clear are the strong limitations to ideas' influence. Ideas will be impotent if they depart from polities' interest in power; they thus have little social power of their own. The realists' general advice to statespersons against pursuing ideals also reveals their skepticism. Stark description converts easily to considered prescription; what may seem like a misanthropic assessment, realists present as wise counsel, as prophetic, tragic, insight.

With realism's canonical teachings about power, anarchy, and ideas, we can sew together a realist account of revolutions in sovereignty. I say *sew together* because revolutions in sovereignty and international constitutions

---

16. "For the past hundred years, and more especially since 1918, the English-speaking peoples have formed the dominant group in the world; and current theories of morality have been designed to perpetuate their supremacy and expressed in the idiom peculiar to them." E. H. Carr, *The Twenty Years' Crisis, 1919–1939* (New York: Harper and Row, 1964), 79–80.

17. See Carr, *Twenty Years' Crisis*, 93; Hans Morgenthau, *Politics Among Nations: The Struggle for Power and Peace*, 6th ed. (New York: Alfred A. Knopf, 1985); Henry Kissinger, *A World Restored* (Boston: Houghton Mifflin, 1957).

are not in the language of Machiavelli, Hobbes, Carr, or other realists. Morgenthau mentions practices of sovereignty, but neither he nor any other realist seeks their genesis. Realists, though, ought to be concerned with international constitutions and their metamorphoses, for to the extent that such constitutions are practiced, they have important implications for material power, a central realist concern.

Sovereignty's three faces—the definition of political authority, the criteria for becoming one of these authorities, and the prerogatives of these authorities—involve strategic stakes of the highest sort. If I am a seventeenth-century German prince, it matters a great deal to my military security whether there exists an emperor who claims control over my territory's religious affairs and regularly sends in his troops over this issue. If I am an imperial metropole, my colonies may provide me with riches and strategic outposts; their independence is not a small affair. States and empires have indeed fought wars over such matters of authority.

If polities have high stakes in international constitutions, then how these constitutions are defined, in a realist explanation, will depend on the strategic power and interests of the economically and militarily strongest polities. In different eras, different polities have found different constitutional practices most conducive to their power. Revolutions in sovereignty, it follows, result from the rise in material power of polities whose interest in preserving (and rationally expanding) this power are served by the new constitutions, and the decline of polities whose interests are served by the old ones. The crucial piece of realist logic is that when means expand, so do ends.[18] When formerly weak polities grow relatively strong, they aspire to more ambitious ends, including new constitutions of international relations, and when strong polities suffer relative atrophy, they become less able to uphold the old order.

At the center of the realist case is the historical fact that revolutions in sovereignty have always followed general wars or sharp shifts in material power—events that consolidate generational power trends. Westphalia, then, resulted from the rise of states and the decline of the Holy Roman Empire, culminating in the Thirty Years' War. The strongest version of the minority-protection treaties came with the military victory of the Allies

---

18. For realists who incorporate this tenet into their thought, see Fareed Zakaria, "The Rise of a Great Power: National Strength, State Structure, and American Foreign Policy, 1865–1908," Ph.D. diss., Harvard University, 1995; and Robert Gilpin, *War and Change in World Politics* (Cambridge: Cambridge University Press, 1981).

in World War I. And decolonization was the product of the decline of Britain and France and the rise of the colonies and their superpower Allies after World War II. For a realist, revolutions in sovereignty are the story of the rise and fall of great powers, the story of changes in the international distribution of power, the realist version of the structure that overrides ideas.

For an ideas account, general wars and crises are undeniably important, but they are more than mere material-power shifts. They are crucial in resolving the contradiction between revolutionary ideas and old constitutions. The crises may themselves be caused by the revolutionary ideas, just as the Reformation was a major cause of the Thirty Years' War. The crises may assist in the creation of revolutionary ideas, just as World War II helped create colonial nationalism. And the crises, by defeating the armies of the old order's defenders, not only weaken them militarily, but hamper their ability to promote the old ideas.

In assessing the role of ideas and structural factors in bringing about revolutions, we must note the historical fact that major crises have always midwifed revolutions. We must further note that in the period leading up to the crises evoking the revolutions, there also occur crises that bring no change in international constitutions at all. The Thirty Years' War was preceded by the great-power wars ending in the Peace of Cateau-Cambrésis in 1559, which failed to usher in a sovereign-states system; Britain's and France's decline after World War II was preceded by World War I, which failed to bring general decolonization. The question confronting each theory is: Why does a certain crisis result in a new constitution of international relations, while an earlier crisis does not?

For the realist, the answer can only be that in the earlier crises, the relative war-fighting power of the polities interested in the new constitution was not yet strong enough, whereas in the later one it was. For an ideas account, the answer can only be that ideas had not yet spread far enough or attained adequate social power in the earlier crises, but had gained greater strength by the time of later one. We can evaluate the two claims by using the crises as milestones, stopping at each one to inspect changes in ideas and structure. If it turns out that between the earlier barren crises and the later birth-giving crisis, ideas have grown while structures (which we can often measure using indices of economic growth, military size, tax revenue, and so on) have either declined or failed to change significantly, then an ideas account will be enhanced.

Sovereign Statehood: The Revolution at Westphalia

When Bodin wrote *On Sovereignty*, he had in mind his own king, whom he hoped would become a true sovereign, the supreme authority within France. For modern international relations to develop, the map of Europe had to become uniformly colored with territories governed by Bodin's monarchs, free from threat within, secure from meddling without, and alike in these capacities. This was not accomplished until 1648, when sovereign statehood became Europe's governing constitution, and when sovereign states became the dominant form of polity. As legal scholar Leo Gross wrote in his classic article on Westphalia, it "represents the majestic portal which leads from the old into the new world."[19]

But if ideas were in important part responsible for sovereign statehood at Westphalia, it was not the idea of sovereignty itself. If scholars precede statespersons, it was not the philosophers of sovereignty whom the powerful followed. The reverse was more likely; those whose position already looked like sovereignty then clothed themselves with the concept for legitimacy. Bodin wrote in the service of the French court. But how these rulers came to have this position, these interests, and in fact much of the reason for which sovereignty was invented, lies in another idea, one that came earlier and answered more basic questions about human life—the Protestant Reformation. When the first reformers began to spread the Gospel as Martin Luther had brought them to understand it, a system of sovereign states was far from their minds. How ideas got transformed into notions of political authority, which led to the defeat of universal Catholic authority and a system of sovereign states, is what I seek to show.

A prior issue, however, is Westphalia's status as the point of origin of modern international relations. This conventional wisdom has recently been challenged; its defense needs to be updated.[20] The traditional argument asserts a historical cleavage: before Westphalia, Europe was still in important ways medieval, whereas afterward it was modern. In the quintessential medieval world, authorities had diverse powers. None of them was sovereign, yet all lived under a common Christian ideal. A pope and

19. Leo Gross, "The Peace of Westphalia: 1648–1948," *American Journal of International Law* 42 (January 1948): 28.

20. The most important critique of Westphalia's importance as a breaking point is that of Stephen Krasner, "Westphalia and All That," in Goldstein and Keohane, *Ideas and Foreign Policy*, 235–64.

an emperor, monarchs, barons, dukes, bishops, and knights all inhabited the arcane world of Christendom's common law, which mutually linked, empowered, and limited them. Nobody was supreme. Like chess pieces, none was alike; each had his own privileges. In the modern world, states are all alike in their privileges, each of them is sovereign, and there is no necessary common ideal that links them except for their very agreement to respect one another's sovereignty. Modernity, then, is more like checkers, where similar units have identical privileges.

This medieval system may never have existed, although something quite like it reigned in the high Middle Ages, between approximately 900 and 1300. After this time, the modern began to infiltrate. By around 1300, British and French monarchs were effectively independent of papal and imperial authority and were developing supremacy within their territories. In fifteenth-century Italy, something like an independent system of sovereign states existed among city-states (which were largely free from transalpine influences). But when Rome was sacked in 1527 by forces of the Holy Roman Empire and Spain, Italy's cities became mere pawns in a European system. This system was not yet one of sovereign states, for in the Holy Roman Empire, the last great medieval entity, the Austrian Habsburgs combined in an intricate family relationship with Spain, the Netherlands, and Burgundy. It was not until this system could be broken up into separate sovereign states that Europe would be a system of sovereign states. To see sovereignty's delayed progress, compare 1648 with the outcome of a previous general crisis: the 1559 Peace of Cateau-Cambrésis, which ended wars between Spain and France. By this time, progress toward sovereign statehood had incrementally advanced. Charles V had abdicated, and since the new Habsburg Holy Roman Emperor was no longer the Spanish king, the two halves of the complex were somewhat severed. Yet sovereign Spain continued to support the emperor in his restoration dream, and the emperor continued to rule as a medieval figure in his own lands, important but not sovereign. Most of all, he disputed the German princes' right to determine the faith of their realms. Although it seemed that they had won this right at Augsburg, when the principle *cujus regio, ejus religio* (whose the region, his the religion) granted princes sovereignty over faith, this settlement proved unstable as the emperor and the princes continued to contest faith through arms, culminating in the Thirty Years' War beginning in 1618. Until princes were authoritative over religion, and the Holy Roman Emperor impotent over it, a system of sovereign states would not exist.

More than any other work, Hugo Grotius's *The Rights of War and Peace,* written in 1625, was a recipe for Westphalia. Grotius describes a world of internally and externally sovereign monarchs, united only by a natural law, which, he argued, was valid even if there was no God.[21] In several ways, Grotius's vision is manifest in Westphalia, not only in the treaties'[22] actual provisions, but in the subsequent practice of international politics. Most important, the Habsburg complex was defeated and broken into sovereign states. Spain and Austria would thereafter no longer act as partners in the restoration of Christendom, but at most as allies.

True, the Holy Roman Empire persisted: the imperial diet, imperial courts, imperial circles, imperial army, and of course the emperor, all remained. These institutions, though, exercised no meaningful executive, legislative, or judicial power in the affairs of the German principalities. The most intrusive form of imperial intervention, that on behalf of religion, never occurred again. In several other respects, Westphalia's provisions evince conscious conceptions of sovereignty. The United Provinces and Swiss Confederation were given full privileges of sovereign statehood. The privileges of the emperor and of the pope were explicitly curtailed. And to regulate relations between Europe's political entities, provisions for treaty making and conflict settlement were included in the treaty and even extended to the German princes, giving them the right to form alliances outside the empire. And the settlement as a whole constructed a European balance of power that did not envision the Holy Roman Empire as a weight on the scale. Although the settlement's provisions did not include the words *sovereign state,* all of the essential provisions for the practice of sovereignty were present. The provisions, admittedly, did not arise ex nihilo, but were the product of centuries of evolution. At Westphalia, though, the last meaningful features of medieval Christendom disappeared, leaving a modern system thereafter.

Behind this transformation was the Reformation. When Luther announced his complaints to the church on the door of the Wittenberg Cathedral in 1517, he meant only to reform the church, not to create a separate church, an independent polity, or anything like a system of sovereign states. Grotian ideas are not in Luther's "Ninety-Five Theses" or John Calvin's *Institutes of the Christian Religion.* Luther's theology is complex and difficult to

21. See Hugo Grotius, *The Rights of War and Peace,* trans. A. C. Campbell (Westport, Conn.: Hyperion Press, 1901).
22. Westphalia consisted of two agreements, the treaties of Münster and Osnabrück.

summarize, but its most central tenets were *sola fide* (faith alone), *sola gratia* (grace alone), *sola scriptura* (scripture alone), and *soli deo gloria* (to God alone be the glory). These, Luther argued, were needed to challenge three prevailing circumstances: the understanding that salvation could be attained through works, the notion that the church was central to the believer's salvation, and what Luther thought was the church's excessive understanding of its divinely sanctioned authority.

In two ways, however, these ideas translated into a Protestant desire for independent states. First, because Reformation theology—the *solas*—was unacceptable to the church, leading the pope to condemn it and the emperor to send troops to eradicate it, Protestants had to seek the protection of their local prince or king and grant him the power to enforce religious affairs that the church and the Catholic emperor then possessed. This usurpation of authority aroused further armed hostility from the church, which required further protection, and so on. Because religion was the key area in which princes and kings still lacked sovereignty, control over this matter would complete their portfolio of powers.

Second, Reformation theology itself entailed political tenets that favored the secular rulers. Virtually every Protestant theologian of the time (and ever since) thought that the medieval church's exercise of secular authority was a corrupting overextension of its spiritual function, and that secular rulers, still governed by Christian principles, ought to perform the duties of taxation, raising armies, and all those functions that we now think of as temporal. These tenets made the reformers all the more willing to support the sovereignty of their prince.

Reformation ideas diffused widely, spreading from town to town, to the countryside, to estates and villages, throughout the hundreds of German principalities and kingdoms, as well as to Sweden, the Netherlands, France, and England. Conversion was more common in the cities and among those with commercial interests, but it was far from restricted to these parties, and the relationship between Protestantism and capitalism remains a complicated one. In many cases, political authorities themselves converted to Protestantism, motivated sometimes by conviction, sometimes by the prospect of seizing church lands and tax revenues. But in all cases, the prince's acquisition of authority over church lands, taxes, and other religious matters was only possible because of the social power of converts to Protestantism. These converts formed new congregations, occupied positions of municipal and legislative authority, and, most important, were willing to join the prince's armies in defeating the Catholic powers.

The pattern by which converts allied with the prince, exerting their social power, and the nature of the resulting political settlement with Catholics varied according to locale. The religious map of Germany became checkered, some regions remaining in Catholic hands. In the Protestant lands, princes enthusiastically became sovereign with the support of Protestant congregations. For more than a century, they fought, on and off, with their Catholic neighbors and with the emperor, until they won their uncontested independence in 1648.

In the Netherlands, which, like Germany, was part of the Holy Roman Empire, lower-class Calvinists rebelled against imperial rulers and finally forced reluctant Dutch nobles to ally with them in the cause of independence. In Sweden, like in England, the Reformation came from above, imposed by the king upon the nobility and eventually spreading widely throughout the country. Sweden was already independent when it became officially Protestant, but its Protestantism resulted in an anti-imperial foreign policy and eventual participation in the Thirty Years' War. France, like Sweden, was already an independent sovereign state at the time of its Calvinist Reformation, but unlike Sweden it remained Catholic. The Calvinist Reformation there never succeeded in capturing the state. But the generation of religious wars that the Reformation brought with it did give rise to a new French political party, the *politiques,* who espoused a new foreign-policy doctrine, raison d'état, which advocated resisting the power of the Catholic emperor more aggressively and fighting for an entire Europe of secular, sovereign states.

The new Protestant polities and their allies eventually came to clash throughout the continent in the Thirty Years' War, which began with a spat over religious privileges in Bohemia, was sustained during its first decade by the combatants' religious passion, but eventually sapped its combatants of their incipient religious motivation and lapsed into a decade-long stalemate fought on German soil between France and Sweden and the Habsburgs. This tug-of-war oscillated in momentum first to one side, then to another, but finally resulted in a settlement when the belligerents decided to preserve their existence and their basic strategic goals. In the end, France, Sweden, the Dutch, and the German principalities prevailed, and sovereign statehood was their victors' terms.[23]

The realists or other structuralists would not dispute that the Reformation

---

23. A good history of the Thirty Years' War is Georges Pagès, *The Thirty Years' War,* trans. David Maland and John Hooper (New York: Harper and Row, 1939); for a sampling of

refashioned both souls and politics within principalities and states. But they would be skeptical that it was a necessary event for Westphalia, that it led the rulers to re-envision and fight for their polities' interests. Actually, to speak of a realist account of sovereign statehood may at first seem somewhat misleading, for does not realism assume the existence of sovereign states? Strictly speaking, this is true, but we can nevertheless imagine a "realist-friendly" account of the road to Westphalia, showing that economic, technological, and organizational change was decisive in the development of "proto-states" that were sovereign in many, but not all, respects, and that these entities came to dominate Europe.

There are several versions of this story. Charles Tilly, for instance, sketches a long evolution in which states became the most effective organizations for coercion and the extraction of capital. Other accounts emphasize the role of the landed nobility or the world capitalist system, but, like Tilly's, leave ideas aside.[24] Through the impersonal unfolding of capitalism and monarchy, states formed. And when states became states, they began to act like states. They extended their territory and wealth as they rationally could, sought to eradicate threats, and when there were enough states in the world, they used the classic tool of states—war—to defeat the last threat to the state, the Holy Roman Empire.[25] Westphalia, then, was the culmination of this centuries-long change in organization and economics.

Religion plays little part in this account. At each juncture where a theorist of ideas finds Protestant influence, the realists point to the inexorable logic of economics and arms. To the assertion that the Reformation brought states to want independence, the realists retort that in fact, adolescent states simply grew up and asked for the independence of their adulthood. Against the emphasis on the desire of Protestant states to defeat Catholic authority, the realists insist that states' collective material power had simply overtaken the empire's.

---

scholarly opinion on the war, see Theodore K. Rabb, ed., *The Thirty Years' War: Problems of Motive, Extent, and Effect* (Boston: D. C. Heath, 1946).

24. Charles Tilly, *Coercion, Capital, and European States, A.D. 990–1990* (Oxford: Basil Blackwell, 1992). See also the accounts of Immanuel Wallerstein, *The Modern World-System: Capitalist Agriculture and the Origins of the European World-Economy in the Sixteenth Century* (New York: Academic Press, 1974); Perry Anderson, *Lineages of the Absolute State* (London: Verso, 1979); and Douglass C. North, *Structure and Change in Economic History* (London: W. W. Norton, 1981).

25. On the "imperial overstretch" of the Habsburgs, see Paul Kennedy, *The Rise and Fall of the Great Powers: Economic Change and Military Conflict from 1500 to 2000* (New York: Vintage Books, 1987), 31–73.

An ideas account must concede the validity of significant aspects of the realists' parsimonious tale. States had indeed evolved economically and institutionally long before the Reformation, and it was with their armies that they defeated the Habsburgs. Spain's decline, Sweden's rise, much of the Netherlands' economic growth, had little to do with the Reformation. The last decade of the Thirty Years' War reads like a realist jeremiad, as the terms of settlement constantly shifted with battlefield fortunes.

The realist story, though, falls far short of accounting for Westphalia. Before the Reformation, sovereign states like France existed but did not desire to eradicate Catholic authority, and polities that had the material power to become sovereign states existed but did not seek sovereignty. Without the German Protestants' desire for political protection against the emperor, without the Dutch Calvinists' iron insistence upon independence, without the French Calvinists and the *politique* ideas to which their armed opposition gave rise, without Sweden's devotion to Protestantism, without the weakening of Spain through the Dutch Calvinists' revolt, Westphalia is difficult to imagine.

After Westphalia, the norm of sovereign statehood was indeed practiced. Above all, European states ceased trying to affect the status of religion within other states' borders; an international equivalent of religious liberty was agreed upon (religious liberty within states still had a way to go). And in the settlement of subsequent conflicts such as the Peace of Utrecht in 1713, Westphalia served as a blueprint. Although, as the next sections show, states would later agree upon limits to sovereignty, the constitutional provisions of Westphalia were more fundamental, for they established the state as the legitimate unit of European politics in the first place. With the significant exception of the European Community, this provision of the international constitution is still valid.

Protection of Nations and Minorities: The Road to Versailles

If in the sixteenth and seventeenth centuries it was the new way of worship preached by Luther, Calvin, and their successors that moved Europeans to challenge old structures of authority, then during the nineteenth century, it was surely nationalism, which I define here as the idea that people living together as a nation ought to have their own state.[26] Many nations, mostly in Eastern Europe, indeed defeated their imperial rulers and gained statehood during the nineteenth and early twentieth centuries. But when these conflicts were over, minority peoples often found themselves stranded within the new states, with the prospect of being just as dominated as any nation still ruled by an empire.

Thus Europeans came to demand two different sorts of constitutional provisions during the nineteenth and early twentieth centuries: minority-rights guarantees and national self-determination, which is simply any legal arrangement that allows a nation greater autonomy to govern itself. That every nation should have its own state is only the most extreme form of the principle; other types include limited autonomy within a federal arrangement or merely certain rights or protections for groups within a state. Both were conditions for becoming states, a revision of sovereignty's second face. Minority rights imposed conditions on new entrants to the European system; national self-determination gave captive nations the right to become states.

When, if ever, were these provisions realized? Nationalists first advocated self-determination during the French Revolution, but their efforts failed. After the energy of Napoleon's revolutionary crusade and the nationalism it inspired was spent, conservative monarchs rejected national self-determination and did not consider alternative guarantees of minority rights.[27] They even agreed to a norm that can only be described as anti-self-determination, by which the great powers would act in concert—the Concert of Europe—to suppress nationalist revolts, within or without their territories. The Concert, however, did not last, and by 1822 the great powers no longer mutually viewed this practice as legitimate.[28]

In the latter part of the same century, Europe's great powers fought, not for the last time, over the Balkans, where nations were liberating

26. This is not an exclusive definition of nationalism. The term could also denote the idea, for instance, that a nation that already enjoys a state has a special destiny to conquer or to otherwise attain greatness.

27. An exception to this is Poland, which was given limited rights of self-government within the territory of a larger power. Inis Claude calls this "the first explicit recognition and international guarantee of the rights of national minorities," in *National Minorities: An International Problem* (Cambridge, Mass.: Harvard University Press, 1955), 7.

28. It is arguable that there was something left of the "Concert of Europe ideal" after 1822, possibly until World War I. But it is difficult to hold that there was a mutually recognized norm that allowed intervention against revolution. See F. H. Hinsley, *Power and the Pursuit of Peace: Theory and Practice in the History of Relations Between States* (Cambridge: Cambridge University Press, 1963), 213–38.

themselves from Ottoman rule. At the Congress of Berlin in 1878, the great powers granted statehood to Romania, Serbia, and Montenegro, with the condition that they agree to protect the right to worship of religious minorities. Although Britain, France, and Russia had, in an 1830 protocol, granted independence to Greece on the condition that it protect the religious rights of Turks, while in the 1856 Treaty of Paris following the Crimean War, the great powers had mandated similar conditions on Moldavia and Wallachia, it was not until the 1878 agreement, aimed at protecting Jews in the new states, that minority protection was mutually approved and sanctioned as a normal condition to be placed on new states. Up through the beginning of World War I, great powers maintained this practice, signing several bilateral treaties patterned on 1878. Although minorities were still persecuted, most glaringly the Armenians, whom the Turks massacred in 1896, the great powers nevertheless continued to regard as legitimate the formula of Berlin.

National self-determination, it is commonly thought, triumphed in the settlement of World War I under the sponsorship of Woodrow Wilson and at the eager behest of freshly liberated Eastern European nations. In fact, however, no lasting constitutional provision emerged. National self-determination cannot be found in the League's covenant, and the League's International Commission of Jurists confirmed its illegitimacy in explaining its 1920 ruling that the Aaland Islands could not secede from Finland to join Sweden. Several Eastern European nations, it is true, acquired statehood, but this simply involved granting de jure status to de facto states, which was no departure from Westphalia.

Several provisions to protect minorities, however, were included. Sheer overlapping complexity and strategic bargains left skewed borders and 25 to 30 million minorities within nations, leading the victors to take corrective measures. Borders were drawn around Poland, Yugoslavia, and elsewhere to protect minorities; plebiscites were held in places like Upper Silesia, Belgium, and East Prussia. And the victorious Allies signed treaties with defeated states (Austria, Hungary, Bulgaria, and Turkey) and the new or enlarged states (Poland, Czechoslovakia, Yugoslavia, Rumania, and Greece) that guaranteed the rights of minorities, while including in the League of Nations covenant a provision to guarantee the rights of "racial, religious, or linguistic minorities" that would be enforced through a judicial arbitration system.[29] In addition to providing a criterion for statehood, the

29. Claude, *National Minorities,* 16–28.

treaty system's regular monitoring function served as a restriction of state sovereignty, at least until Hitler took power, when it finally ceased to function. During its actual operation, the system amounted to a revision of sovereignty's third face, the prerogatives of states, the legitimate polities.

Why did minority treaties come to be accepted while national self-determination came to be rejected? Both outcomes, to the realist, were in states' strategic interests. At the Congress of Vienna, the conservative monarchists—Prince Metternich of Austria; Lord Castlereagh, the foreign minister of Britain; Talleyrand of France; and Czar Alexander I of Russia—wanted to contain France, which had threatened their past existence, and suppress the nationalist revolutionary fervor unleashed by Napoleon's European conquests, which would threaten their future existence. Thus they rejected national self-determination and for a short time practiced collectively approved intervention against revolution, until Castlereagh died and was replaced by Canning, whose strategic vision was noninvolvement on the continent.

Can an ideas account add to or improve upon the realist account of this outcome? It might focus on the ideas of monarchs and their domestic supporters, pointing to their conservativism. But while their ideology no doubt influenced their approach, it did not give them an interest substantially different from one that a realist might predict. They wanted primarily the protection of their regimes from threats that might weaken it, from within and without. And this explains not only why they would not countenance a norm protecting nations or minorities, but also why they temporarily adopted an interventionist norm. The real claim of an ideas account is that ideas—nationalism or liberalism—were not yet strong enough to elicit national self-determination or minority rights as an international constitutional provision. This claim, though, cannot be sustained by looking at 1815, but only by showing that in a later power shift in which a norm protecting minorities did result, liberalism had grown and was influential.

Such a power shift would occur in the Russo-Turkish War of 1878. Indeed, both nationalism and sympathy for minority rights had grown remarkably, especially in the Western liberal states, Britain and France. But behind the minority-protection treaties, the realist would find less sublime motives. The territory of Russia, Austria, and the Ottoman Empire bordered the Balkan region, as did the vital trade routes of Britain and France. Each power was intensely concerned with the encroachments of the other in the region; each of them welcomed any pretext for the well-placed intervention; and their common involvement in the Crimean War and the settlement of the Russo-Turkish War at the Congress of Berlin gave each of them an opportunity to take for themselves a clause in the treaty that would allow for such action.

The trouble with such a realist explanation is that it does not account well for the pattern of agreements that the powers actually signed. Unlike previous protection treaties, in which a particular power aimed at a gain in a particular region, these were multilateral and the powers understood them to govern the international system.[30] Bilateral treaties, allowing focused application and unilateral enforcement, were most plausibly great-power instruments. On some occasions, the great powers indeed applied threats of force or diplomatic pressure when egregious violations of religious freedom had occurred. Evidence also exists that people and governments within Western states, especially Britain, developed a conscience sympathetic to religious freedom and ready to be plucked when religious minorities were massacred in Balkan wars of liberation.[31] In this way, identities were changed.

In 1914, nationalism in the Balkans was the spark, if not a chief cause, of the next European general crisis, World War I. Since the nineteenth century, both nationalism and liberalism had continued to grow, and the former had helped bring about the general clamor for statehood in Eastern Europe at the end of the war. By the end of the war, the Western Allies were not only willing to grant Eastern European nations statehood, they were advocating a lasting principle of self-determination.

For the realist, the most important aspect of this advocacy was its timing. Both the United States and Britain failed to advocate the liberation of nations within the Austro-Hungarian conglomerate until it was clearly breaking up. The reason was their belief that they could induce the old Habsburg dynasty into signing a separate peace, thereby quickening the pace toward victory. In the final settlement, the Allies rejected self-determination, largely on account of realist interests in France, which wanted strong allies against Germany in the east and feared that self-determination would only weaken them. The effort to protect minorities was also compromised by strategic necessity: large groups of Germans were stranded in Poland, Czechoslovakia, and France; the province of

30. On the consensus surrounding the Congress of Berlin, see Raymond Pearson, *National Minorities in Eastern Europe, 1848–1945* (London: Macmillan, 1983), 133.

31. C. A. Macartney, *National Minorities in Eastern Europe, 1848–1945* (London: Russell and Russell, 1968), 164.

Alsace-Lorraine was taken by France without a plebiscite; the Danzig Corridor was given to Poland without consulting its inhabitants; and several other regions were left within foreign borders that they did not choose.[32]

Yet despite the agreements' failure to render self-determination a lasting norm, many important provisions for minorities were incorporated into the treaty. Any assessment must begin with an appreciation of the difficulty of the task: national peoples and ethnic groups overlapped so much and were so mixed that any settlement would have left a great number of them unsatisfied. Despite this complexity, a large number of borders were drawn and plebiscites held in order to accommodate national groupings. In several instances, they countered what seemed to be the strategic interests of the Western powers.[33]

Who were the couriers of these liberal ideas? How were they socially empowered? Woodrow Wilson, of course, was the most enthusiastic. In his plan to bring about a revolution in international affairs, for which he thought he had a popular mandate, Wilson considered self-determination a central tenet. He wanted to leave "no odor" of the Treaty of Vienna, which had rejected the aspirations of national peoples in its enthusiasm for balance-of-power politics.[34] He was also deeply committed to the minority-protection system and campaigned to see it realized.

32. On the content and negotiation of Versailles, see "The Peace Settlement of Versailles," in *The New Cambridge Modern History,* vol. 12, ed. C. L. Mowat (Cambridge: Cambridge University Press, 1968), 209–41; Alan Sharpe, "Britain and the Protection of Minorities at the Paris Peace Conference, 1919," in *Minorities in History,* ed. A. C. Hepburn (New York: St. Martin's Press, 1979), 170–89; Victor S. Mamatey, *The United States and East Central Europe, 1914–1918* (London: Kennikat Press, 1972); Arthur Walworth, *America's Moment: 1918* (New York: W. W. Norton, 1977); Arno J. Mayer, *Political Origins of the New Diplomacy* (New Haven: Yale University Press, 1958); Arno J. Mayer, *Politics and Diplomacy of Peacemaking* (New York: Alfred A. Knopf, 1967).

33. For instance, although it was in the interests of the victors to have as strong a Poland as possible, Lloyd George insisted upon plebiscites in the districts of Upper Silesia, Allenstein, and Marienwerderland, which could easily have gone to Poland. And, despite Clemenceau's protests, it was agreed that Western Germany's Saar Valley would be allowed a plebiscite in fifteen years, rather than being annexed by France or remaining under indefinite Allied control. Beyond this, many other plebiscites were held and nationalities placed in a way that did not simply reflect Allied strategy or local power. See "Peace Settlement of Versailles," 200, 215, 217, 223.

34. In his "Peace Without Victory" speech to the American Congress on 22 January 1917, Woodrow Wilson spoke of the principle, and a year later, he included self-determination for many of Eastern Europe's peoples in his famous statement of war aims, the Fourteen Points. See Mamatey, *United States and East Central Europe,* 49.

But Wilson was only one man; he needed allies. Of course, part of his success resulted from a starkly realist factor: the United States was now the strongest state on earth, and it had provided vital force in winning the Great War. Now, European states relied on it to guarantee the settlement. But Wilson also had ideological allies at many levels. Among the heads of state, British prime minister David Lloyd George was the most sympathetic. Although not as enthusiastic about the League of Nations, and more strongly in favor of punishing Germany than was Wilson, Lloyd George was nevertheless enthusiastic about both self-determination and the minority-treaty system. In the negotiations over Poland, he in fact fought even harder than Wilson for many plebiscites.

Heads of state were also supported at the conference by entourages of intellectuals who helped lay the groundwork for self-determination through behind-the-scenes advocacy and extensive research into the situations of various nationalities.[35] Aside from these central elites, Wilson was assisted—socially empowered—by publics, parties, and lobbyists. In Italy, he appealed to the Italian people to support his program on self-determination, an effort that failed to modify Italian borders but that awakened the negotiators in Paris to the strength of public passions. In various Western states, he was also assisted by what Arno Mayer calls the "forces of movement," political parties, sections of parties, and coalitions between parties such as the United Democratic Coalition in Britain, which had decided to favor progressive war aims in 1917, including self-determination for Europe's captive states. Although these parties generally suffered defeats just before the negotiations, they still provided political support for advocates of liberalism at the peace conference.[36] Finally, we should not overlook the role of transnational networks of interests, including representatives of the Eastern European nations who developed contacts in Western states during the war, and Jewish lobbies that worked hard for the minority-treaty system.

On the question of national self-determination, the outcome for ideas is

---

35. Wilson was assisted by a commission headed by Colonel Edward House. In Britain, Sir Robert Cecil, Lloyd George's key assistant at the Versailles Conference, was a strong advocate of self-determination, and the Political Intelligence Division under Sir James Headlam-Morley promoted the minority treaty system tirelessly. See Mamatey, *United States and East Central Europe;* and Sharpe, "Britain and the Protection of Minorities." Even in France, the intellectuals on the Comité d'Études of the Ministry of Foreign Affairs mitigated Clemenceau's opposition to self-determination. See Kalevi J. Holsti, *Peace and War: Armed Conflicts and International Order, 1948–1989* (Cambridge: Cambridge University Press, 1991), 192.

36. See Mayer, *Political Origins of the New Diplomacy.*

at best indeterminate. An ideas account would claim that sympathy for nationalism was not strong enough in the victor states to overcome Clemenceau's opposition, but since self-determination was advocated forcefully both at the bargaining table and in the public discussion, one must ask how strong ideas must become before they can overcome realist considerations. This we cannot know unless a successful outcome occurs. The verdict for ideas here is ambiguous at best, negative at worst. The minority treaties, however, are hard to conceive without the role of liberal ideas.

The Freeing of Colonies

Although self-determination was rejected at Versailles, later in the century, in a different locale, in a different context, it would finally win acceptance. In 1960, the United Nations declared colonies free: "All peoples have the right to self-determination," and "inadequacy of political, economic, and social and educational preparedness should never serve as a pretext for delaying independence." Colonialism was condemned as "alien subjugation, domination, and exploitation . . . a denial of fundamental human rights."[37] In roughly the decade surrounding 1960, the colonial powers also granted independence to the preponderance of their remaining colonies. The British spurt began in 1957 with the release of Ghana. By 1960, France admitted the sovereign rights of its sub-Saharan colonies, and not long after, of all of the rest.[38] Like Westphalia, the transition was not neat: colonies had already been released before this period and would trickle into independence during the next two decades. But in the eyes of the United Nations and the vast majority of its member states, including now the former colonial powers, for a state to have governing authority over a colony was illegitimate; decolonization was now a provision of the international constitution, a revision of the second face of sovereignty, the terms upon which polities could become states.

In 1885 it was quite different. At the Berlin Conference, where Bismarck had assembled the colonial powers to settle the map of Africa and set the

---

37. UN General Assembly Resolution 1514 (XV), 14 December 1960.

38. David Strang points out the concentrated time period in which colonies were released in quantitative terms in "Global Patterns of Decolonization, 1500–1987," *International Studies Quarterly* 35 (1991): 429–54.

ground rules for colonialism, they espoused a paternal colonial ideal. The world was divided into two kinds of entities: civilized European states, and barbarian peoples who could not participate as equal law-abiding members of the international community until they had learned the art of governing. Such was the powers' "standard of civilization," which specified who could be a state and who could not.[39]

At the end of World War I, after the colonial states had suffered massive losses in armies, economy, and population, they decided to retain their colonies, but they relaxed their approach to self-government somewhat by creating a mandate system making it possible for some of the more advanced colonies to move toward independence under colonial "stewardship." Thus, under the general principle of self-determination, article 22 of the League covenant prescribed a mandate system in which colonies were to be held under a "sacred trust of civilization" and divided up into categories, A, B, and C, according to their level of development and prospect of becoming a viable independent state.[40] The mandate system legitimated an aspiration for some colonies under some circumstances and represented an advance in thinking on the issue of self-government, but in terms of actual self-governance or changes in the international constitution, it changed little. No independence was granted, no authority transferred.[41]

At the end of World War II, Britain and France had once again lost military and economic might. Would they keep their colonies? Britain's decision to grant independence to its largest colony, India, was a major colonial concession, but aside from this, the colonial powers retained virtually all of their empires as well as their tutelary justification. The UN charter endorsed self-determination but also noted in article 73 that regions not ready for self-government would be treated as a "sacred trust." And they

39. See Gerrit Gong, *The Standard of "Civilization" in International Society* (Oxford: Clarendon Press, 1984).

40. William Roger Louis explains it well: "The colonial settlement of 1919 in effect defined three classifications of mankind: the 'A' peoples of the Middle East, who in a relatively short time would be able 'to stand alone'; the tribal 'B' peoples of tropical Africa, who would require an indefinite number of years or decades of economic and political advancement under European tutelage; and the 'C' 'primitive' peoples of the Pacific and the 'hottentots' of South West Africa, who probably would remain European subjects for a period of centuries, if not forever." "The Era of the Mandates System and the Non-European World," in *The Expansion of International Society*, ed. Hedley Bull and Adam Watson (Oxford: Claredon Press, 1984), 201.

41. On the history of the mandate system, see Quincy Wright's voluminous *Mandates Under the League of Nations* (Chicago: University of Chicago Press, 1930).

regarded the capacity for self-government as being decades away.

It is remarkable, then, that both Britain and France almost completely reversed their approach to their colonies within only fifteen years. The relative importance of ideas and material power at the end of the World Wars is indeterminate: one could argue both that the colonial powers had the resources to hold onto their colonies while still deriving profit from them, and that ideas were simply not strong enough to change their minds about the legitimacy of their colonies. It is between 1945 and 1960, rather, that we must look for evidence of change, both in ideas and in material power. I concentrate mostly on the case of Britain and less on France, for it is these powers that set the trend and on which we have the best information.

For the realist, the fact that the United Nations and the colonialists came to declare colonialism illegitimate is not what is important. These were only legitimations for strategic retreat, a retreat decided upon when the colonies had come to be, on balance, burdensome cargo, rather than a source of booty. They were "too weak," Hedley Bull writes, "to maintain old kinds of dominance."[42] The growing costs of colonies, in fact, was a trend that had begun during the Great Depression, when the metropolitan powers not only found their strength sapped, but also found the profitability of their empires eroded by an unfavorable alteration in the terms of trade.[43] After the war, the argument runs, Britain and France were militarily and economically weary, and their hopes for a quick and steady recovery faded. Only with voluminous infusions of cash from the United States could they avoid collapse. As a result, "it came to be questioned whether colonial dependencies were a source of material gain: the old liberal thesis, that the true interests of the metropolitan peoples lay in nonintervention and avoidance of empire, was revived, and appeared to be confirmed by the economic triumphs of Germany and Japan, achieved without military pre-eminence of colonies."[44]

Military struggles with their colonies also weakened the will and resources of metropolitan powers. This was especially true for France, which suffered humiliating defeats in Indochina and Algeria, but it was

42. Hedley Bull, "The Revolt of the West," in Bull and Watson, *Expansion of International Society*, 224.

43. J. D. Hargreaves, *Decolonization in Africa* (London: Longman, 1988), 32–48.

44. Bull, "The Revolt of the West," 224–25. On the growing perception that colonies were too economically burdensome, see R. F. Holland, *European Decolonization 1918–1981: An Introductory Survey* (London: Macmillan, 1985).

also the case for Britain, whose involvement in the 1956 Suez Crisis severely tarnished its image in the Third World. The debacle in Egypt brought to the prime ministership Harold Macmillan, who was more sympathetic to decolonization than his predecessor, Anthony Eden.

The international power equilibrium was also crucial. In several respects, the rise of the Cold War aided the colonies against their masters. First, the Soviet Union, now a superpower, established alliances with the Third World against the West. Second, the competition between the West and the Soviet Union for the favor of the Third World allowed the colonies to play the two camps against each other. And finally, the United States, on whom the colonizers depended for their security needs, pressured them to decolonize, in part to open up new markets.

It cannot be disputed that the perception of relative decline contributed to the decision for decolonization. Yet, there are several flaws in such an explanation. For instance, many in the upper echelons of foreign policy in Britain and France were firmly committed to their respective colonial empires well into the 1950s, and in both parliaments, colonialism still had firm support. Especially in France, colonies were seen as a vital sign of national greatness.[45] Although some questioned the cost, the view that colonies were unsustainable was hardly dominant, and economic recovery during the 1950s helped diminish the sense of crisis. And if colonies had clearly become too costly, it is also not clear why the metropolitan powers, again, especially France, fought costly wars to keep them. For that matter, since only a few colonies had the ability to put up a fight, why not keep the rest, which could be easily dominated?

While important to decolonization, realist factors are hardly sufficient for explaining it. As Robert Jackson insightfully argues, what realists have the most trouble explaining is the timing of decolonization.[46] If it was material power that was most at stake, then we would expect decolonization to be piecemeal and gradual, independence given to each colony as it became too costly, with perhaps an accompanying rationalization stating that it was now in fact ready for independence. Yet liberation came in a sweeping moment, suddenly and comprehensively.

Within metropolitan societies, equality came to be strongly advocated by several important factions, a product of changing identities. From

45. Tony Smith, "A Comparative Study of French and British Decolonization," *Comparative Studies in Society and History* 20 (1978): 70–102.

46. Robert Jackson, "Weight of Ideas in Decolonization: Normative Change in International Relations," in Goldstein and Keohane, *Ideas and Foreign Policy*, 111–38.

1945 to 1951, the Labor Party held power in Britain and, although not all Laborites favored decolonization, the party generally led opinion toward equality, both domestically and within the empire. Although in both Britain and France decolonization occurred under conservative governments, in Britain the Labor Party helped to change opinion toward it. In addition, as Robert Jackson points out, in the 1950s many domestic activists who had not been active in the 1930s began to pressure elites. Opposition to colonialism was not totally new among intellectuals and activists, but in the early 1950s, it reached a significantly larger scale.[47] World War II itself was significant for discrediting the old "sacred trust of civilization" justification for trusteeship. The experience of Nazism, for instance, smeared racial doctrines in a way that few protests from the colonies themselves ever could have.[48]

In France the experience of fighting for the empire in Algeria in the late 1950s did much to rob colonialism of its allure. More than simply weakening the French military, it touched off great division and protest within French society, contributing to the fall of the Fourth Republic and Charles DeGaulle's rise to power, which brought rapid decolonization. Again, the defeat of the French military forces hardly meant that France did not have the capacity to hold on to her colonies elsewhere. But at home, where society had fractured between opponents of the war and the army, who favored the war and opposed the republic's constitution altogether, the war could not be politically sustained.[49]

As for the role of the United States, the notion that it was only economic or strategic power that led the country to pressure its allies, Britain and France, to decolonize, is inadequate. The source of the United States's leverage was its position as the superpower that opposed the Soviet Union. But the fact that it used power for decolonization resulted not just from its desire for free trade, but also from its commitment to self-determination, dating back to its own revolution and reinforced by Woodrow Wilson. The country's own struggles with civil rights during the 1950s also strengthened its commitment to global racial equality.[50]

47. Neta Crawford, "Decolonization As an International Norm: The Evolution of Practices, Arguments, and Beliefs," in *Emerging Norms of Justified Intervention,* ed. Laura Reed and Carl Kaysen (Cambridge, Mass.: American Academy of Arts and Sciences, 1993), 37–62.

48. R. J. Vincent, "Racial Equality," in Bull and Watson, *Expansion of International Society,* 252.

49. On the role of political parties and the Algeria conflict, see Miles Kahler, *Decolonization in Britain and France: The Domestic Consequences of International Relations* (Princeton: Princeton University Press, 1984).

50. See Jackson, "Weight of Ideas in Decolonization," 128–29, 136.

One cannot ignore growing support for independence within the colonies, either. Ferment for separation grew as the colonized became more imbued with European ideas of nationalism and self-determination. Most of the colonial nationalist leaders had been educated in European universities, where they had become persuaded that the European model of the state was their own country's future. Thousands of colonial soldiers who had fought for the Allies in World War II also came back to Africa as proponents of independence. Sociologist David Strang shows that colonies that were the most self-governing and that had the highest proportion of European settlers were more likely to seek and gain independence, evidence that they had learned Western patterns of governance.[51]

Finally, criticism from the United Nations and other international organizations most likely made a difference as well. During the 1950s, Third World states, which were being admitted in increasing numbers to the United Nations and that organized themselves into the Afro-Asian bloc, the Non-Aligned Movement, and the Group of 77, spoke out more and more strongly. This overhauling of international discourse resonated deeply in imperial domestic societies.[52] Whereas in the early 1950s France was able to quiet UN debate over the fate of Morocco, as the decade progressed, the Third World's voice in international organizations grew ever louder and more irrepressible.

Conclusion

What can we generally say about ideas and the evolution of sovereignty? In all cases, it took both a shift in material power and the spread of intellectual ideas to produce changes in the constitution of international relations. War, or a sharp change in relative material power, was necessary not only to defeat resisters of change but to strengthen its proponents. However, we should not look at these "general crises" solely as shifts in economic and military fortunes, for often the crises themselves were agents of change in ideas. In each case, war also had an effect on ideas about justice.

51. See David Strang, "From Dependency to Sovereignty: An Event History Analysis of Decolonization," *American Sociological Review* 35 (1990): 854–56.
52. Bull, "The Revolt of the West," 227.

The razed villages and scorched fields of the Thirty Years' War led leaders and philosophers of the time to favor a settlement that would make religion no longer a matter of international contention, a matter that could only be fought to the death. In World War I, the adoption of self-determination as a war aim by the Allies gave the idea support both in Eastern Europe and among Western publics. World War II helped to create colonial nationalism; France's colonial wars in Indochina and Algeria brought many French to have greater moral sympathy for colonial independence.

More generally, without the Reformation, the revolution at Westphalia would not have occurred. Without growing liberalism, the minority treaties would never have come about. Without anticolonial ideas, colonial independence would not have resulted. In each case, revolutionary ideas arose that rejected the existing terms of authority, converted hearers into adherents, led adherents to make speeches, write pamphlets, join protests, vote, and take up arms against the old order's defenders, and finally to overthrow the old order itself. International constitutions, then, are the products of the contradictions created by iconoclastic ideas about legitimate authority.

Different ideas operated in different historical contexts and wielded different kinds of power. May we conclude anything generally about the historical direction of these revolutions in sovereignty? With due caution, we may indeed discern a telos in the progression of the constitutions—a telos of liberalism. Westphalia protected the religious practice of a state against outside intervention, although it did little to guarantee freedom of worship for the dissenting individual. Minority treaties advanced religious freedom by seeking to protect the rights to worship of minorities in Eastern Europe. The norm of colonial independence provided freedom from imperial control for colonial peoples. And today, the norm of humanitarian intervention asserts protection for human rights in potentially any state.

Any celebration of moral progress, however, must be tempered by the memory of the moral cost at which new constitutions have come, for revolutions in sovereignty have typically arrived on the heels of the worst sort of moral disasters: the death of at least a quarter of the German population in the Thirty Years' War, the World Wars and the Holocaust of the twentieth century, the costs and destruction of the Cold War.

2

Pan-Islamism, State Sovereignty, and International Organization

Sohail H. Hashmi

Of the many forces operating in international politics today, perhaps the most devalued and least studied is religion. In the vast literature on sovereignty in particular, works focusing on the role of religious ideologies in either buttressing or undermining the legitimacy and power of the sovereign state are rare indeed. This scholarly neglect belies the increasingly important and assertive role that religious ideologies and organized religious movements play in the domestic as well as the international politics of every region in the world. One need only consider the prominent role of the Catholic Church in influencing the antiauthoritarian movements in Latin America and Eastern Europe, the religious enmities and solidarities enormously complicating the Balkans conflict, the role of expatriate Hindu groups in financing and directing the Hindu nationalist movement in India, and, of course, the turbulent politics of Islam in the modern world.

The paucity of studies of the religious impact on contemporary international politics—and on issues of sovereignty, specifically—is understandable in light of the historical origins of the sovereign nation-state in

European practice and theory. For the emergence of the modern nation-state occurred precisely through the diminution and ultimately the elimination of the idea of the *civitas dei,* the united community of Christians under the authority of the church and its temporal arm, the Holy Roman emperor. As J. N. Figgis has observed: "Christendom, the union of various flocks under one shepherd with divine claims, divine origins, and divine sovereignty, had to be transformed into Europe, the habitat of competing sects and compact nations, before the conditions of modern politics arose."[1] But once this transformation had been achieved, the religious factor in international relations receded to the periphery of statecraft and state theory.

For many students of contemporary Islamic political thought, the process of European evolution is evident in the twentieth-century evolution of the Muslim world. The Muslim world, in its attempts to reconcile traditional societies with the conditions of modernity, has replicated—willingly or unwillingly—the Western model. It has in fact and in theory become "the habitat of competing sects and compact nations." As in Europe, so in the Muslim world, according to this view, "premodern" religious universalist aspirations are loath to vanish altogether and indeed resurface periodically before they too are ultimately marginalized.[2] These views were certainly the scholarly consensus from the end of World War I until the late 1970s. The Iranian Revolution, and the Islamic resurgence of which it was the most dramatic manifestation, has necessitated a reappraisal.

This chapter examines challenges to the sovereign nation-state emerging from Islamic political thought. It argues that while the notion of state sovereignty has been embraced as the juridical basis for international relations among Muslim states, the norms of sovereign statehood have yet to be assimilated in either Islamic political thought or Islamic behavior. Islam continues to be used in a number of different ways that serve to undermine the essential norms of external state sovereignty. In particular, our focus here will be upon challenges to the contemporary state system that arise from the Islamic ideal of the single, unified Muslim community. How are pan-Islamic ideologies manifested today, and how have they pressured

1. J. N. Figgis, *Political Thought from Gerson to Grotius: 1414–1625* (Cambridge: Cambridge University Press, 1923), 21.
2. See, for example, T. Cuyler Young, "Pan-Islamism in the Modern World: Solidarity and Conflict Among Muslim Countries," in *Islam and International Relations,* ed. J. Harris Proctor (New York: Praeger, 1965), 205.

Muslim states toward the evolution of transnational, if not yet supranational, international institutions?

Since the emergence of Muslim states after World War II, pan-Islamic ideologies have been and are currently being used to fulfill a number of instrumental ends, each of which we shall consider in this study. First, they are used to generate alliances by states threatened by a hostile or potentially hostile regional milieu, the most prominent example being that of Pakistan in the first decade of its existence. Second, they are used to legitimate traditional regimes against domestic and foreign challenges, the most prominent example being Saudi Arabia's financial support of international Islamic organizations and Islamic groups scattered from the Middle East to South and Southeast Asia. Third, they are used to justify the export of revolutionary movements beyond state borders, the most obvious example being the case of Iran, whose government has actively supported or morally bolstered militant Islamic groups throughout the Muslim world.

While some of these methods can be seen as attempts to serve various state interests and to bolster the power of the state, others must be considered as emerging from Islamic ideology itself. In other words, the instrumental explanation is only a partial explanation of the continuing presence of pan-Islamic urges in international politics. Such explanations cannot adequately account for the ideational motivations underlying many of the challenges to the sovereign state. In short, the idea of the unified Muslim community that transcends state borders and challenges conceptions of state sovereignty remains very much a point of discussion and debate for Muslim theorists and very much an aspiration for Muslim activists, for reasons intrinsic to Islamic ethics. The fact that the sovereign state would be challenged on ethical grounds is inevitable, given the explicit moral value that the Qur'an invests in the unified Muslim community and the condemnation it reserves for those who favor any moral worth to essentially linguistic, tribal, or ethnic attributes.

Pan-Islamism and Islamic Political Thought

The evolution of European thought to accommodate the emergence of distinct territorial units, sovereign and independent in their domestic and international relations, was neither swift nor continuous. As F. H. Hinsley has chronicled, for centuries after the de facto emergence of the European state system, political and legal theorists were loath to abandon the notion of the essential unity of Christendom.[3] The comparison with the current controversies in the Muslim world is indeed striking, although, as we shall have occasion to see, it should not be stretched too far. The aftermath of the disintegration of the Ottoman Empire in the early twentieth century and the Soviet empire in the late twentieth century, along with the retreat of British, French, Italian, Spanish, and Dutch colonialism in between, has resulted in the emergence of some fifty sovereign states in which Muslims constitute the majority population. These states, without exception, have acceded to the principles and conditions of the contemporary sovereign-state system. All of them, for example, are members of the United Nations.

Thus the Muslim peoples have by no means departed from the traditional pattern of postcolonial Third World states; instead of rejecting the imposed territorial divisions of the colonial powers, they appear to have embraced them as the organizing principles of modern political life.[4]

And yet challenges to the sovereignty and to the very legitimacy of the Muslim states had begun to emerge even before they were born and continue unabated to this day. The challenges were logical, given the historical conditions for the emergence of the states, that is, the strong involvement of colonial powers in the dismemberment of Muslim empires and their promotion of secular, nationalist identities and political elites. The resulting stigma attached to the state led inevitably to attempts at "reversing" the colonial legacy through supranational unity. In the Arab world, these attempts were manifested in the emergence of two sometimes complementary, sometimes opposed movements, pan-Arabism and pan-Islamism. Pan-Arabism witnessed its heyday in the late 1950s and early 1960s, and finally met its demise in the late 1960s. The abject failure of pan-Arabist schemes could not but give impetus to its rival supranationalist ideology, pan-Islamism. The revival and strengthening of Islamic movements in the Middle East and throughout the Muslim world was very much related to the inability of secular Muslim states to deliver either political stability and economic development at home or progress on Islamic issues abroad.

---

3. F. H. Hinsley, *Sovereignty,* 2d ed. (Cambridge: Cambridge University Press, 1986), 168.
4. This is the argument advanced at length by James Piscatori in *Islam in a World of Nation-States* (Cambridge: Cambridge University Press, 1986).

Political and economic explanations of the Islamic-oriented challenges to the sovereign state are, however, only partially correct. They seriously diminish the importance of the ideational factor underlying the Islamic challenge to the contemporary state system, the factor that gives these religiously motivated attacks more universal and broad-based appeal than pan-Arabism or other secular, nationalist ideologies have been able to generate. State sovereignty, simply put, is perceived as representing a fundamental challenge to certain core ethical values of the Islamic tradition, one of the principal being the idea that Muslims belong to a single universal community endowed with moral purpose—the *umma* referred to by the Qur'an.

The umma as a unified political community of the faithful ceased to exist in reality within decades of the Prophet Muhammad's death in 632 C.E. The fractured nature of the political community was, however, only gradually absorbed into juristic elaborations of Islamic constitutional law. Centuries after the umma had been divided along a number of confessional and political lines, jurists such as al-Mawardi (d. 1058) and Ibn Jamaʿa (d. 1333) continued to insist on the legitimacy of a unitary caliphate to govern the entirety of the Muslim community. Only in the fourteenth century, in the writings of Ibn Taymiyya (d. 1328), and subsequently in the works of Ibn Khaldun (d. 1406), do we find attempts to reconcile the historically fractured state of the Muslim umma with the political theory of the caliphate. Nevertheless, the legal reinterpretation of the caliphal institution could not alter the essence of the ethical ideal. As a normative goal, the umma paradigm, as outlined by the Qur'an and as realized under the Prophet's charismatic leadership, has remained a goal that could never quite be renounced.

The reasons are intrinsic to Qur'anic ethics. Several verses refer to the Muslims as constituting a single community. Others warn against the dangers of fragmentation: "And hold fast, all together, by the rope which God [stretches out for you] and be not divided among yourselves" (3:103). "Be not like those who are divided against themselves and fall into disputations after receiving clear signs. For them is a dreadful penalty" (3:105).

Modernist interpretations of these verses in the age of the nation-state have assigned exclusively spiritual and cultural significance to the concept of the umma, removing from it any effective political content. Instead, in their attempt to reconcile the reality of existing states with Qur'anic injunctions, the modernists invariably focus on other verses that they claim establish the legitimacy of a plurality of Muslim states: "Had God willed He could have made you one community. But that He may try you by that which He has given you [He has made you as you are]. So strive as in a race in all the virtues" (5:48). This verse, and several others that refer to the disunity of mankind on the issue of faith in God as being God's will, are frequently cited in the modernist literature as Qur'anic proof-texts for legitimate political divisions. Yet those who make this claim cannot escape the obvious fact that each of these verses refers to the division of mankind along confessional and not political lines. One leading writer, Mohammad Talaat al-Ghunaimi, comes to precisely this conclusion: "It may be argued that the oneness or division referred to in these verses relates to religion. But if we consider the close and indispensable relation between the religious and the political in the Islamic theory we will come to the conclusion that the ideas expressed by the said verses apply to political aspects as well. Thereby the verses postulate the division of the world community into separate political communities as the normal state."

So far, al-Ghunaimi's argument is theoretically sound. The Qur'anic verses obviously imply the political division of mankind as a consequence of religious differences. However, al-Ghunaimi continues in the next sentence to argue: "If Islam tolerates the division of the Islamic community into different states, Islam, a fortiori, must accept the division of the world community among different states."[5] The last sentence is particularly indicative of the strained logic that characterizes much of the modernist discourse. Nothing in the verses cited by al-Ghunaimi provides support for his claim that the Qur'an accepts the division of the Islamic community into different political entities. Indeed, the verses in their proper context are intended only to absolve the Prophet and the Muslim community as a whole for the failure of earlier scripturaries to heed Islam's universalist appeals. Clearly implicit in the verses is the view that while the religious plurality of mankind is God's will, the unity of mankind within the Muslim umma is God's true purpose.

The problems inherent in his analysis are recognized by al-Ghunaimi himself. Toward the conclusion of his work, he writes that "Islam assumes a certain degree of solidarity among the Islamic states. . . . We believe that Islam binds Islamic states together in some sort of commonwealth, not excluding any stronger form of federation or unity as circumstances may

---

5. Mohammad Talaat al-Ghunaimi, *The Muslim Conception of International Law and the Western Approach* (The Hague: Martinus Nijhoff, 1968), 195.

necessitate for the welfare of the faith."[6] Thus even the modernist attempt at legitimating the present division of the Muslim world into sovereign states is ultimately qualified by the recognition that the nation-state cannot be embraced as the summum bonum of Islamic political life. In other words, even the modernists must acknowledge that Muslim states should constitute in some form a separate community of states within the international system of sovereign states. This subsystem should be governed by Islamic ethical principles of solidarity and cooperation among Muslim peoples, regardless of their political arrangements. The end result of such concessions is to undermine the very concept that the modernists espouse: the compatibility of sovereign states with Islamic ethics and law.

In addition to its Qur'anic bases, the ideal of a unified Muslim community finds expression in the Prophetic traditions (*hadith*). The *hadith* literature has been challenged for its authenticity throughout Islamic history, and traditions dealing with political issues have in particular been the focus of Muslim modernist apologetics or of rejection. These challenges and reinterpretations have, however, generally failed to alter the essential conception of the umma as representing a single Muslim community. The reasons again stem from fundamental causes. The essence of the Prophet's mission was to reform the tribal loyalties and racial barriers that underlay pre-Islamic Arabian society. Outside the Prophet's own family and immediate circle, the earliest converts to Islam were the Meccan underclass, that is, members of the less-distinguished tribes, foreigners, and slaves. Islam's appeal to these people lay precisely in its transcendence of tribal, class, and racial divisions.

When the Prophet relocated from Mecca to Medina in 622 C.E., he contracted an agreement with the tribes of Medina that established the political and social basis for the nascent Islamic state. The first clause of this so-called Constitution of Medina declared the Muslims to be "a single umma apart from all other men."[7] This statement was intended on the one hand to unite the Muslim migrants with the local Medinan inhabitants under the leadership of the Prophet, and on the other hand to establish the only relevant source of identity as religious faith. The Jewish tribes of Medina were recognized under this agreement as representing a separate umma of their own in alliance with the Muslims.

This original "social contract" established the pattern of Muslim relations

6. Al-Ghunaimi, *Muslim Conception of International Law,* 206–7.
7. For the text of the Constitution of Medina, see Ibn Ishaq, *The Life of Muhammad,* trans. Alfred Guillaume (Karachi: Oxford University Press, 1967), 231–33.

with non-Muslims that characterized Muslim states well into the late nineteenth century. The original model was replicated on much larger scales as Muslim empires were consolidated in the Middle East and South Asia. The Ottoman Empire, for example, officially recognized separate *millets* of non-Muslim communities that enjoyed a sphere of political and legal autonomy within the Ottoman provinces. The Muslims, of course, were all viewed as subjects of the Ottoman state irrespective of ethnic or racial background. It was the decline and ultimate fall of this Ottoman model that unleashed the state of anarchy that characterizes Islamic political thought today.

Pan-Islamism As Islamic Solidarity

In the first three decades of the twentieth century, as the Indian independence movement began in earnest, the largest Muslim population in the world, that of India, was at best ambivalent concerning its nationalist aspirations. The central issue agitating Indian Muslims was not the future independence of India, but the integrity of the Ottoman Empire and the preservation of the symbol of Muslim unity, the caliphate. These twin concerns had animated the earlier opposition of most of the Indian Muslim elite to the Arab revolt against the Ottomans. The leaders of this revolt, Sharif Husain (the Ottoman governor of the Hijaz) and his sons, were generally perceived and criticized as puppets being manipulated by the British for the destruction of the Ottoman Empire.

The defeat of Turkey by the Allies and the imposition of the Treaty of Sèvres brought the Indian agitation on the caliphate to a climax. In 1919 began the Khilafat movement, largely under the direction of the Oxford-educated journalist Muhammad ʿAli. The following year he led a deputation to London, where, in meetings with British prime minister David Lloyd George, he argued for the Turkish caliph's retention of sovereignty over the Arabian peninsula, Syria, Iraq, and Anatolia, because this territory constituted the Islamic heartland, with its spiritual and historical centers of Mecca, Medina, Jerusalem, Damascus, Baghdad, and Istanbul.

The abolition of the caliphate by the Turkish Grand National Assembly in 1924 dealt the final blow to the Khilafat movement, whose enthusiasm had already begun to dissipate by this stage due to disillusionment and internal quarrels. When a conference was convened in Cairo in 1926 to discuss the prospects of reviving the caliphate, neither the Khilafatists nor the Indian religious scholars (ʿulama) were represented.

Nonetheless, an issue such as the caliphate, which had genuinely stirred a broad section of the Indo-Muslim population, could not immediately disappear. It continued to be the focus, if not of agitation, of public discourse, long after the institution had ceased to exist. The concern with the caliphate, as Aziz Ahmad has observed, was motivated not by any loyalties to the actual incumbents of the office, but to the institution itself, or rather what that institution symbolized to Indian Muslims.[8] The symbol of the caliphate satisfied various ideological and psychological needs of the different elements within the Muslim community. For traditional elements, defense of the caliphate against the European threat was religiously inspired. The institution, despite its corruption, continued to represent the modern Muslim's link to the period of Islam's glory as well as the ideal of the united Muslim umma. For the modernists and secularists, the Khilafat agitation was foremost a means of mass mobilization in the Indian nationalist struggle against British rule. The irony of these nationalist leaders' position is that they were so absorbed in their own nationalist campaign that they failed absolutely to perceive or comprehend the trends of Turkish and Arab nationalism, which were running counter to their own pan-Islamic ambitions. This failure in understanding continued to dog Arab–Indo-Muslim relations well into the beginning of the Pakistan movement and the partition of the subcontinent.

The different ideological positions that were actively engaged in the Pakistan movement may be divided very broadly into the following three categories: (1) Islamic modernism, represented by the poet-philosopher Muhammad Iqbal; (2) secular Muslim nationalism, represented by the leader of the Muslim League, Muhammad ʿAli Jinnah; (3) Islamic traditionalism and fundamentalism, represented respectively by the ʿulama and by the revivalist scholar and founder of the Jamaʿat-i Islami, Abu al-Aʿla Mawdudi.

Muhammad Iqbal began his intellectual odyssey at the turn of the twentieth century very much as an Indian nationalist. His early Urdu poetry resounds with the fervor of resurgent Indian nationalism, a nationalism

---

8. Aziz Ahmad, *Islamic Modernism in India and Pakistan: 1857–1964* (London: Oxford University Press, 1967), 123.

whose principal objective was the maintenance of Hindu-Muslim solidarity against the perceived threat of British-instigated communal antagonisms.

The turning point in Iqbal's thought appears to have been the four years (1905–9) he spent pursuing graduate studies in philosophy and law at Cambridge and Munich. Upon his return to the subcontinent, Iqbal began to express profound reservations about the compatibility of secular Western nationalism, as it had been adapted to fit the Indian environment by the Indian National Congress Party, with the ethical principles of Islam.

In the diffusion of nationalist aspirations within the Muslim world, Iqbal saw a European assault on Islamic civilization more invidious than any military campaign. Nationalism threatened to weaken permanently the Muslim world because it challenged the core of Islamic teaching, belief in the oneness of a community of believers worshipping one God.[9] In a letter to his friend R. A. Nicholson, the British scholar of Persian literature, Iqbal wrote:

> Since I find that the idea of nationality based on race or territory is making headway in the world of Islam, and since I fear that the Muslims, losing sight of their own ideal of a universal humanity, are being lured by the idea of a territorial nationality, I feel it is my duty as a Muslim and a lover of mankind to remind them of their true function in the evolution of mankind. Tribal or national organizations on the lines of race or territory are only temporary phases in the unfoldment and upbringing of collective life, and as such I have no quarrel with them; but I condemn them in the strongest possible terms when they are regarded as the ultimate expression of the life of mankind.[10]

Such a condemnation of tribal or ethnic divisions would appear to contradict Iqbal's own advocacy of an autonomous Muslim homeland in India. How to reconcile this statement with subsequent declarations that "We are 70 millions, and far more homogeneous than any other people in India. Indeed, the Muslims of India are the only Indian people who can fitly be described as a nation in the modern sense of the word"?[11]

    9. Parveen Feroze Hassan, *The Political Philosophy of Iqbal* (Lahore: Publishers United, 1970), 197.

    10. Quoted in Hassan, *Political Philosophy of Iqbal,* 203–4.

    11. Syed Sharifuddin Pirzada, ed., *Foundations of Pakistan: All-India Muslim League Documents, 1906–1947* (Karachi: National Publishing House, 1969), 2:169.

The theoretical justification for this apparent self-contradiction is found in the final line of the passage cited above. Iqbal's condemnation was not of nationalism per se, but only when it was viewed as the "ultimate expression" or aspiration of a people. Indo-Muslim nationalism, which meant the struggle against both British and Hindu domination, could thus be countenanced only if it was seen as the first step toward the realization of a universal Islamic community. In the *Reconstruction of Religious Thought in Islam,* first published in 1934, he wrote: "For the present every Muslim nation must sink into her deeper self, temporarily focus her vision on herself alone, until all are strong and powerful to form a living family of republics. . . . It seems to me that God is slowly bringing home the truth that Islam is neither Nationalism nor Imperialism, but a League of Nations which recognizes artificial boundaries and racial distinctions for facility of reference only, and not for restricting the social horizon of its members."[12]

Thus the formation of an independent Muslim state in northwestern India, in Iqbal's view, did not represent the culmination, but the beginning of the Indian Muslims' struggle. The Muslim homeland was to be a state with a moral mission; Indian Muslims were to be exemplars for their coreligionists throughout the world. Without the ultimate goal of a Muslim League of Nations—whose powers and organization Iqbal never elaborated—Muslim separatism could not be legitimate.

Iqbal's death in 1938 precluded his participation in the actual formation of the separate Muslim homeland in India that he had evoked. That task fell to the Muslim nationalist leadership organized as the Muslim League. At the head of this group was Muhammad ᶜAli Jinnah, a successful and tenacious barrister who came to be in the 1930s and 1940s the spokesman for the "two-nations theory" espoused by the Muslim League, that is, the argument that Muslims and Hindus represented two distinct national groups within British India, and each was entitled to a separate state.

Jinnah and the Muslim League campaigned for Pakistan on the mobilizational power provided by Islamic ideology. Yet the meaning of an Islamic state appears never to have seriously occupied Jinnah's thought. For him the prime motivating interest clearly appears to have been a nonreligious concern for the preservation of Muslim upper- and middleclass interests, which he and the Muslim League leadership perceived to

---

12. Muhammad Iqbal, *Reconstruction of Religious Thought in Islam* (Lahore: Shaykh Muhammad Ashraf, 1977), 159.

be seriously threatened in an independent India ruled by their Hindu counterparts.

The secularism that characterized Jinnah's approach to the organization of the Pakistani state determined his approach to external relations as well. His limited involvement in the international affairs of his time was motivated by the objective of advancing the Pakistan movement by soliciting foreign support, particularly and most logically from the Arabs. At no time was Jinnah motivated, nor did he ever claim to be motivated, by the Muslim universalism of Muhammad Iqbal. Indeed, when Burmese Muslims of the Arakan region neighboring Bengal rebelled in 1948 against their rulers in favor of joining East Pakistan, Jinnah's reaction was to deny categorically Pakistani encouragement for the rebellion and to encourage the Muslims to give allegiance to their own state.[13]

The quest for a separate Muslim state on the subcontinent was actively resisted by the Indian ᶜulama, organized politically since 1919 under the rubric Jamiyyat-i ᶜUlama-yi Hind (Organization of Indian ᶜUlama). The ᶜulama were joined in their opposition to the Pakistan movement by the Jamaᶜat-i Islami (Islamic Assembly), a well-organized, revivalist group founded by Abu al-Aᶜla Mawdudi. The Jamiyyat's opposition was based primarily on the pragmatic objection that the Muslim separatism espoused by the Muslim League fragmented and thus weakened the Indian nationalist movement. Mawdudi, on the other hand, challenged the idea of Indo-Muslim nationalism in principle.[14] For him, nationalism represented an explicit abnegation of the fundamental Islamic principle of divine sovereignty over the whole of the Muslim umma. Acceptance of even an Iqbalian synthesis of Islam and nationalism was for him unacceptable, since in such an attempted theoretical reconciliation he saw the initial encroachment into Islamic political life of that perfidious Western notion, secularism.

As it happened, when the Pakistan movement proved successful in partitioning India in 1947, Mawdudi decided to relocate to the Muslim state that he had ideologically opposed, where he joined the more traditional ᶜulama in ensuring that Pakistan—now that it existed—lived up to its Islamic credo, domestically as well as internationally.

Throughout the period that the Muslim League was mobilizing foreign support for its partition demand, the Pakistan movement appears

---

13. Arif Hussain, *Pakistan: Its Ideology and Foreign Policy* (London: Frank Cass, 1966), 89.

14. Marietta Stepaniants, "Development of Concept of Nationalism: The Case of the Muslims in the Indian Subcontinent," *Muslim World* 69 (January 1979): 36–37.

to have aroused little interest and even less active support beyond the rhetorical in the Arab world. The problem was partly the league's own fault; its leaders were so absorbed in trying to realize their goals within India that few resources could be diverted to an international lobbying effort.

A more fundamental problem, however, was that the two-nations theory—far from generating even a modicum of enthusiasm—had been received with suspicion and hostility by Arab leaders, who, like the Indian ʿulama, saw in the Pakistan movement the hand of British imperialism. Indian partition, they feared, would establish a precedent for the partition of Palestine, leaving in both areas weak states dependent upon Great Britain. In the Arab response was a bitter irony for Muslim separatist leaders; just as many of them had earlier urged Arab leaders not to join European imperialists in fragmenting the Ottoman Empire, so now the Arabs were urging them not to contribute to the prolongation of British colonialism by dividing the Indian nationalist movement.

The rebuff suffered by Muslim League leaders at the hands of Arab leaders prior to partition did not diminish their campaign to elicit external Muslim support after partition. The motivation was partly pragmatic: Pakistan was immediately at war with India over Kashmir. Security concerns, however, were not the only factors. An ideological commitment to fostering a community of Muslim states motivated many within the Muslim League leadership and, of course, was a consistent feature of the Islamic groups. In the first national constitution adopted in March 1956, the first of the "directive principles of state policy" was that "the State shall endeavor to strengthen the bonds of unity among Muslim countries." Over the previous nine years of Pakistan's existence, this directive principle had been pursued along two tracks: (1) Pakistani sponsorship of international Islamic conferences within the country, and (2) Pakistani leadership on behalf of Arab issues, particularly Palestine, within the United Nations.

The overtly pan-Islamic phase of Pakistani foreign policy was manifested in a number of official and semiofficial attempts to forge a united Islamic front. Among the earliest such efforts was the eventful Middle East tour of Chaudhri Khaliq al-Zaman, then president of the All-Pakistan Muslim League. Khaliq al-Zaman embarked upon his tour in September 1949 with the avowed aim of sounding "public opinion for the formation of a people's organization, 'a World Muslim League,' representing all Muslim countries in the world with a view to discussing common factors among themselves and also evolving if necessary a common policy which may benefit Islam and the Muslim world as a whole."[15]

The Pakistani's two-month tour took him to Iran, Syria, Iraq, Saudi Arabia, and Egypt, giving him an opportunity to appraise Iranian and Arab views on the future of Muslim cooperation. Somewhere along his tour, Khaliq al-Zaman decided to espouse openly the idea of creating an "Islamistan." In Cairo he presented his concept as an "Atlantic Pact of the Muslim world," which, "if and when Islamistan is formed, will be an iron curtain against foreign ideologies." Apparently untroubled by any con-tradictions between his vision and his actions, he then proceeded from the Middle East to Britain in order to discuss his plans with "responsible British officials."[16]

Khaliq al-Zaman's Islamistan proposal met with an icy reception among Arab leaders both because of its substance and because of the manner in which the Muslim League leader had presented it. Pakistan was openly mocked as an upstart attempting to assume leadership of the Muslim nations through this scheme for unity. Moreover, Khaliq al-Zaman's depar-ture for London aroused suspicions that his campaign was nothing more than a Western maneuver to undermine the nascent Arab League.[17]

The Pakistani government under Prime Minister Liyaqat 'Ali Khan was swift to dissociate itself from the entire Islamistan idea. *Dawn*, the princi-pal organ of the Muslim League and the largest English daily in the coun-try, declared in an editorial that Khaliq al-Zaman's campaign had been approved by neither the Muslim League nor the government.[18]

Notwithstanding government declarations, it is highly unlikely that the Muslim League president had been sent without the government's fore-knowledge of and approval of his Islamic unity campaign. Indeed, on 30 May 1949, four months prior to Khaliq al-Zaman's tour, *Dawn* reported that the government had issued invitations to members of the Arab League and other Muslim states to attend an Islamic conference in Karachi for the purpose of signing treaties of formal alliance. The proposed meeting was not widely publicized and in the end never convened. Nevertheless, between 1950 and 1951, Pakistan did sign treaties of friendship with seven Middle Eastern states, although these arrangements went little beyond

15. Cited in S. M. Burke, *Mainsprings of Indian and Pakistani Foreign Policies* (Minneapolis: University of Minnesota Press, 1973), 135.

16. Burke, *Indian and Pakistani Foreign Policies,* 135.

17. Burke, *Indian and Pakistani Foreign Policies,* 136.

18. Ibid.

establishment of friendly diplomatic relations and securing rights of nationals to travel, reside, and trade in the signatory states. Moreover, both Liyaqat ᶜAli Khan and his foreign minister, Zafrallah Khan, would continue to issue statements of Islamic cooperation in the international arena that were highly reminiscent of Khaliq al-Zaman's Islamistan proposal.

The failure of the government's initial attempt to convene a political conference of the Muslim world led to a shift toward sponsorship of so-called private pan-Islamic conferences. The first Islamic Economic Conference met from 25 November to 5 December 1949 in Karachi and was attended by twenty-one delegations. The idea for the conference was attributed to Jinnah himself, who had reportedly suggested to the finance minister, Ghulam Muhammad, that steps be taken toward Muslim cooperation in economic development.[19] The conference concluded with a declaration on the desirability of concerted action toward cultural and economic progress. Despite the general enthusiasm with which the meeting ended, the participating states never succeeded in establishing the institutional framework enabling the joint efforts envisaged by the final declaration. Nor was much progress made toward this goal in successive meetings of the economic conference held in Syria in 1951 and again in Karachi in 1954.

Prior to his departure for the Middle East, Khaliq al-Zaman had initiated the convening of the Mu'tamar al-ᶜAlam al-Islami (Conference of the Islamic World) in Karachi on 18–20 February 1949. The conference's purpose was ostensibly apolitical: it was billed as a forum for linking Muslims socially and culturally in an attempt to realize the ideal of Muslim fraternity. The first meeting concluded with the declaration that to achieve its goal, the conference had first to strive for the liberation of all Muslim peoples still under colonial rule.

The first conference was followed by a much grander affair held in Karachi two years later. The second conference was attended by over 120 delegates from thirty-six Muslim states and chaired by Amin al-Husaini, the well-known mufti of Jerusalem. In the course of the four-day convocation, the conference adopted over thirteen resolutions. These ranged from declaring that aggression against any Muslim state would be viewed as an aggression against all to expressing support for Muslims in Kashmir, Hyderabad, and Junagadh (all territories with large Muslim populations

19. *Economist*, 3 December 1949, 1228.

inside India), as well as in Palestine, North Africa, South Africa, Eritrea, Somaliland, and Yugoslavia.

At the final session of the second conference, the delegates decided to establish a Propagation of Islam Organization, which would work "to create a strong Islamic public opinion, thereby cementing the ties of Muslim unity and directing their entire abilities toward one goal—the exaltation of Islam and the service of humanity through application of its ideals." Amin al-Husaini brought the proceedings to a close by diplomatically affirming that Pakistan was "very dear to every Muslim of the world" and that all were prepared to support it. "The Muslim world," he declared, "is pinning her hopes on this newly born biggest Islamic state of the world."[20]

The Pakistani government could not have been more pleased with the outcome of the second conference. Prior to the meeting, it had conducted a press campaign stressing its "unofficial" nature. Nonetheless, the government's active role in convening this conference, as in the previous economic conference and first Mu'tamar, was apparent as soon as it began. Liyaqat ʿAli Khan delivered the inaugural address, in which he took the opportunity to propound the notion of a "commonwealth of Muslim nations," an idea his government was concurrently pushing quietly through diplomatic channels in the Arab world. Such an association, the prime minister argued, would be the Islamic world's response to both the Western and the communist blocs. Islam would be shown to have an ideology unique among the contending ideologies of the world, one "capable of addressing the challenges of the modern world."[21] During the first Islamic conference, a Pakistani brochure entitled *Muslims of the World Unite!* had been circulated, arguing the logic of Pakistan's initiatives in forging a non-aligned Muslim bloc, since Pakistanis "do not subscribe to the theory that a nation is based on geography or race, but whose country's very foundation is laid on the theory of Religious Nationality."[22]

The flurry of international conferences in Karachi was aimed by the Pakistani elites primarily at the Arab states, whose formation of the Arab League in 1945 was seen as an initial step toward wider Islamic cooperation and unity in international affairs. And, indeed, the Arab states during this period did reciprocate in some measure to Pakistani efforts. For example, Arab representation was prominent in all of the international

20. *Dawn* (Karachi), 14 February 1951, 1.
21. Hussain, *Pakistan: Ideology and Foreign Policy,* 136–38.
22. Department of State, File 845F.404/2-2549 (National Archives, Washington, D.C.).

conferences. In addition, a steady stream of high-level deputations from Egypt as well as from the nationalist movements of Tunisia, Morocco, and Algeria passed through the Pakistani capital, expressing gratitude for Pakistan's support for their causes. Nevertheless, official relations never warmed beyond the diplomatic level of cordiality, nor passed beyond the realm of rhetoric. No Pakistani leader ever established a close personal rapport with any Arab head of state.

The problem was rather fundamental and stemmed from the general Arab rejection of the partition demand that we have noted earlier. Despite concerted efforts by Muslim League propagandists to establish the Islamic "necessity" of partition, the Arabs were never quite convinced. Among the emerging Arab leaders of the time, Islamic ideology was not the basis for the nationalist movements they led. Islamic ideology, in their perception, was not sufficient to provide a source of identity and a national consciousness in the anticolonial struggles that were under way. The basis of Arab nationalism, articulated quite often by Christian Arab intellectuals, was the very much Western appeal to a common historical and cultural heritage and an affinity for the homeland, translated into Arabic as *watan.* Even the word *umma,* which in its religious meaning clearly defines a community according to faith and not ethnicity or race, was now being appropriated in the nationalist cause with references to the "Arab umma."

Opposition groups within the Arab world who rejected this nationalism on Islamic grounds were deeply suspect and often suppressed. Similarly, Pakistan, whose creation was justified on Islamic rationalizations and whose leaders continued to declare its pan-Islamic mission, was deeply suspect among Arab leaders. The view of Pakistan as a Trojan horse of British imperialism that had been left in partitioned South Asia, just as Israel had been left in a partitioned Palestine, lingered in the Arab world.[23] The fervor with which Pakistanis pursued the cause of Islamic solidarity, and their frequent declarations of Pakistan's destiny to lead the Muslim world because of its large population and central location, compounded the suspicion with annoyance. This was particularly the case in Egypt, where Pakistani ambitions collided with similar Egyptian designs.

Thus Pakistan-Arab relations became enmeshed from the very beginning in a paradox. The fundamental aims of the Arab and the Pakistani leadership were identical: cultivation of a national identity and the securing of national interests against external challenges. The Pakistanis, given

---

23. Sangat Singh, *Pakistan's Foreign Policy* (New York: Asian Publishing House, 1970), 38.

the explicit ideological foundations of their state, sought to realize these goals by resort to Islam; the Arabs sought to realize them by marginalizing Islam. The more Pakistanis pressed the Arabs to reciprocate for Pakistan's manifest expressions of its Islamic solidarity with their causes, the more recalcitrant the Arabs became. For Pakistan demanded in reciprocity an Arab commitment to its position in its dispute with India. This was a commitment that the Arabs, for both pragmatic and ideological reasons, were unwilling to make.[24] The Egyptian foreign minister, Salah al-Din Pasha, expressed the general Arab attitude when he declared in November 1951 that Egypt looked to India for "moral support in her struggle for national liberation."[25]

Disillusionment at the fruits of Pakistan-Arab relations was quick to develop within the Pakistani leadership. It hardened into publicly expressed resentment at perceived Arab ingratitude in the summer of 1952. The catalyst was provided by an abortive Muslim prime ministers' conference planned for Karachi. Although the conference's failure was not the first example of a government setback in its attempts to promote political cooperation among Muslim states, it certainly was among the most publicized and controversial.

The conference appears to have been the inspiration of Foreign Minister Zafrallah Khan. During a visit to Turkey in February 1952, the foreign minister stated that no specific proposals were being contemplated by the Pakistani government for the formation of a Muslim bloc, but "as so many countries with the same faith and culture have achieved their independence, [there is] bound to be a tendency toward closer relations."[26] Prior to returning to Karachi, Zafrallah stopped in a number of other Middle Eastern capitals, reportedly in accordance with directions given him by Prime Minister Khwaja Nazim al-Din.[27]

In Karachi, Zafrallah stated that he had broached the possibility of a high-level conference of Muslim leaders during his tour and had found "a general desire for closer collaboration."[28] Therefore, the Pakistani government had extended invitations to the governments of Afghanistan, Egypt, Indonesia, Iran, Iraq, Jordan, Lebanon, Libya, Saudi Arabia, Syria,

---

24. Keith Callard, *Pakistan: A Political Study* (New York: Macmillan, 1957), 314.
25. Quoted in S. M. Burke, *Pakistan's Foreign Policy: An Historical Analysis* (London: Oxford University Press, 1973), 67.
26. Quoted in Hussain, *Pakistan: Ideology and Foreign Policy,* 140–41.
27. Hussain, *Pakistan: Ideology and Foreign Policy,* 141.
28. Quoted in Hussain, *Pakistan: Ideology and Foreign Policy,* 141.

Turkey, and Yemen to attend the conference scheduled to be held in Karachi in early July 1952. The talks, Zafrallah declared, would be "for the purpose of meeting together to devise a system of mutual consultation on problems of common interest." He further moved to answer charges that Pakistan was engaged in active efforts to supplant the Arab League by denying that any decisions would be taken that would be binding on the participants. Nevertheless, Zafrallah does appear to have envisioned the founding of a more permanent organization at the conference, for he reportedly suggested in Iraq the creation of machinery for ongoing consultations.[29]

By April the government had announced that Egypt, Iraq, Jordan, Libya, Saudi Arabia, Syria, and Yemen had accepted the invitations to attend. However, Turkey, being wary of the conference's pan-Islamic overtones, promptly rejected the proposal. It was followed in May by Lebanon and Afghanistan, while Iran and Indonesia had expressed little interest. As May drew to a close, Zafrallah conceded that he had received "repeated requests for clarification" of the conference's aims, even from those Arab governments that had earlier been reported to have accepted the invitation.[30]

On 24 May 1952, the *Economist* published an article under the title "Pakistan Comes Back to Earth," which dealt at length with the failure of the prime ministers' conference. The conference, the article claimed, had "at once provoked a certain amount of jealousy and suspicion," which, though concealed at the official level, was evident in private reactions to the proposal. As an example, the article cited the comment of the rector of Cairo's Al-Azhar University, who was quoted as dryly observing that recently, too many Islamic conferences had been called in Pakistan. Disappointment over the conference's failure, the article concluded, "has brought about the rebirth of the spirit of realism which was so characteristic of the Dominion's [Pakistan's] early years. In those days the struggle to make good . . . left the government little time for ideological experiments."[31]

The *Economist* article was reprinted in the *Evening Times* of Karachi on 28 May as well as in several Urdu papers. The controversy that was generated forced the foreign minister to make an unprecedented point-by-point refutation of the press report during the Constituent Assembly session of

29. Foreign Office, File 371/101198 (Public Record Office, London).
30. Ibid.
31. *Economist*, 24 May 1952, 522.

2 June. Zafrallah heatedly denied that Pakistani policy had ever been aimed at assuming leadership of the Muslim world or at weakening the Arab League. Pakistan's policy had remained constant, he declared, and its basis remained close cooperation with Muslim countries.

Despite the government's concerted attempts to have the conference fade into oblivion, the matter refused to die. In November of that year, a foreign-office spokesman, responding to press inquiries, stated that no date had yet been set for the proposed meeting of Muslim prime ministers due to the "pressing domestic problems existing in the countries concerned." He further stated that the government could not predict how soon it would be able to "recommence efforts to call a conference."[32]

Why did the Pakistani government undertake when it did, and with such publicity, the convening of an official conference of Muslim heads of government? Since the conference appears to have been largely the initiative of Zafrallah Khan, supported by Prime Minister Khwaja Nazim al-Din, a number of both personal and political factors may have been involved. Prior to this period, Zafrallah Khan's personal prestige had steadily risen in international forums, most notably in the United Nations, where his advocacy of the Palestinian and North African causes had made him the principal Muslim figure in the General Assembly. His standing at home, however, had steadily deteriorated. As the most prominent member of the Ahmadiyya sect in the government, he had become by 1952 the focal point of anti-Ahmadiyya agitation provoked by certain conservative religious groups, among them the Jamaᶜat-i Islami. These groups had increased their opposition to the secular tendencies at home of the Constituent Assembly, and in foreign affairs of the alleged Western orientation of Pakistani policy under Zafrallah Khan. The major demand of an All-Muslim Parties Convention held that year was for his removal from the government.

By initiating the prime ministers' conference, Zafrallah may have been attempting to counter many of the Islamic-based charges directed at the government and at him specifically. As the *Economist* observed: "It must, in fact, have been difficult for the government to close its ears to the urgings of those sections of the Pakistani public, represented by the *mullahs* and others, who wanted to see the chief emphasis laid on the Islamic character of the state and believed that, abroad and at home, victory lay in the sign of the crescent."[33] A British Foreign Office report noted as well that

---

32. Department of State, File 790D.21/11-1552 (National Archives, Washington, D.C.).
33. *Economist*, 24 May 1952, 522.

"since [the death of Liyaqat ʿAli Khan in 1949] pressure has increased and orthodox Muslim opinion now appears to be more firmly entrenched in the Cabinet."[34]

Moreover, the general enhancement of Pakistan's position in the Arab world as a result of its activities in the United Nations, as well as the enthusiastic note on which the three Islamic conferences had ended, may have convinced Zafrallah and Nazim al-Din that the moment was propitious for a major political initiative toward forging Muslim unity to be undertaken by the government itself.

Though the significance of the conference and its failure to materialize was constantly downplayed by Zafrallah Khan and the Foreign Office, it was readily exploited by many political leaders already disenchanted with the lukewarm response that Pakistan's Islamic overtures had aroused in other Muslim capitals. The newly defiant, yet obviously insecure, mood of the Pakistanis was reflected in a lengthy 4 May 1952 *Dawn* editorial: "Pakistan is not adding to its prestige in the international field by running after certain other countries which are economically and otherwise in a far less stable position than Pakistan itself and which can really be of little help to us. Pakistan constitutes a Muslim World in itself."[35]

The secular, nationalist elements within the government felt so emboldened by the turn of events as to bring Pakistan's quest for Western military hardware, which had begun in early 1951, into open discussion. Talk of Islamic unity was now replaced by declarations of the need for a pragmatic Pakistani foreign policy, a policy based on the primacy of Pakistan's "national interests." In other words, if the Arab states would not support Pakistan in its cold war with India despite its steadfast support for Arab causes, then Pakistan would look for that support in the West.

In April 1954 Pakistan and Turkey concluded a mutual-assistance agreement, paving the way for the signing of the Mutual Defense Assistance Agreement by Pakistan and the United States in May. In September Pakistan became a signatory to the Manila Pact establishing the Southeast Asia Treaty Organization (SEATO). The following year, on 23 September 1955, Pakistan followed Iraq, Turkey, and the United Kingdom into the Baghdad Pact. Iran joined in October.

Pakistan's repeated attempts during the 1950s to forge a Muslim bloc can be viewed as primarily motivated by strategic considerations, by the isolation and insecurity that its leaders felt in their rivalry with India.

34. Foreign Office, File 371/101198 (Public Record Office, London).
35. *Dawn*, 4 May 1952, 7.

According to this explanation, when the Pakistani elites realized that their pan-Islamic strategy was yielding little or no practical benefits, they disavowed their "idealistic" foreign policy and turned to a realpolitik alliance with Western powers. This explanation has, however, two problems: first, no abrupt shift in Pakistani foreign policy is in fact discernible. The search for Western arms had begun long before 1955 and was pursued simultaneously with Pakistan's pan-Islamic activities. Second, the search for Islamic unity must also be seen as an outgrowth of the ideological basis of the state itself. Pakistan's only rationale for existence was the claim that the Muslims of British India constituted a distinct nation apart from all others by virtue of their Islamic faith. Thus Pakistan's governing elites, pressured by religious elements within the new state, could not but turn to other Muslim states for support, collaboration, alliance, and, in a more fundamental sense, for national identity. True to its Iqbalian idealistic origins, Pakistan could not be Pakistan without embracing a pan-Islamic vision. It was to be the ideological vanguard for the revitalization of the Islamic umma. It was to be the expression of the vitality and viability of political Islam in the modern world. Of course, what the Pakistani elites failed to appreciate was the degree to which utilization of Islamic rhetoric and symbols would be resisted by Arab leaders. In the ideology of pan-Arabism, pan-Islamist schemes were viewed as both diversionary and utopian.

Pan-Islamism As International Organization

The bitterness surrounding the Islamic conferences of the 1950s prevented the reconvening of the Mu'tamar al-ᶜAlam al-Islami until 1962. Although the headquarters continued to be in Karachi, Pakistan was no longer interested in hosting the international gatherings. As a result, the 1962 conference was held in Baghdad. Another session was convened in 1964 in Mogadishu, under the patronage of Somali president Adam ᶜAbdallah ᶜUthman. Encouraged by the attendance of delegates from thirty-three Muslim countries, ᶜUthman urged moving beyond the unofficial framework of the Mu'tamar to "the ideal of building up a commonwealth of Muslim countries . . . and to convene an Islamic Summit Conference."[36]

36. Quoted in Noor Ahmad Baba, *Organisation of Islamic Conference: Theory and Practice of Pan-Islamic Cooperation* (Dacca: University Press, 1994), 36.

His statement reflected a growing interest among other Muslim leaders in establishing an intergovernmental organization. Among these, Saudi Arabia's King Faisal would play a decisive role.

Faisal came to the throne in 1964 at the height of what Malcolm Kerr has described as the "Arab Cold War."[37] This period was marked by increasing acrimony between the so-called Arab radicals and the moderates. The radical camp had been immensely bolstered by a rapid succession of events: the 1956 Suez crisis that had catapulted Nasser and Nasserist pan-Arabism to new heights of public adulation; the February 1958 merger of Egypt and Syria into the United Arab Republic; the bloody July 1958 overthrow of the Hashemite monarchy in Iraq; the civil unrest created by news of the UAR and the Iraqi revolt in fragile states such as Lebanon and Jordan, leading to intervention by the United States and Britain; and, finally, the September 1962 coup against the Yemeni monarchy, which touched off a protracted "hot war by proxy" over the next five years. Secular, socialist, republican Arab nationalism—whether of the Nasserist, Ba'athist, or communist variety—seemed poised to overrun the remaining monarchies of the region.

Saudi Arabia under Faisal soon emerged as the leader of the conservative camp. Faisal brought to the Saudi throne not only a highly developed acumen for power politics but also a counter ideological vision to that of secular pan-Arabism. He viewed Arab nationalism as a foreign import that could only succeed in the Arab-Muslim environment through coercion and intimidation. For it to gain popular support, Arab nationalism had to be part of a broader movement for solidarity and cooperation among all Muslims. Faisal thus became the leading spokesman for pan-Islamism during the 1960s. Unlike previous advocates of Islamic unity, however, he had the growing financial resources of the Saudi state to back his vision.

Faisal took the first step in his pan-Islamic campaign in 1962 by convening a conference of prominent Muslim scholars in Mecca during the annual pilgrimage. Out of this meeting emerged the Rabitat al-ʿAlam al-Islami (World Muslim League), whose ostensible purpose was to provide a forum for the discussion and dissemination of Islamic viewpoints on issues facing Muslim societies. Yet, with its headquarters in Mecca and with significant Saudi financial backing, the league was immediately

---

37. Malcolm Kerr, *The Arab Cold War: Gamal ʿAbd al-Nasir and His Rivals, 1958–1970,* 3d ed. (London and New York: Oxford University Press, 1971).

perceived as Faisal's instrument for combating secular ideologies in the Arab world.

By 1965 Faisal had begun lobbying among Muslim leaders for an intergovernmental organization that would move Islamic cooperation and unity beyond the nongovernmental level. From December 1965 to September 1966, he toured nine states, stressing in each the need for an Islamic summit conference: "Muslims in general and Arabs in particular must keep in touch with each other and help in each other's problems so that, holding firm to God's rules, they must not be dispersed and can protect themselves and their future from the threatening dangers, whether religious or political."[38]

Faisal's tour revived the old controversies surrounding the idea of a permanent Islamic organization. Most of the states he visited, most importantly Iran, Pakistan, Morocco, and Jordan, expressed polite support for his initiative. Turkish leaders demurred, citing their country's secular basis. From the Arab countries that were not included on Faisal's itinerary came immediate and harsh denunciations. Egypt, Syria, and Iraq castigated the proposal as nothing more than a reactionary Saudi attempt to undermine Arab nationalism and Faisal himself as an agent of Western imperialism.

Faisal's call for Islamic unity in the mid-1960s may have met the same fate as the Pakistanis' ventures in the 1950s had it not been for the crushing Arab defeat by Israel in June 1967. For the Arabs, the war came to symbolize the abject failure of secular Arab nationalism to deliver any tangible rewards, domestically as well as internationally. For Muslims throughout the world, the war's most significant casualty was the loss of Jerusalem to Israeli control. To compound the shock of the loss of the city came news in August 1969 of arson at al-Aqsa mosque, located near the Dome of the Rock. This event provided the catalyst necessary to galvanize Muslim states toward the creation of an international Islamic organization. The level of public outrage at events transpiring in Palestine was so great that not even the most recalcitrant states, such as Egypt and Turkey, could avoid the pan-Islamic momentum. On 26 August 1969, the Arab League Foreign Ministers' Conference endorsed Faisal's call for an Islamic summit conference and charged Saudi Arabia and Morocco to prepare the meeting in Rabat.

Most studies of Faisal's pan-Islamic campaign during the 1960s empha-

---

38. Quoted in Baba, *Organisation of Islamic Conference*, 50.

size as the basic motivating factor Saudi security concerns arising from radical challenges.[39] Indeed, Saudi Arabia was a principal target of Nasserist-Ba'athist subversion throughout the early decade. But such explanations are much less credible for the latter half of the decade, when Faisal most energetically pursued the cause of Islamic solidarity. By this time he had consolidated his reign, Saudi Arabia's economic power and self-confidence were clearly evident, and the radical challenge was markedly declining following the breakup of the UAR and the quagmire of the Yemeni civil war.

What the security emphasis misses is the crucial ideological role played by Faisal's vision of Islamic international behavior. Imbued at an early age with the Wahhabi ethos of his ancestors, Faisal more than any other modern Arab leader attempted to implement a consciously Islamic policy.[40] As the birthplace of Islam, Saudi Arabia could, in his mind, pursue no other course. Advocacy of Islamic unity and solidarity was foremost for him a moral obligation. Like the Pakistani leaders who had espoused Islamic solidarity in the previous decade, Faisal obviously saw no contradictions between Islamic unity and enhanced state security. The contradictions would, however, soon emerge.

Pan-Islamism As Supranational Integration

The Organization of the Islamic Conference emerged in September 1969, when representatives of twenty-four countries meeting in Rabat declared that "Muslim governments would consult with a view to promoting among themselves close cooperation and mutual assistance in the economic, scientific, cultural, and spiritual fields, inspired by the immortal teachings of Islam."[41]

Subsequently, the OIC charter, which was adopted in 1972, declared the member states' conviction that "their common belief constitutes a strong factor for rapprochement and solidarity between Islamic people"; the

---

39. See, for example, Baba, *Organisation of Islamic Conference,* 38–55, 255–56.

40. See David E. Long, "King Faisal's World View," in *King Faisal and the Modernisation of Saudi Arabia,* ed. Willard A. Beling (Boulder, Colo.: Westview, 1980), 173–83.

41. ʿAbdullah al-Ahsan, *OIC: Organization of the Islamic Conference* (Herndon, Va.: International Institute of Islamic Thought, 1988), 18.

charter stated as well their commitment to "preserve Islamic spiritual, ethical, social, and economic values."[42]

Both declarations are significant for three reasons: First, the OIC was to be an association of sovereign states. In fact, all five of the operating principles of the organization, as enumerated in the charter, constitute an affirmation of the principles of state sovereignty. These include the specific declaration that the members agree to respect "the sovereignty, independence, and territorial integrity of each member state." Second, the statements conspicuously avoid mentioning political or military cooperation in any specific way. This again reinforces the sovereign character of the member states. Third, the ideological basis for cooperation is declared to be the teachings of Islam.

To observers and critics of the OIC, the organization has labored since its founding under the contradiction of adhering to state sovereignty as its fundamental principle while embracing Islamic ideology as the basis for cooperation. The contradiction—and the criticism—was perhaps inevitable, for most of the Muslim leaders who created the OIC sought to achieve at the international level what they were attempting to realize at the national level, namely, the appropriation of Islamic ideology in the service of realizing their specific, national agendas. However, the problem confronted by these elites at the international level is essentially identical to the one they have faced at the national level. Simply put, Islamic ideology does not lend itself to easy appropriation in the service of the secular national state. By evoking religious terminology in their declarations and in the charter, most importantly the frequent references to the Islamic umma, the OIC founders ensured that the organization's goals and activities would be open to the competing claims and myriad interpretations of Islam in the modern world.

The issue that most illuminates the tension between the professed Islamic goals of the OIC and its organizational basis is its role in conflict management. Despite its founders' unwillingness to so declare explicitly, the OIC has ineluctably emerged as an organization for political and military cooperation—or at least strong pressures have been exerted upon it to become such.

In acknowledgment of the central role that the 1967 Arab defeat by Israel played in the creation of the OIC, the charter includes a specific reference to the Palestinian-Israeli dispute in its stated objectives: "To

---

42. For the text of the OIC charter, see al-Ahsan, *Organization of Islamic Conference*, 127–34.

coordinate efforts for the safeguard of the Holy Places and support of the people of Palestine, and help them to regain their rights and liberate their land." In the next clause (as a result of pressures from non-Arab members) the charter expands the scope of the OIC's commitment to include support "of all Muslim peoples with a view to safeguarding their dignity, independence, and national rights." Beyond these rhetorical commitments, however, the charter is silent on the actual mechanisms whereby these goals may be realized. There is certainly no attempt to institute any collective-security mechanism for the "safeguarding" of Muslim peoples' "dignity, independence, and national rights."

It is precisely because the OIC failed to implement any collective-security mechanism that it has been subjected to severe attacks by its critics. For many Muslim activists, the Qur'anic ideal of the umma requires as its political counterpart a resurrection of the institution of the caliphate. As the first institution since the abolition of the caliphate in 1924 to claim universal Muslim loyalty, the OIC has emerged in the minds of many Muslims as a proto-caliphate, and as such the modern bearer of the classical institution's obligation to ensure the security of Muslims from both external and internal aggression. Certainly, its performance has been judged according to such expectations, despite the organization's explicit disavowal of any such role. Thus the repeated failure of the organization to undertake collective intervention in conflicts, ranging from Palestine to Afghanistan to Bosnia to Chechnya, has sharpened its critics' attacks.

The most strident criticism of the organization and the greatest challenges to its structure as an association of sovereign states have arisen from its response to intra-Muslim disputes. Among the operational principles enumerated in the charter is the "settlement of any conflict that may arise by peaceful means, such as negotiation, mediation, reconciliation, or arbitration." Since this principle was adopted, it has been violated most egregiously by Iraq in its two wars in the Persian Gulf.

During the first conflict, the OIC sought to play a significant mediating role under the leadership of Pakistan's Zia al-Haq. These efforts were repeatedly rebuffed by Ayatollah Khomeini, who argued that collective action against Iraq and not arbitration was demanded according to the strictures of Islamic law. He based his argument primarily on one Qur'anic verse that commands Muslims to undertake collective intervention in a dispute involving two Muslim parties when one of the parties "transgresses beyond the bounds established by God" (49:9). Iraq's aggression against Iran, and the avowedly antireligious character of its regime, argued Khomeini, necessitated united Muslim action against Iraq.

Khomeini's arguments received wide support from the Islamic opposition movements in virtually every Muslim country. Yet they failed to move the OIC states to undertake any military action against Iraq. Indeed, the OIC became effectively paralyzed when most of the Arab regimes, specifically the Gulf states, including Kuwait, undertook to finance Iraq in its war against what they feared would be a wave of Islamic revolutionary agitation throughout the region should Iran succeed in overthrowing Saddam Hussein.

Khomeini's hostility toward the OIC stemmed not just from differences over the Iran-Iraq War, but from a more fundamental opposition to the structure of the organization itself. For Khomeini, the Iranian Revolution was merely the first phase in the broader Islamic revolution that he envisioned would in time sweep away all other un-Islamic regimes. This revolution would be achieved, he argued, not through violence or external conquest, but through internal implosion of the regimes through loss of popular support. Iran's revolution was to be the vanguard and the model. As such, Iran's international obligation was to lend moral as well as material support to Islamic movements everywhere. The fact that such assistance would be interpreted as a violation of state sovereignty (and of the principles of the OIC charter) was meaningless in his worldview, since the very notion of sovereign territorial states violated the cardinal principles of the universal umma. Thus the Iranian foreign minister, 'Ali Akbar Velayeti, declared quite candidly in 1985 that "we do not accept the current configuration of the OIC and have fundamental objections to the way it works."[43]

When Saddam Hussein turned against his erstwhile ally Kuwait in August 1990, the OIC once again quickly emerged as a forum for intense debate on the appropriate "Islamic" response to the crisis. The Iraq-Kuwait dispute was one of the items on the agenda of the nineteenth meeting of the OIC Council of Foreign Ministers when news of the Iraqi invasion reached Cairo, the conference site. By a vote of thirty-seven to five, the OIC session adopted a resolution calling upon Iraq to withdraw immediately and unconditionally from Kuwait. This vote is significant in being the first indication of the division of the Muslim governments on the Gulf crisis. It was also among the last formal statements issued by the OIC, because soon thereafter, with the injection of American-led Western forces

---

43. *Impact International* (London), 11–24 January 1985, 6.

into the Gulf dispute on 8 August, the crisis moved beyond the level of an Arab or Islamic dispute. It remained thereafter a conflict directed from Washington with the imprimatur of the UN Security Council.

The broadening of the conflict did not, however, end the controversy within the OIC states on the appropriate means of resolving the issue. Indeed, the presence of Western troops so close to the spiritual center of Islam exacerbated the dispute. In the first weeks of August, the prevailing mood in the Muslim countries and particularly among the most active fundamentalist groups was generally anti-Iraq. While few groups rushed to the verbal support of the ousted al-Sabah family, Saddam Hussein was also no favorite of Muslim activists because of his brutal campaign against Islamic opposition movements within Iraq and his eight-year war against Iran. This anti-Iraq consensus began to shift quickly, however, following George Bush's declaration of American military intervention.

In the four-and-a-half month interval separating the Iraqi occupation of Kuwait and the launching of the allied air campaign, the anti-Iraq coalition was largely on the defensive, steadily justifying the presence of non-Muslim forces in the Arabian peninsula. The focus of the debate now shifted decisively away from the Iraqi invasion of Kuwait to the American intervention in the dispute. The very verse (49:9) that Khomeini had repeatedly cited as requiring Muslim collective action against Iraqi aggression during the Iran-Iraq War was now frequently cited by the same ʿulama who had opposed Khomeini earlier. This fact was not lost upon the critics of the coalition. Moreover, these critics pointed out that the verse commanded *Muslims* to resolve disputes among themselves with justice; the Qurʾanic injunction made no mention of involving external parties, particularly those who had clearly demonstrated their antipathy for the Muslims. The Saudi regime was especially condemned for having invited non-Muslim forces into lands so close to the sacred cities of Mecca and Medina.

As early as September 1990, a conference of ʿulama convened by the World Muslim League under Saudi auspices had urged the formation of an "Islamic army" to respond to the security threat caused by the Iraqi aggression. This military force, the ʿulama suggested, was to be under OIC supervision in order to prevent foreign troops from being used in hostilities against Iraq.[44]

44. *Rabita* (Mecca), October 1990, 27.

The Muslim coalition partners seem to have been unprepared for the scope of the massive allied air bombardment of Iraqi targets that began on 17 January 1991. General unease with the conduct of the war is evident from numerous attempts by several coalition governments as well as by a number of Muslim nongovernmental organizations to convene an emergency meeting of the OIC foreign ministers in order to achieve an immediate cease-fire. Popular sentiment against the allied air campaign intensified when both the Saudi and the Egyptian governments blocked such moves.

The OIC's handling of the Gulf War has had ramifications that are still being felt at both the international and domestic levels. For example, the first postwar OIC summit conference that met in Senegal during December 1991 ended in bitter recriminations over the organization's statements, policies, and omissions during the crisis. It was the object of vociferous attacks from numerous sources for its inability to mount a purely Islamic response to the Iraqi invasion. The inability of ruling governments to undertake effective action without Western support has also contributed significantly to the increased popularity of Muslim fundamentalist groups in Pakistan and Algeria, to name just two cases.

The Muslim debate on the war also emphasized the continuing ambivalence of most Muslim theorists with regard to the legitimacy of the contemporary international system. The foremost issue here still remains the status of the sovereign national state according to Islamic ethics. It is instructive that the most frequently given Islamic rationale for repelling the Iraqi aggression was not the inviolability of territorial frontiers or noninterference in the domestic affairs of sovereign states, but the sedition and strife within the Muslim community that the Iraqi invasion precipitated. The disappearance of Kuwait from the political map of the Middle East was not the chief concern of most of the Islamic arguments against the Iraqi aggression. Rather, it was the prospect that Kuwait would be conquered by another state that was equally inimical to Islamic goals.

The immediate consequence of the Gulf War was a further tarnishing of the OIC's image. In the long term, the Gulf War may well prove as significant a milestone in the development of Islamic international organization as was the 1967 defeat by Israel. Far from altogether renouncing the OIC as an Islamic organization, Islamists have concluded from the Gulf War that it remains the most effective basis for supranational integration. Sudan's principal Islamic ideologue, Hasan Turabi, has summarized succinctly this vision: "Even if regional and international official Muslim organisations are devoid of significant Islamic or functional utility, they serve as token and frame to encourage the popular unionist drive. . . . Just as earlier Muslims achieved an extensive measure of multinational unity, by working from the particular and immediate towards the general and the universal, the emergence of Muslim unity will proceed through the opening of state frontiers towards the emergence of trans-national regional conglomeration and beyond to the pan-Islamic commonwealth in due course."[45]

Conclusion

The Islamic impact upon the sovereign state has thus far been quite mixed. This is not at all surprising given the wide differences in Muslim opinion on the relationship of Islam to the modern state. Even the advent of Islamic regimes committed to Islamization of domestic and foreign policy has not yet produced any serious alterations in the structures of the sovereign state. Indeed, if the Iranian, Pakistani, and Sudanese examples are any evidence, regimes committed to Islamization are simultaneously committed to state building. As Sami Zubaida has pointed out with reference to Iran, "the Islamic elements of the republic fit in very well with the nation-state model, both in terms of state organization and of the structure of the political field and its discourses."[46] Islamic fundamentalism, like the secular-nationalist authoritarian state it is most often pitted against, has as its initial goal state centralization. Only through the coercive apparatus of the modern national state can the Islamist program of social and legal reform be enacted. The Islamic state—just as much as any other state—has proven itself to be quite resilient against domestic threats.

This chapter has argued that Islamic pressures upon the sovereign state are rarely felt in a downward, subnational direction.[47] Rather they consistently push in an upward direction, beyond the territorial state to broader transnational or supranational aggregations. Thus the Islamic challenge to

45. Hasan Turabi, "Islam As a Pan-National Order," *Impact International,* 12 June–9 July 1992, 6.

46. Sami Zubaida, *Islam, the People, and the State: Political Ideas and Movements in the Middle East* (London: I. B. Taurus, 1993), 179.

47. I have discussed the resistance to subnational fragmentation in "Self-Determination and Secession in Islamic Thought," in *The New World Order: Sovereignty, Human Rights, and the Self-Determination of Peoples,* ed. Mortimer Sellers (Oxford: Berg Publishers, 1996), 117–51.

state sovereignty is most likely to be felt in the near future at the level of external sovereignty, in interstate interactions. As for the longer term, we can only speculate on more radical transformations of the Muslim state system or on the further evolution of Islamic international institutions should the Islamist movements triumph in other Muslim states. Such an evolution of existing international organizations like the OIC from their current (sometimes) cooperative nature to increasingly transnational and eventually supranational institutions is clearly a significant part of the Islamist agenda. Until the day when the Islamic movement triumphs in other Muslim states—and if it indeed proves capable of realizing the visions of its ideologues—the politics of the Muslim world will continue to be shaped by irony: As the international community moves beyond traditional conceptions of state sovereignty toward a more universalist ethic, the Muslim states continue desperately to inculcate the notion of the sovereign state in the face of Islam's universalist ethics.

3

Sovereignty, Self-Determination, and Security

New World Orders in the Twentieth Century

Beatrice Heuser

The nations and peoples of the United Nations are fortunate
in a way that those of the League of Nations were not. We
have been given a second chance to create the world of our
Charter that they were denied.
—Boutros Boutros-Ghali, *Agenda for Peace,* July 1992

The end of the Cold War has provided us with a new opportunity to
transform the international system into one more able to prevent war and
injustice and to foster peace and justice. For the third time in this century,
we have the opportunity to create what President George Bush in those
euphoric, golden months after the end of the Cold War called a "new world
order." And for the third time we are faced with a paradox, which may
well, once again, prove the fundamental structural flaw in this order, preventing it from working in anything but at best an erratic way. It is the
paradox of the rule of international law on the one hand and the absence
of a reliable, impartial executive charged with its compulsory enforcement
on the other. It is the tension between justice and immunity to the enforcement of justice. It is the tension, also, between justice and the right to with-
hold help for its enforcement. In short, it is the sovereignty of states.

Sovereignty, as will be argued here, is an impediment to the global rule
and application of law in three ways: first, it is not stated explicitly in the

UN charter or in any subsequent UN resolution that the United Nations has the right to intervene in the internal affairs of a sovereign state, even if this state's government or a group unchecked by the government is breaking that state's commitments to the observation of the UN charter and the human-rights covenants. In fact some such interventions have occurred, most notably in Cambodia, Iraq, and Somalia. But they have been carried out on an ad hoc basis, emphasizing the Security Council's rights under chapter VII as opposed to the sovereign rights of a state under article 2(7). And no steps have been taken to ensure a universal and consistent application of such intervention if the government of a state is clearly disregarding its engagement to uphold human rights.

Second, any UN resolution has to be reached by the Security Council, whose permanent members, as states more sovereign than others, so to speak, have a veto power. Third, the enforcement of a UN resolution, if one is ever passed, depends ultimately on the free choice of the governments of all the other sovereign member states to help implement it. The United Nations has no means to extort the assistance of member states in this process.

The problem is not a new one, but one that has become increasingly pronounced since World War I. There has never been a system of international law that was enforced through an effective supranational executive. Laws have been enforced within countries and within empires. But obligations incurred by sovereign entities have only been enforced against their will if it happened to be in the direct interest of other sovereign entities to do so, and if these were willing to apply the necessary pressure—and bear the cost of doing so.

As E. H. Carr has argued, one of the fundamental problems underlying all attempts to enforce international law is the divergence between the ideal of justice and the reality of power.[1] While idealists (or utopians) have long postulated the creation of a nonpartisan executive for the enforcement of international law, realists have pointed to the facts of the distribution of power: the sovereign great powers cannot be made to obey international law (or even to execute it against a third-party offender) except in extreme cases in which other great powers compel them to do

The author would like to express her thanks to Professor Adam Roberts and B. M. for their critical comments on earlier drafts. All errors and opinions expressed here, unless otherwise attributed, are nonetheless the author's.

1. E. H. Carr, *The Twenty Years' Crisis,* 2d ed. (London: Macmillan, 1991), 170–207.

so, willing to incur the costs of applying force. If great powers happen to be unanimously opposed to the behavior of a smaller power, they can usually threaten it sufficiently to force it to comply with the rules dictated by them. If the great powers are not in agreement, however, small powers can usually play them off against each other and thus evade the enforcement of the rules.

The Concert of Europe: Oligarchy

The system most often cited as resembling the one supposedly developing after the Cold War is that of the Concert of Europe set up in 1815 at the end of the Vienna peace conferences. Essentially, this was a system of voluntary collusion among an oligarchy of great powers. The powers had fundamental interests in common—resistance to any revolutionary movement that might have questioned their internal monarchic systems and resistance to hegemonic aspirations by any one of them or by any power not included in the oligarchy. If these two principles clashed, consensus could not be reached. Was the Greek revolt against Turkish rule thus to be opposed by Britain, Austria, Prussia, and Russia, as it carried within it the spirit of revolution? Was it to be encouraged, as it would limit the powers of the Ottoman Empire, the centuries-old rival of Christian Europe? Or would its encouragement by Russia—if successful—result in the extension of Russian power and thus in Russian hegemony in Eastern and Southeastern Europe, upsetting the internal balance of the oligarchy?

The oligarchy thus worked as long as collusion happened to be in the interest of all the powers concerned. Once more complicated situations arose, consensus was eroded, and in the extreme case the members of the oligarchy would even go to war with each other. But even when it worked, the rule of the oligarchy was certainly not anything akin to an impartial, reliable institution administering justice. For the Greeks, or even for the Belgians, let alone for the Tyroleans or religious minorities throughout Europe, the hope of being granted what people on the other side of the Atlantic already regarded as their inalienable rights depended on the accident of great-power consensus on what might, or might not, be in the great powers' interest.

The League of Nations: Collective Security

If the Concert of Europe was the realist approach to the management of European security (to stay with E. H. Carr's terminology), the system set up a century later took a step toward the utopian approach, without the realistic means to ensure its workability. Instead of leaving the fate of Europe in the hands of an oligarchy of powers "more equal" (because more powerful) than others, by the end of World War I the concept of the sovereignty even of lesser states had triumphed in Western thinking.

Essentially, the postulate of sovereignty for all members resulted in a system that functioned even more erratically than the exclusively oligarchic system. Without going into the details of all the shortcomings of the League of Nations, the following ones are relevant to our argument.[2] In its preamble, we read: "The High Contracting Parties, in order to promote international cooperation and to achieve international peace and security by the acceptance of obligations not to resort to war . . . Agree to this Covenant."

But the obligations were so ill defined that it was considered necessary to conclude the Kellogg-Briand Pact of 1928 to make this engagement more explicit, and even then, it applied only to the signatories of the pact. According to article 16(4) of the covenant of the League, each member had to decide for itself if a breach of the covenant had been committed. While the League sought to facilitate decision making among its many members through the establishment of a council (not unlike the later UN Security Council), this council was not seen as having executive and enforcement powers itself.[3]

Moreover, the League at crucial times in its history did not count the major aggressors among its members, and it proved impossible to turn the mutual-security commitments of the peaceful members of the League into a defensive pact. Germany and Japan simply left the League when they launched wars of conquest, and the League had never really addressed the problem of how collective security and compulsion by peer-group action should operate against states who were not members of that collective.

Nor was it possible to enforce the mutual-defense clauses of the League

2. Admittedly, the League also had some early successes. See Evan Luard, *A History of the United Nations*, vol. 1, *The Years of Western Domination, 1945–1955* (London: Macmillan, 1982), chap. 1, "Lessons of the League."

3. See art. 15 of the League's covenant.

against transgressing members, as Ethiopia had to learn painfully. In both cases, the basic problem was that there was no supranational organization, no judicature, and no executive, that could have enforced sanctions or mutual defense commitments or anything else. The League was nothing but the sum of its members, feebly guided by a council that was nothing but a moral authority (and as such in steady decline in the 1930s). Moreover, the League's members could not force each other to honor the commitments they had made in signing the covenant (such as to impose automatic sanctions on any aggressor, article 16[1]).

Admittedly, had the political will to take action existed, the Western powers Britain, France, and the United States could have used the framework of the League to take action together. But domestic problems, the massive economic crisis starting in 1929, and their own lack of martial ambitions, made war avoidance, not hard-line intervention, the hallmark of their policies. As none of these fully sovereign, independent nation-states could count on each other, they were consequently (and self-defeatingly) reluctant to be the first to oppose aggression. France's treasured independence, the "non-automaticity" of her commitment to the defense of anybody (sacrosanct until this day), directly contributed to the successes of Hitler. The same was true for the United States's proud protection of its sovereignty and distaste for "entangling alliances," for Britain's resigned willingness to come to gentlemen's agreements with dictators, for Belgium's decision for neutrality, and so on.

The League was thus—not accidentally—the result of a Quaker-like belief in the good in man, in the force (presupposing the unanimity) of "world opinion," in the universal desire for peace.[4] These beliefs were exposed as dangerously naive and erroneous by subsequent events and have gently but firmly been refuted by academics since.[5] Aggressive nationalism, national egotism, vainglory, and the manic quest for predominance easily crushed the brittle defenses of collective goodwill.

The League thus lacked the machinery to enforce any decision, if indeed decisions or resolutions could be achieved at all among its multitude of equal members (which was rarely the case). Even the Concert of Europe

4. For the intellectual debt owed to the Quakers and their peace movement, see, for example, F. H. Hinsley, *Power and the Pursuit of Peace: Theory and Practice in the History of Relations Between States* (1988; reprint, Cambridge: Cambridge University Press, 1963), 16–18, 39–41, 93–118 passim.

5. Hans Morgenthau, *Politics Among Nations: The Struggle for Power and Peace,* 4th ed. (New York: Alfred A. Knopf, 1967), 250–60.

had, arguably, worked better, because the four or five powers involved could at least take action once they all felt like it. Within the League, it was infinitely harder to translate consensus into action.

At the same time, the League erred on the side of emphasizing the freedoms and the sovereignty of states, and not the freedoms and rights of individuals. The emphasis of the League's covenant was on a mix of sovereignty and nation-statehood, building on the Wilsonian motto of self-determination, in a continent where this mix could only be pernicious. It naively presupposed a world in which territory could be neatly partitioned into countries with homogeneous populations, cultures, and histories, who would happily stand together to determine their own fates in an entirely rational, democratic, and tolerant fashion. Because the Wilsonian emphasis was so much on self-determination (as the remedy of what was seen as the evil of interference and domination by colonial powers), the road to law enforcement within states was blocked. Knowledge in the West of the massacres of the Armenians by the Turks before and during World War I invalidates the argument that it took the even vaster atrocities committed by the Germans during World War II to show that violence within a state might be just as evil as external aggression. But Colonel Edward M. House and Woodrow Wilson and many others with them had failed to understand the lesson of the Armenian genocide. Their highest ideal was one of democracy, but it was somehow assumed that it would be guaranteed by the self-determination of nations. They did not imagine that majorities within nations might wittingly or unwittingly (but democratically!) exchange democracy for an authoritarian system that was racially and ideologically (or religiously) intolerant of "otherness." As a result of the Wilsonian emphasis on sovereignty (rather than on the universal respect for human rights), the system of the League of Nations had inviolable sovereign nation-states as building blocks.

Thus collective security was no help to minorities within a state who were persecuted by their own government. The German people could freely elect a president who could legitimately appoint the racist leader of one of the largest political parties to form a government that would then legitimately introduce a state of emergency, legitimately suspending the rule of law and democracy within that state. There were no internal constitutional checks against this: this specific chain of developments had not been foreseen by the creators of the Weimar constitution. Nor were there any external restraints, no international law that could act as a check and that could have been enforced for the protection of human rights within Hitler's Germany.

One of the painful lessons slowly learnt by the champions of Western liberal democracy and human rights was that there is an inherent link between the ability to persecute minorities internally and the ability to commit an act of aggression externally. Both cases indicate the absence of internal checks by law, of an impartial judicature, of government opposition, of a press, and of public opinion. Thus a government or an individual tyrant who can build a huge conventional army in defiance of peace treaties or who can secretly develop nuclear weapons in defiance of the Non-Proliferation Treaty, who can invade Bohemia or Kuwait, who can have dissenting members of government executed or imprisoned, is also technically capable of gassing minorities within the boundary of the territory he controls.[6]

In other words, a government that is not subject to internal democratic and legal (let alone budgetary) checks and balances cannot be trusted.[7] To say that the inverse may not always be true does not invalidate the conclusion put forward here: as long as such autocratic regimes exist or could come into existence, other states, and indeed their own minorities, will not be safe from them unless there is a credible outside force ready to check transgressions. The League of Nations was not able to be such a force, as it was neither a supranational organization nor a powerful alliance, for there was nothing to guarantee its cohesion and thus its credibility.

The United Nations: Oligarchy in Collective Security

The authors of the charter of the United Nations sought to address some of the League of Nations' shortcomings. But once again, they did not question the sanctity of the sovereignty of the nation-state. External aggression, imperialist interference in the domestic affairs of another power, political fifth columnism were the dangers against which the United Nations sought to guard by insisting on the inviolability of another nation's

6. I have argued this point in "Stalin As Hitler's Successor," in *Securing Peace in Europe, 1945–1962: Thoughts for the Post–Cold War Era,* ed. Beatrice Heuser and Robert O'Neill (London: Macmillan, 1992).

7. Arguably, detailed parliamentary scrutiny of defense budgets in view of electorates' interests in keeping taxation to a tolerable minimum makes it structurally impossible for governments to prepare aggressive wars through massive arms buildups.

sovereignty.[8] The United Nations thus outlawed "the use of force against the territorial integrity or political independence of any state" (article 2[4]) from the beginning, although it took almost three decades to gain recognition by the General Assembly of a definition of *aggression*.[9] And while the United Nations charter and various declarations on human (and political) rights emphasize the freedom of the individual, the contradiction of this imperative with that of the upholding of sovereignty is usually decided in favor of the sovereign state.[10]

The charter's framers did, however, seek to render the United Nations more capable of taking action than was the League, by strengthening the leading oligarchy within the community of member states. The result was one in which some members were given greater powers than others, despite some cosmetic assertions that all members were equally sovereign.[11] Thus the United Nations' founders settled for a paradoxical fusion of realism and idealism, for a ruling oligarchy, for a concert of powers within a system of collective security, ostensibly among equals.

One of the crucial errors of this step was soon exposed (and is still not fully understood): the permanent members of this oligarchy (the UN Security Council) had even less in common than the members of the Concert of Europe in the nineteenth century, with all their nationalist egotism and self-interest. For the Security Council included first one, and then two permanent members whose basic ideology and hence interests were completely incompatible with those of the other permanent members. And of course every permanent member could (and can) veto a decision. Consequently, the Security Council was paralyzed for as long as that other ideology was thriving. And it is no coincidence that once again, the different ideology confronting the liberal democracies and paralyzing the Security Council (and thus the United Nations as a system of collective security) was an authoritarian, indeed a totalitarian one. Moreover, the

8. See, for example, the *Declaration on the Inadmissibility of Intervention in the Domestic Affairs of States and the Protection of Their Independence and Sovereignty,* of 21 December 1965, UN Doc. A/6014, 1966. See also Boutros Boutros-Ghali, *An Agenda for Peace,* UN Doc. A/47/277 and S/24111, paras. 10, 30, 1992.

9. Again phrased almost exclusively in terms of the use of force between states. UN General Assembly Resolution 3314 (XXIX), UN Doc. A/9631, 1975.

10. See the excellent article by Jarat Chopra and Thomas G. Weiss, "Sovereignty Is No Longer Sacrosanct: Codifying Humanitarian Intervention," *Ethics and International Affairs* 6 (1992), which identifies the twin paradoxes of the United Nations as those of sovereignty versus human rights and peace versus justice.

11. Art. 2(1) of the UN charter, which reads: "The Organization is based on the principle of the sovereign equality of all its members."

danger of paralyzing the Security Council by the veto of one of the big five continues to exist as long as these five do not have a common interest in a given issue.

The realistic recognition that there were greater and lesser powers, and that the strength of the great powers had to be harnessed to the new system to provide for the enforcement of its resolutions, inevitably undermined the principle of the equality of the member states. The "normal" members of the United Nations bound themselves in the UN charter to enforce the resolutions passed not by them, but by the chosen few in the Security Council. Moreover, from the perspective of the 1990s the composition of the Security Council's permanent membership is quite arbitrary. It is held today not primarily by the most populous nations of the world, although three of these are represented, and it is held by only three of the seven strongest economic powers of the world. Criticism of the United Nations as dominated by an all-powerful group in the Security Council, irrespective of the wishes of the unrepresented majority of the world's population, is thus all too easy to make.

Nor is it an irrelevant or unjustified criticism. The Security Council system is in every respect an extraordinary concept. Not only are the "jury" and the executive largely identical, they are also not answerable to anybody (except, if they happen to be democracies, to their own parliaments and publics, with their national preferences). Yet they cannot enforce compliance with requirements stemming from their resolutions by the rest of the UN members any more than the League of Nations could; the United Nations has no more power than to "ask," or "invite" members to help.[12] Nor is the United Nations able to take action directly against a permanent member of the Security Council, which is unlikely to forego its veto power to defend itself.[13] This means that ultimately the permanent members are above the law. And, if they wish, they can also protect their clients through their veto.

Thus, instead of combining the most useful aspects of the Concert of Europe and collective security from the point of view of the ultimate aim

12. Art. 43 of the charter specifies that all members should undertake "to make available to the Security Council . . . armed forces, assistance, and facilities, including rights of passage," but it is nowhere specified how the members should be forced to do so if they are unwilling.

13. The Korean War is no exception, as no direct action was taken against the Soviet Union. Inis Claude argues that many of the minor powers were glad that this arrangement would spare them any possibility of collective action against any of the great powers. See Inis Claude, *Power and International Relations* (New York: Random House, 1962), 158–62.

(the protection of peace and human rights), the UN machinery in some respects incorporates the worst of both world orders. Instead of adopting the greater equality among the member states that could de facto be found in the League, it has adopted the clear two-tier system of the Concert, with the most powerful sovereign states holding each other in check inside and outside the United Nations, as the United Nations has little influence on their underlying relations. Nor can the United Nations take any action against the most powerful sovereign states, as their own veto power can block that.

Instead of going further along the logical path of declaring a set of laws and rights to be universally valid and applicable and next taking steps to enforce them universally, the United Nations, like both former mechanisms, leaves the enforcement of law to accidental consensus among the great powers and to voluntary support for action on the part of every individual member state. The problem with both is that only sovereign governments are represented, and expecting them to recognize unequivocally the United Nations' right to enforce human rights and international law against the opposition of a sovereign government comes close to expecting the House of Lords to vote for its dissolution and for the transformation of the United Kingdom into a republic. Thus, like both older systems, the United Nations has left technically unchallenged the sovereignty of its member states.

This last point needs some qualification. With its repeated restatements of human rights, and above all the Genocide Convention, the United Nations has in theory committed all signatories to obey the rules stated therein.[14] But the Genocide Convention, for example, can only be invoked by a state, which is to say that a persecuted minority cannot appeal to the United Nations for help against the government that is executing or condoning the persecutions.[15] Equally, it is only a state that can protest against the

---

14. "Universal Declaration of Human Rights" (10 December 1948), UN Doc. A/810, at 71, 1948; "Convention on the Prevention and Punishment of the Crime of Genocide" (9 December 1948), 78 United Nations Treaty Series (hereafter UNTS) 277; "Convention relating to the Status of Refugees" (28 July 1951), 189 UNTS 137; "Convention on the Political Rights of Women" (31 March 1953), 193 UNTS 135; "International Convention on the Elimination of All Forms of Racial Discrimination" (7 March 1966), 660 UNTS 195; "International Covenant on Civil and Political Rights" (19 December 1966), UN Doc. A/6316, 1967; "International Covenant on Economic, Social, and Cultural Rights" (entered into force 3 January 1976), UN Doc. A/6316, 1967.

15. Art. 35: "A state which is not a Member of the United Nations may bring to the attention of the Security Council or the General Assembly any dispute to which it is a party . . ."

infringement by other states on other human-rights clauses.

Thus in the context of the Gulf War (1990–91), Security Council Resolution 688 of 5 April 1991, concerning the immediate cessation of repression of the Iraqi Kurds, was imposed on a defeated Iraqi government.[16] One year later, repressive actions by the Turkish government, also against its Kurdish minority, only led to a row between Ankara and one of its principal arms suppliers. The latter suspended deliveries of weaponry and protested against the Turkish government's use of tanks that had been supplied to protect NATO territory against external aggression for such acts of internal violence. The Turkish government responded that it was only defending its country's stability against internal rebellion, a sovereign right on its part. The United Nations kept well out of this story, and two permanent members of the Security Council rushed to conclude arms deals with Turkey, filling the gap left by the suspension of military deliveries.[17]

This is only one of many examples of national or even alliance considerations being uppermost in the minds of members of the Security Council, which are thus hardly the impartial judges needed to administer justice universally and equitably. But this example also shows very typically that the observance of the various charters and conventions is not enforced with regard to members of the United Nations whose sovereignty is otherwise intact. Also in the cases of Cambodia and Somalia, a sovereign central government had effectively ceased functioning, and it is in the absence of a sovereign agent that the United Nations intervened, precisely in order to re-create an independent sovereign entity, as Gregory Fox has so persuasively shown in chapter 4 of this volume.

The sovereign UN member state thus continues in practice to be immune to the enforcement of international law, unless it either voluntarily honors it or has directly challenged the national interests of the Security Council oligarchy to the point where one or more of these great powers will go to war against it and defeat it. Only then, as an afterthought, may the Security Council, for good measure, add some further resolutions, charging the offending state to bring its house in order. Only

16. For excerpts of the text, see *Survival* 33 (May–June 1991): 274–78.

17. Anna Tomforde, "Germans Suspend Arms to Turkey," *Guardian,* 27 March 1992; John Murray Brown, "Turkey Signs $2.8 bn. F-16 Deal with U.S.," *Financial Times,* 27 March 1992; Arnaud Rodier, "Un marché de 200 helicoptères," *Le Figaro,* 13 April 1992. This last deal also profited German industry, as the helicopters offered to Turkey by President Mitterrand are produced by the Franco-German consortium Eurocopter.

then, as they happen to be "at it," will forces under UN command be used if necessary to enforce the observance of human rights.

As Iraq had invaded Kuwait (i.e., committed an act of external aggression), and as, exceptionally, the Security Council could reach a post–Cold War consensus on this point, the coalition forces could go to war against Iraq with the blessing of the United Nations. Had Saddam Hussein confined himself to gassing the Kurds within his own country, no government would have gone to war against him. Equally, before the recognition of the various republics of Yugoslavia as independent states, the United Nations found it very difficult legally to devise a leverage enabling it to authorize intervention in the Yugoslav civil war.

But even with regard to the relative success of UN-sanctioned operations against Iraq, we must keep in mind how fortuitous it was that the Security Council could reach the necessary consensus for these operations to be authorized. The government that had ordered the Tienanmen Square massacres was coaxed into playing along with an exhausted, morally defeated Soviet Union and three Western industrialist nations whose oil supplies were at risk. It is not altogether surprising that Saddam Hussein thought it would never happen, and it is highly questionable whether one can rely upon the Security Council to take such action in future, whenever it is required.

Indeed, the early history of the Yugoslav war shows a different pattern: arguably, the Soviet Union and then Russia blocked UN action a number of times, while U.S. disinterest proved obstructive in its own way. Similarly, quite apart from the problems of legal leverage and other technicalities, the United Nations initially displayed considerable hesitancy to become involved in Somalia; none of the permanent five had a national interest in the situation, until President Bush discovered here the potential of a good deed for the historic record of his administration's final days.

The Cold War: Non-War Between Integrated Alliances

What other security systems are available in the absence of a reliably functioning Security Council? One is of course well known to us, as it secured peace in Europe throughout the Cold War. The strange balance of deterrence that was created through the establishment of two integrated, profoundly antagonistic alliances, each led by a superpower, both in possession of nuclear weapons and thus of the capacity to annihilate each other, has been analyzed many times over. For our purposes it is important to note that the Western powers, unable to find protection through the United Nations, opted for two new forms of close peacetime cooperation and alliance. Both had conceptual roots in previous centuries but were quite new in their actual realization.

One, the North Atlantic Treaty Organization, was a wartime alliance in peacetime, but for a peace that came to be thought of as a special sort of war and that on several occasions came dangerously close to turning into an actual war even in Europe. NATO united the free countries on both sides of the Atlantic and on the northern shores of the Mediterranean against the military-cum-ideological threat posed by the Soviet Union, its satellites, their joint armed forces, and their dangerous ideological challenge. This defense union was rooted in the right of individual and collective states' self-defense against aggression (UN charter article 51). It was built under the looming shadow of a commonly perceived giant threat, and with the building material provided by common values that the members of this alliance wished to defend against it.

For the sake of defending against this threat, the members of NATO—most of them, a good deal of the time—were willing to surrender a part of their freedom of action (and thus, arguably, some degree of their sovereignty) and of their national pride to the common endeavor. While each member of this alliance made a valid contribution to the overall defense effort, the alliance was based on an important degree of mutual dependence. Admittedly, for some the dependence was greater than for others. Nevertheless, the culture of defense cooperation, of transparency of defense policies, planning and thinking, the joint discussions, the joint exercises, and the knowledge of mutual dependence if war ever broke out, fostered what is perhaps today a unique degree of mutual trust and familiarity among the key members of this alliance. And strangely, two of these key members have been, since 1949 and 1955 respectively, the very countries that were the enemies in Europe of the liberal democracies less than ten years earlier.

This special importance of the integration of Germany and Italy, of the enemies-turned-friends, was and is even more notable in the other new institutional creation of post–World War II Europe, the European Community, since 1 November 1993 the European Union. Although this scheme too had its conceptual roots in earlier centuries, its espousal was even more strikingly ingenious. What enormous faith it must have taken, only shortly after the recognition of the full extent of the German crimes, to start working for a new structure that would unite the former enemies in what was designed, from the beginning, as an integrated Europe. While this scheme has to this day not been carried out to the extent that the founding fathers of European integration would have liked, it proved to be astonishingly successful in bringing about harmonious cooperation (and even integration) among nations deeply scarred by two centuries of fratricidal wars. At times, oddly enough, within the European Community relations between the former enemies (e.g., France and Germany, Britain and Germany, France and Italy, Britain and Italy) were even closer than between some of the former Allies (France and Britain).

In addition, the outside pressure on Western Europe stemming from the ideological and military threat of communism became a catalyst for this development. It is therefore not surprising that some of the momentum for further integration strongly felt in the last years of the 1980s was lost with the crumbling away of the Berlin Wall and of the Warsaw Pact. Nevertheless, after considerable soul-searching, the governments of Western Europe remembered the central reason for European integration: to create a sphere of prosperity and peace through ever-closer union with their neighbors, lest the renationalization of politics (above all, defense policies) should lead the countries on either side of the Rhine back to the strife and wars of the past.[18]

The logical conclusions of Bernardin de Saint-Pierre and Immanuel Kant thus finally found their acceptance in Western Europe: the assurance of peace is sought in the establishment of a single economic and political system. The logic of European integration is ultimately federation. The logic of the prevalence of European legislation and the European Court of Justice over national legislatures and judicatures, the logic of the voluntary acceptance of the verdict of the European Council's Commission of Human Rights within this context, are that of a partial cession of sovereignty to a supranational entity.

But it is unprecedented that nation-states voluntarily and in peacetime should cede part of their sovereignty, and the boldness of this move has caught up with the daring drafters of the Treaty on European Union (how-

18. Jan Willem Honig, "The 'Renationalization' of Western European Defence," *Security Studies* 2 (Autumn 1992): 122–38.

ever cowardly the product of the Maastricht Conference seemed to some idealists at the time). As the French and the two Danish referenda on the treaty demonstrated, almost half of the populations of the countries concerned still cling to sovereignty and independence in preference to interdependence, even if this means closing their eyes to the economic realities of the present.

Even the Treaty on European Union itself, as a halfway house (with options for return) between distant ideals and present realities, is an exceptional accomplishment in a world of resurging nationalism and of old and new nation-states fiercely defending their sovereign rights. It must be remembered how special the circumstances were in which Western Europe gradually and organically grew closer, and how strong (and again exceptional) the common cultural and intellectual heritage is that the members of the European Union now largely share. It requires great faith to think that these common values and norms will by themselves spread to other parts of the globe, finding acceptance by sheer osmosis among peoples of other cultural and religious backgrounds.

Options for Post–Cold War Security

The end of the Cold War has shaken up the existing security structures. The West is left with an operational military alliance with uniquely close relations of mutual trust existing within its organization, a factor that in itself, as we have noted, stabilizes the relations between the members of this alliance. But it is left without the giant enemy against whom it was conceived, and thus without the tasks (both in deterrence and in war) for which it was created. Nevertheless, it is the only integrated, multinational, well-equipped military organization left anywhere in the world, presently undergoing structural changes to adapt it to a wide array of possible future tasks.

In the Gulf War some of the coalition forces drew to a considerable extent on normally NATO-assigned equipment and on the cohesion and familiarity fostered by years of joint exercises. But it was only the Yugoslav war that catalyzed the transformation of NATO into an agent of the UN Security Council. While this is a fundamental change for NATO, which had hitherto confined its mission purely to that of collective self-defense in a precisely circumscribed region (to which Yugoslavia does not belong), it would be rash to argue that the way is now open for NATO to accept any mission arising anywhere outside its treaty area. Repeated and exclusively Euro-American joint action outside NATO's area could easily become the focus of Third World opposition to perceived Euro-American domination, militarism, and neo-imperialism.

Second, there is the European Union, where a common culture of integration, cooperation, and nonviolence has grown. Its leaders are hoping to extend this culture, and with it, one day, the confines of this bloc, to include countries that had previously been part of the Soviet empire. But this process will take time, and there will be geographical limits beyond which the European Union cannot be extended easily. At present, the economic plight, the revival of nationalism and of bellicosity in important sectors of Eastern Europe, only serve to emphasize the differences in political culture and the economic obstacles that have to be surmounted first. Indeed, there is the danger that the revival of nationalism and racism could spread to the West before the norms of the West have time to spread to the East.

If the Maastricht review process in 1996–97 is successful, the European Union might appropriate the European elements of NATO and form its own defense arm under the West European Union, provided the political will and consensus exist among its members. But even if a greater convergence of views and interests among EU members were to make this possible, this would take time. Accordingly, in a crisis that is of greater direct concern to Western Europe than to its transatlantic partners—the wars in what used to be Yugoslavia—the European Union and its potential defense arm hesitated to take action alone, even though individual EU member states favored such a course. It must be added here that neither NATO as a whole nor its European members alone, prior to the Yugoslav war, had the expertise or shape to be useful tools in peacekeeping operations or in interventions of limited intensity.[19]

Third, there is the United Nations, partly freed from its Cold War paralysis but still as imperfect and prone to impasses as it was in its youth. As noted above, there is no way of saying for how long the precarious consensus established on some subjects in the Security Council can be maintained. And, as also noted above, the enforcement of justice continues to

---

19. This discussion of organizational structures and "world orders" has deliberately excluded the entire dimension of the military translation of political will. The resultant picture is, of course, a distorted one. The discussion of this dimension would, however, have blurred the focus of this essay.

depend on the erratic and selective interest taken by the Security Council in certain issues.[20] The observance of human rights will thus continue to depend on whether individual governments feel like observing them, and, if not, on whether the permanent five of the Security Council feel like authorizing or even themselves taking action against offenders.

Further, the United Nations has come into sharp conflict with the limits hitherto imposed on its own blue-beret or -helmet forces. The problem has arisen of whether blue-helmet forces can be used for peacemaking, for which they hitherto have no mandate, as opposed to peacekeeping. How far can the United Nations actually go in intervening in a civil war? The problem was not satisfactorily resolved in UN operations in Somalia. The reevaluation necessitated by this operation of the United Nations' military mission is akin to that which NATO and the Western European Union are facing.

The post–Cold War conflicts have thus already brought into sharp focus the shortcomings of the existing security structures. The arbitrariness of Security Council interests and resolutions, the unwillingness of members to commit resources and forces to issues of limited or no direct interest to them, the problems posed by sovereignty—the United Nations' inability to enforce a greater commitment of resources, its inability to come to the aid of an ethnic group as long as it has not been recognized as a separate state and as the clear victim of external aggression—all have become glaringly obvious.

Toward a New Model

In each of three international systems discussed above—leaving aside NATO and the European Union—law is enforced, if at all, in an arbitrary fashion. If the oligarchy or the crucial great powers happen to be in agreement, and the issue at hand seems to them to merit the cost it takes to set it right, law may be enforced. If either of these factors is absent, the only means of doing so are thoroughly problematic: self-help under article 51 (one should think of Tibet's inability to defend itself against China),

20. Even though it must be said that the United Nations, in having the decision-making mechanism of the Security Council, is of course far more capable of taking action than are most other international organizations.

unilateral vigilante action (the U.S. invasion of Grenada), or assistance given unilaterally to a friendly nation under article 51 (the Soviet Union's answering the call for help of the "legitimate" government of Kabul in 1979).

E. H. Carr summarized the early-twentieth-century discussions on this problem by stating: "Law cannot exist except in a political society," i.e., there must be a society ruled over by an authority that can enforce the law.[21] In the absence of this political society and this executive authority, whether at or above the state level, law does not cease to exist, but it ceases to be effectively binding. As Boutros-Ghali noted in his *Agenda for Peace:* "The principles of the Charter must be applied consistently, not selectively, for if the perception should be of the latter, trust will wane and with it the moral authority which is the greatest and most unique quality of that instrument."[22]

It would seem that in order to make the UN charter, the respective human-rights covenants and resolutions, binding, an enforcement agency must be created that does not depend on the accidental consensus and goodwill of an oligarchy, nor on their or any other states' voluntary (and thus arbitrary) decision to commit their national resources for the execution of justice. It must also be an enforcement agency that does not stop at the borders of an undefeated sovereign state for fear of interfering with its domestic affairs—if these domestic affairs involve the clear breach of commitments to the United Nations and to other human-rights charters. The prevalence of this system of international law over national law, and thus the sovereignty of its guardians over national judicatures and executives, must be established in theory and in practice, universally and not arbitrarily. In other words, the only logical answer can be the establishment of a supranational judicature with its own means for law enforcement that is essentially similar to those operating on national levels within an *État de droit*, a state governed by the rule of law.[23]

Admittedly it took European societies centuries to arrive at systems in which the enforcement of justice, indeed, in which the use of force became an essential state monopoly. In military terms, the world today resembles

---

21. Carr, *Twenty Years' Crisis*, 176–78.

22. Boutros-Ghali, *Agenda for Peace*, para. 82.

23. Boutros-Ghali seems to be moving in this direction when he writes in *Agenda for Peace*, para. 39 (a): "All Member States should accept the general jurisdiction of the International Court under Article 36 of its Statute, without any reservation, before the end of the United Nations Decade of International Law in the year 2000."

feudal France, before King Charles VII at the end of the fifteenth century made the possession of a standing army a crown monopoly. It is therefore not surprising that this monopoly of the central, sovereign government, next to the legislature the very essence of sovereignty, is particularly jealously defended by any sovereign state. Nor is it surprising that the quest for a just and peaceful international system has already lasted several centuries, and that the past systems sketched above are still so far from what it really takes to set up an international society guaranteeing both peace and justice.[24] But if this historical analogy holds, there is no reason, as yet, to abandon the quest. The existing UN framework is already concrete enough for it to be discernible where changes would have to be made to realize this ambitious scheme.

For example, the International Court of Justice could be extended to take on the functions hitherto held by the Security Council.[25] Alternatively, a new UN supreme judicature could be established. The UN secretary-general should be given the role of prosecutor. Groups, even individuals, not just states, should be allowed to bring their cases before him.[26] Thus during the Yugoslav civil war, the Croats, before an independent Croat state was recognized, could have brought their grievances before the UN, as could have the Kurds, who still do not and never have had a separate state.

The UN supreme judicature, formed perhaps by judges advised by a jury composed on similar lines as the Security Council (to insert an element of "realism"), should pass resolutions. But it should also have the means of enforcing them, i.e., a police force. The United Nations should therefore have whatever military forces are necessary to reverse unjust actions by state governments or by groups unchecked by governments, which is a mission broader still than that of "peacemaking," let alone "peacekeeping." The United Nations should command substantial standing forces in peacetime for this purpose. This, in embryo, is what Boutros-Ghali proposed in 1992 when he called for permanent UN forces, and, pending the acceptance of this proposal, for volunteer peace-enforcement units.[27]

24. See Chopra and Weiss, "Sovereignty Is No Longer Sacrosanct," 116.

25. At present, the Security Council can decide upon measures of enforcement—again at its will—depending on consensus among the Permanent Five. See art. 94(2).

26. *Statute of the International Court of Justice,* chap. II, art. 34(1).

27. Boutros-Ghali, *Agenda for Peace,* paras. 43–45. See also his "Empowering the United Nations," *Foreign Affairs* (Winter 1992–93), in which he somewhat retracts his earlier formulations.

The members of the United Nations should be forced to make further forces available to the United Nations' executive through an automatic system of trade sanctions (including a complete cutoff of fuel supplies) against any country trying to evade this obligation. In other words, compliance with the UN charter's chapter VII (articles 41–49) should be made compulsory.

Automatic sanctions should also be enforced against any state that evades sanctions against the offending states if such have been imposed by the United Nations. Particular hardship that is caused to individual states by the compliance with these sanctions should be eased by other states who are less or not affected (article 16[3] of the covenant of the League of Nations).

Further details of procedure need to be amended. For example, even provisional measures, pending final verdict by the new UN judicature, should not insist excessively on being enforced "without prejudice to the rights, claims, or position of the parties concerned" (article 40 of the UN charter). In the past, this has effectively guaranteed preliminary equal treatment to aggressors and victims. While in civil-war situations it is difficult to identify whole parties as guilty or guiltless, individual groups can much more easily be identified as aggressors. If a group of people indiscriminately shells a city filled with its civilian population (in obvious breach of the Geneva Conventions), then the United Nations should be entitled to authorize the use of force to take action against that group. In this case it is clear who is using force and who are the victims of this act.

Of course, even these solutions, particularly the compulsory cooperation with the United Nations in exerting pressure on a third party, require a certain degree of voluntary compliance by the member states. A central institution is incapable of enforcing these regulations against the will of a reluctant majority; perhaps even a recalcitrant minority would be enough to obstruct the functioning of this machinery. Even these reforms, therefore, presuppose a more general acceptance of the ideals on which the UN charter is based than can hitherto be found. As in Plato's Republic, and as in the European Union, the functioning of the mechanism ultimately depends on the general acceptance of its values and its laws.[28]

28. Boutros-Ghali is optimistic in discerning a "global phenomenon" of transition from "authoritarian regimes" to "democratic forces and responsive Governments." *Agenda for Peace*, para. 8.

Unresolvable Problems?

Having sketched this model for a solution, it is only fair to face up to the problems that will exist in realizing it. It will immediately become clear why it seems to many as utopian now as were the ideas of Saint-Pierre and Kant in the eighteenth century.

The key problem is likely to remain that of gaining general, global acceptance of the pacific and humanitarian ideals on which both the League of Nations and the United Nations were founded. Even today they are upheld only by a minority of countries—albeit a substantial and powerful one. How can this minority persuade the rest of the world of the validity of these values? While it is true that all members of the United Nations signed its charter, and most are signatories to its resolutions, it must be remembered that an important factor in their compliance was the desire to gain entry to a club, and to economic aid. It may even be the reflection of the London School of Economics, Somerville, or Harvard education of some of the Third World's key diplomats and state leaders. But as subsequent events have demonstrated in far too many cases and in far too many countries, these small elites were more often than not unrepresentative of their own cultures. As the Yugoslav civil war shows, one does not have to travel far from EU territory to reach that greater part of the world where human lives are valued little. But it is not as though the old liberal democracies presented no problem. The reform of the United Nations is most practicable; for its success, all that is required is the consent of the sovereign states and a few similar trifles, to paraphrase Frederick the Great.[29] In order to effect such changes within the structure of the United Nations, one would have to persuade its members, and above all the permanent members of the Security Council, to surrender part of their sovereignty. This is no mean undertaking, as, on the whole, states are only willing to surrender power—and above all their sovereign rights—if forced to do so by defeat, or if it is clear beyond any doubt that they stand to gain much more than they will lose.

The European Union, once the reason for hope, is now mainly a reminder of how difficult this transition is. Even the limited cession of sovereignty in military matters by its members is hotly disputed. This in spite of the value system largely shared among its members and their shared attitudes toward concepts like legitimacy, the use of force, and the rejection of the use of violence to further one's own interests.

29. See Hinsley, *Power and the Pursuit of Peace*, 45.

What, then, is the way forward? The obstacles to a reform of the United Nations may well prove insurmountable. On the side of the status quo powers—the sovereign states of the democratic world—there is inherent conservatism, the fear of exchanging a highly imperfect system for one as yet untried. On the side of the young nation-states of Eastern Europe and throughout the rest of the world, the list of impediments is even longer. There are the grievances against the Western industrial nations—the former colonial powers—harbored by the underdeveloped peoples and by the West's industrial competitors in Asia and Latin America. There is the deep skepticism of any values and ideology imposed by the rich and the powerful, which must surely be designed to work in their favor only, and against the underprivileged. For countries that have only within the past fifty years acquired their national independence and sovereignty, the mere idea that they should subscribe to the supremacy of international law over their country's laws, and accept the enforcement of it by a supranational authority, must be deeply objectionable. Finally, as Sohail Hashmi demonstrates in chapter 2, there are religious beliefs that make difficult the divorce between "church" and state and that lay claim to universal applicability, seeing any laicistic approach as the worst sort of danger to the spiritual health of their followers.[30]

Nevertheless, some analysts see signs of hope. Some think that the self-regulating forces of trade and investment will help spread the realization that transparency in government and internal economic management will help trade. As Richard Rosecrance argues optimistically, "The lesson 'if you want to trade with us, be stable, open, and democratic' is a very powerful one."[31] Others put their faith in the discernment even by skeptics of the benefits to be accrued from a truly secure and stable international environment, in which change can be sought by peaceful means. They trust in the ability of the North American and West European powers to radiate their values, to serve as models, to influence through economic, cultural, and political contacts the thinking in other states and other regions.

But even if these ideas are overoptimistic, the general conclusion stands: The only clear and honest answer to the problem of the enforcement of law,

---

30. It is deeply and sadly ironic that some Algerian freedom fighters of the 1950s and 1960s who fought for the sovereign independence of a laicistic Algeria from French tutelage are now political refugees in France, having been driven out of their country by Islamic fundamentalist harassment.

31. Richard Rosecrance, "Regionalism and the Post–Cold War Era," *International Journal* 46 (Summer 1991): 390.

the respect for human rights, and the renunciation of the use of force is the establishment of a supranational judicature with its own, independent executive. Its power must be unchecked by national sovereignties at either end and must be applied universally and not merely selectively.

The only alternative would be for the North Americans and West Europeans to turn their own regions into fortresses, turning a blind eye on atrocities and aggression committed outside NATO area or indeed within the sovereign territory of at least one of their own NATO allies. But as their economic links with other parts of the world cannot be severed, they will time and again find that isolationism cannot work. Should they feel compelled to intervene, and should they be unable to gain Security Council approval, their operations will be legally little better than vigilante action. It will be as difficult to present such action as lawful and protective of the universally accepted principles and values enshrined in the United Nations as it was to explain the American invasions of Grenada and Panama. Such actions will be seen in Third World countries—obsessed with their own sovereign immunity against outside intervention—as the acts of big bullies, not of *defensores pacis*. Ultimately this will increase and sustain differences in outlook and mentality between the Third World and the West, not help overcome them.

Nor may it be possible for Western governments to continue indefinitely a policy of sending expeditionary forces on a national basis to fight in faraway regions without fear of retaliation against their own countries. The spread of weapons of mass destruction and their means of delivery may soon make the populations of Western Europe hostage to aggressors in the Middle East and North Africa, which could easily tie the hands of Western governments. For some European government leaders, this was already a consideration during the Gulf War.[32] Again, it is difficult to see how the proliferation of such weapons can be stopped without much greater power being given to a supranational institution that has the right to enforce the observance of any commitments that have been made. The United Nations has taken a first step in this direction with Security Council Resolution 687 of 3 April 1991, with regard to the elimination of weapons of mass destruction and the means of producing them in Iraq.[33]

32. During the French debate on the merits of French involvement in the Gulf War, the Chevènement faction within the French Socialist government made this point very forcefully, even though the only means available to Saddam Hussein to frighten the French was terrorism.

33. For excerpts of the text, see *Survival* 33 (May–June 1991): 274–76.

This gave executive clout to the feeble protests of the formerly powerless International Atomic Energy Agency.

With this final argument, then, for giving a reformed United Nations the power to check the proliferation of weapons that make the boundaries of sovereign states and the distances between them meaningless, we must face up to the urgency of the problems ahead. And we have not even touched on the need for supranational enforcement of measures to protect the environment, to fight diseases, to curb the traffic in drugs and arms. As we have shown, the obstacles on the way to success are enormous. Nevertheless, this seems to be the only logically consistent way toward a peaceful, just, and reliable new world order.

4

New Approaches to International Human Rights

The Sovereign State Revisited

Gregory H. Fox

In a lecture on trends in modern British literature, Virginia Woolf remarked that "In or about December 1910, human character changed."[1] Her words, no doubt meant partly in jest, should nonetheless have resonance for our times. Without exaggeration it is possible to say that on or about 3 December 1992, the character of the international community changed, or at least that portion of the community studied by people likely to read this chapter.

On that date the United Nations Security Council authorized the deployment of troops into Somalia.[2] The initial mandate issued by the Council was to "use all necessary means to establish as soon as possible a secure environment for humanitarian relief operations in Somalia."[3] Several

---

1. "Mr. Bennett and Mrs. Brown," in *The Collected Essays of Virginia Woolf,* vol. 1 (New York: Harcourt, Brace and World, 1967), 320.
2. UN Security Council Resolution (hereafter S. C. Res.) 794 (1992).
3. S. C. Res. 794, operative para. 10.

months later that mandate was expanded to include such tasks as the confiscation of weapons, the training of a new civilian police force, and the rebuilding of the county's infrastructure.[4] The UN troops that replaced the vanguard American force, unlike any previous peacekeeping mission, were given the power to use force to maintain the peace. [5] And the peace in question was that within Somalia, not between Somalia and another state. The UN's long-term goal in Somalia, according to Secretary-General Boutros Boutros-Ghali, was nothing less than "to initiate the process of rebuilding a civil society."[6]

Of course, the Somalia mission encountered numerous difficulties, some avoidable and some perhaps inherent in interventions by foreign troops in countries whose political institutions have wholly ceased to function. Yet the very initiation of the Somalia mission is a remarkable precedent in three ways. First, it marks the first time the United Nations dispatched troops on a humanitarian mission without the explicit consent of the target state's government. Second, it was also the first time the Security Council interpreted its jurisdiction under chapter VII of the UN charter—which allows it to respond with force to "threats to the peace"— to include a purely humanitarian crisis. And third, it was the first time the United Nations undertook the revamping of a state's domestic political institutions without an initial negotiation with the relevant local factions as well as with other powers having influence over the state.[7]

Taken together, these factors suggest that the United Nations is prepared to discard both substantive and procedural barriers to intervening in humanitarian crises. These barriers—in this case, the requirement of prior consent, the exclusion of domestic crises from the definition of "threats to the peace," and the existence of a negotiated settlement— derived from a traditional conception of the state as a legal entity possessing certain immutable rights of sovereignty. The Somalia mission

4. S. C. Res. 814 (1993).

5. *Further Report of the Secretary-General Submitted in Pursuance of Paragraphs 18 and 19 of Resolution 794* (1992), UN Doc. S/25354, para. 91, 1993.

6. *Letter Dated 29 November 1992 from the Secretary-General Addressed to the President of the Security Council,* UN Doc. S/24868, at 2, 1992.

7. In this respect, the Somalia operation is to be contrasted with the Cambodia mission, which was authorized only after a highly detailed peace agreement had been negotiated by all major political parties, the relevant regional powers, and other nations with strategic interests in the area. *Final Act of the Paris Conference on Cambodia,* UN Doc. A/46/608 and S/23177 (Annex), 1991. See generally Steven R. Ratner, "The Cambodian Settlement Agreements," *American Journal of International Law* 87 (1993): 1.

evinced little regard for those traditional rights, expressing instead a direct concern for the welfare of individual Somalis.

One might view the Somalia mission as simply a culmination of prior trends rather than a sharp break with past practice. The international community has in fact promulgated an increasing number of legal rules directed at individuals rather than states. I shall discuss several of these rules shortly. But the Somalia mission represents as no other single undertaking the extent of the international community's involvement in issues previously reserved to the domestic jurisdiction of states. As such, it should force scholars to begin thinking differently about how and why that jurisdiction has been changing; in other words, to think differently about state sovereignty. Sovereignty is best understood as an allocation of decision-making authority between national and international legal regimes. The Somalia mission, in which the international community acted through a central institution according to legally constituted procedures, suggests that there is now a real choice to be made: Should primary authority over humanitarian issues be located at national or at international levels?

There seems to be a conventional wisdom about the nature of changes in state sovereignty brought about by the human-rights movement. This conventional view holds that international bodies are rapidly acquiring authority over an increasing number of issues previously considered solely domestic in nature.[8] Many also describe an informal, noninstitutional process of interdependence that functions as a de facto limit on states' discretion to order their domestic affairs as they see fit. As President Bill Clinton has remarked, "in this global economy there is no such thing as a purely domestic policy."[9] This conventional wisdom might be described as the "one-way street" view, with change in authority flowing only in one direction, from the domestic to the international level. Proponents point out that in the field of human rights, recent international agreements have been explicit in asserting that a claim of exclusive domestic jurisdiction will no longer be accepted.

8. See Anthony D'Amato, "The Concept of Human Rights in International Law," *Columbia Law Review* 82 (1982): 1110; Louis Henkin, "Human Rights and Domestic Jurisdiction" in *Human Rights, International Law, and the Helsinki Accord,* ed. Thomas Buergenthal (Montclair, N. J.: Allanheld, Osmun, 1977); Myres McDougal, Harold Lasswell, and Lung-Chu Chen, *Human Rights and World Public Order* (New Haven: Yale University Press, 1980), 211.

9. *New York Times,* 27 February 1993, 6.

For example, in the 1991 Moscow Document, the member states of the Council on Security and Cooperation in Europe (which includes virtually every European state, East and West), "categorically and irrevocably declare that the commitments undertaken in the field of the human dimension are matters of direct and legitimate concern to all participating States and do not belong exclusively to the internal affairs of the State concerned."[10]

In this chapter I would like to challenge the normative assumptions of this conventional view. I will suggest that the international community's concern with an expanding list of essential human rights, culminating in the Somalia operation, should be seen as an attempt to strengthen, not weaken, the state as a political unit. Advocacy of human rights, and in particular the selection of leaders through democratic elections, is designed to produce a broadly inclusive political process that the mass of citizens perceives as legitimate. The international community has indicated in numerous ways that it views such liberal states as more stable, both internally and externally, than illiberal regimes.[11] As a consequence, the policy choices of liberal states are accorded substantial deference in a variety of contexts. This is to be contrasted with the policies of illiberal regimes, which are increasingly scrutinized, condemned, and used as the basis for forcible and nonforcible intervention.

Understanding and Defining Sovereignty

The "conventional view" makes claims about changes in the content of state sovereignty. In order to evaluate the merits of these claims, it is first important to establish a frame of reference that clarifies and defines the nature of sovereignty itself. This requires a conceptual distinction to be drawn between the content of state sovereignty and the form of sovereign rights. The form of sovereignty serves as the constant factor in this inquiry:

10. *Document of the Moscow Meeting of the Conference on the Human Dimension of the CSCE* (3 October 1991), reprinted in *International Legal Materials* 30 (1991): 1670, 1672.

11. For example, the Organization of American States General Assembly proclaimed in its 1991 *Santiago Commitment to Democracy and the Renewal of the Inter-American System* a "firm political commitment to the promotion and protection of human rights and representative democracy, as indispensable conditions for the stability, peace, and development of the region." Reprinted in OAE/Ser.P/XXI.O.2, vol. 1, 3 (4 June 1991).

it describes how sovereignty functions as a constitutive element of the modern international order, including, most important for our purposes, how sovereign rights are established. The content of sovereignty is the variable factor: it describes the attributes of states as political units that define limits on their decision-making authority. If the form of sovereignty remains constant, one can then construct a "time line" of substantive changes in the content of sovereign rights.

The argument I would like to suggest here is that sovereignty is in form a legal concept, embodying the normative order governing relationships among states and between states and international organizations.[12] The antithesis of this view—and one that must be addressed if a legal paradigm is to be accepted—is the realist conception of sovereignty as ultimate and unlimited power within a political community. This notion was first used to describe rulers' consolidation of power within national communities. When these entities began to resemble modern states, the sovereignty-as-power theory came to be used to describe the international order as well. According to realists, a state that is sovereign owes allegiance to no higher authority and is thereby free to act up to the point at which other states react by protecting their own sovereign prerogatives. In the spheres of influence that result from these clashes of might, the realists contend, one finds the limits of sovereignty defined. The exercise of sovereign discretion, in other words, is limited by nothing more than a state's capacity to impose its will on other states. Anything a state can do, it is, by sovereign right, permitted to do.

This is an extreme position that is normative only in the most superficial sense. Realists must retain some normative content in their definition of sovereignty for the reason that states constantly make rule-based claims about the permissible limits of sovereign discretion.[13] In modern times, the assertion of such claims has taken on a highly formal character in the process of treaty formation and implementation; one scholar estimates that more than forty thousand treaties have been concluded in the twentieth century.[14] Such an ongoing dialogue concerned with permissible limits of

12. Ian Brownlie, *Principles of Public International Law,* 4th ed. (New York: Clarendon Press, 1990), 287.

13. As D'Amato observes, "much of the content of intergovernmental communication is self-consciously grounded in legal terminology." Anthony D'Amato, "Is International Law Really 'Law'?" *Northwestern University Law Review* 79 (1984–85): 1293, 1302.

14. Hurst Hannum, *Autonomy, Sovereignty, and Self-Determination* (Philadelphia: University of Pennsylvania Press, 1990), 22 n. 62.

action implies the existence of ascertainable standards in which those limits are set forth.

Yet if states may alter those limits through an exercise of pure power, the rules last only as long as the lulls between the confrontations in which a new set of sovereign rights are fought over and defined. Thus, a realist might describe international norms as nothing more than data points on a graph charting the ebb and flow of states' capacity to effect their interests. Such norms hardly seem worth analyzing, let alone positing as fundamental organizing principles of the international community.

The realists are surely correct that states frequently impose their will on each other in defiance of the norms embodied in the growing roster of international agreements. But it would be a mistake to equate these examples of coercion with the notion of political obligation embodied in the concept of state sovereignty.[15] This is not to say that questions of power are irrelevant to a definition of sovereignty, only that the power in question is de jure not de facto power. Even the realist's necessary nod to a normative component of sovereignty suggests that the concept goes beyond a pure capacity to act and encompasses some notion of an entitlement to act.

A theory of sovereignty that ascribed no independent force to claimed limits of sovereign discretion—such as is provided by a legal rule—would wholly ignore such questions of entitlement. As Middleton puts it, "A true theory of power would seek to explain not political obligation but political obedience, and questions of law would be irrelevant to it except in so far as they may be a psychological factor influencing human behavior."[16]

If sovereignty, therefore, must retain at least some normative content, the question becomes whether it contains more than the minimal amount implicit in the realist view. There are at least two reasons to think that it does. First, assertions by rulers of sovereign entitlements often serve not a descriptive function of identifying actual limits on power but a propagandistic function of staking claim to more power than the ruler is able to exercise at that moment. In the late Middle Ages, for example, the term *sovereignty* was used as "a political slogan by territorial princes in their quest to emancipate themselves from or resist the claims to universal temporal jurisdiction made by pope or emperor, to replace the medieval medley of overlapping personal jurisdictions with an exclusive territorial

15. K. W. B. Middleton, "Sovereignty in Theory and Practice," in *In Defense of Sovereignty,* ed. W. J. Stankiewicz (New York: Oxford University Press, 1969), 133.
16. Middleton, "Sovereignty in Theory and Practice," 133.

jurisdiction, to curb and eliminate rivaling powers of nobility and estates, and to establish a relationship of immediate obedience between ruler and individual subjects."[17]

This "constitutive" function of the term continued on in such claims of entitlement as the right to acquire colonial territory without papal approval, the designation of certain non-European states as "half" or "partial" sovereigns, and, in the postwar era, the claim by developing countries of a right to expropriate foreign-owned property without the traditional obligation to pay "prompt, adequate, and effective" compensation. Today, some states claim sovereign authority on issues of human rights over which they previously renounced exclusive jurisdiction in binding legal instruments.

These rulers use the rhetoric of legal entitlement to win acceptance of a notion of sovereign authority that is still in the process of gestation. It is important to note that staking a claim to new rights is not an uncommon act; it is, in fact, part of the dialectic from which new customary law emerges.[18] But the possibility of developing new norms does not automatically invalidate those then in force. When regimes engage in deliberate overreaching, therefore, scholars should hesitate in accepting their claims of sovereign entitlement at face value—the practical consequence of a pure sovereignty-as-power theory. In fact, blatantly expansive claims of sovereign right are frequently challenged. The International Court of Justice, the European Court of Justice, the UN Security Council, and panels of the World Trade Organization all regularly adjudicate claims that states' domestic legal standards, and not those of the international community, should control a particular dispute.[19]

The process of evaluating such claims against preexisting standards is a legal process. If a claim of exclusive domestic competence is rejected, the adjudicating body effectively denies that the state's capacity to act

17. Helmut Steinberger, "Sovereignty," in *Encyclopedia of Public International Law*, vol. 10, ed. Rudolf Bernhardt (Amsterdam: North-Holland, 1987), 399.

18. Customary law arises through repeated state action accompanied by statements that the actions are taken pursuant to legal right (*opinio juris*). Anthony D'Amato, *The Concept of Custom in International Law* (Ithaca: Cornell University Press, 1970). Because customary rules only emerge over time—after practice has evolved into habit and claims of right have been accepted by a critical number of states—in the initial stages, practice will run afoul of pre-existing norms.

19. As a general matter, if international standards exist, the tribunal will reject a claim that domestic norms should prevail. "Vienna Convention on the Law of Treaties" (1969), 1155 UNTS 331, art. 79: "[a] party may not invoke the provisions of its internal law as justification for its failure to perform a treaty."

defines the limits of its sovereignty. Rather, the limits are defined by the international law that the state has been held to violate. If the claim is accepted, the dialectic of norm formation has still advanced, but not by virtue of the acting state's capacity to impose its will on the international community.

On the contrary, legal validation of the state's assertion of exclusive jurisdiction is granted by the international community, which has found insufficient expression of interest by other states to hold the objecting state accountable to international standards. In other words, the process of ascertaining the content of a state's sovereign rights (even if they are found to be substantial) is itself an international legal process. Final discretion in this process lies with the international community and not with individual states.

Second, the realist view posits a highly misleading tension between its conception of sovereignty as pure pursuit of state interest and the legal view, which it describes as a system of rules externally and unnaturally constraining state action. This is a distortion of the legal view. International law is not forced upon states in disregard of prerogatives they would otherwise enjoy. Rather, norms arise solely through state consent. Each state—by its nature juridically equal to every other[20]—has the right to consent or not consent to new law governing its actions.[21]

Such formal equality does not counteract the disparities in power that inevitably skew the lawmaking process toward the interests of larger and wealthier states. Yet there is surely no legal system in which questions of power are irrelevant to the creation of norms. In the United States, for example, the influence of large campaign contributions is a source of heated debate. A critique of the international system based on the argument that state consent to new norms is distorted by power thus proves little that is unique. But realists frequently overlook even the existence of legally guaranteed access to lawmaking procedures. The point is worth

20. UN charter, art. 2(1): "The Organization is based on the principle of the sovereign equality of all its Members."

21. New states are generally held to enter the international community fully bound by the norms then in force. Oscar Schachter, "State Succession: The Once and Future Law," *Virginia Journal of International Law* 33 (1993): 253, 256. An exception is made in the case of former colonial territories, which did not have an opportunity to pass on their rulers' treaty commitments. For these new states, international law has developed the "optional blank slate" doctrine, under which former colonies have the option of renouncing certain treaty commitments. "Vienna Convention on the Succession of States in Respect of Treaties," art. 16, reprinted in *International Legal Materials* 17 (1978): 1488.

emphasizing: The process of consensual lawmaking is neither an erosion of nor an imposition on the state's sovereignty, but a positive exercise of sovereign rights.[22]

Given this framework, realism is further misleading in characterizing the construction of normative regimes as something other than states pursuing their interests. Every party to every legal dispute, domestic or international, pursues its own interests. Those short-term interests, however, are distinct from an ongoing interest in the integrity of the legal process itself, which states (like individuals) find useful not because it guarantees a favorable result in each case, but because it provides a consistent and peaceful means of dispute resolution. Few states are so dedicated to subverting international standards that they expect to lose most or all disputes that are judged according to international law.

Rather, most states believe that most of their actions are justified most of the time, and so they expect at least some success in international forums. Realism ignores the benefits of having such legal forums available—the sense of order, predictability, and fairness they foster in an environment where might would otherwise make right. No state expects the rule of law to dominate international affairs to the same degree as it does domestic affairs. But as the international community becomes both more interdependent and more complex, the resolution of disputes by force or coercion becomes increasingly untenable. These trends have created tangible incentives for states to submit disputes to legal resolution. Thus, realism's juxtaposition of state interest versus legal process as competing definitions of sovereignty rings false. For reasons realism is apparently unable to explain, states regard their interests as well served by defining sovereign rights through a network of legal rules.

Sovereignty, as a legal concept, represents the interaction of these international rules and the rules of national legal systems.[23] The line of demarcation between the domestic and international orders is often described territorially: a sovereign state has the exclusive power to regulate activity occurring within its borders, while international law governs without. But

---

22. *The S. S. Wimbledon (Great Britain, France, Italy, Japan, and Pol. v. Ger.)*, 1923 P C I J (ser. A) No. 1, at 25 (Aug. 17). There may come a point, however, at which a state has ceded away so much of its decision-making authority that it loses certain essential attributes of sovereign statehood. Such cases are extremely rare. Robert Jennings and Arthur Watts, *Oppenheim's International Law,* 9th ed., vol. 1 (Harlow, Essex: Longman, 1992), 122 n. 9.

23. Hans Kelsen, "Sovereignty and International Law," in Stankiewicz, *In Defense of Sovereignty,* 117.

in the modern era, this description is doubly inadequate: it fails to account both for international regulation of domestic conduct in fields such as environment and human rights, and for states' increasing willingness to project their domestic laws extraterritorially.[24] A better definition would simply refer to the norms themselves, wherever applied. In Brierly's words: "Sovereignty is not a metaphysical concept, nor is it part of the essence of statehood; it is merely a term which designates an aggregate of particular and very extensive claims that States habitually make for themselves in their relations with other States."[25]

Viewing sovereignty as a legal concept does not make ascertaining its content any easier. If sovereignty represents the totality of prerogatives claimed for national legal systems, then the concept must be defined in relation to the entire body of international law, against which such claims are measured.[26] And such an inquiry must be ongoing in order to permit "a continuing readjustment of inclusive and exclusive competences as conditions may require."[27] But for any given issue, the international legal process does provide a fairly well-established framework for ascertaining whether a rule has emerged and binds a particular state. The drafters of the UN charter presumed that the content of sovereign rights was ascertainable when they forbade the organization from intervening in matters "which are essentially within the domestic jurisdiction of any state."[28] And indeed much of the history of the United Nations has consisted of issues being "taken off the table" of domestic jurisdiction as consensus develops on their status as binding international rules. Examples range from decolonization to apartheid to the existence of democratic political processes.

As new issues become subject to international rules, a legal concept of sovereignty allows for a rational ordering of the process of change. It allows policy makers to separate the rhetorical excesses of self-interested rulers from legal entitlements established by formal agreement or practice-

---

24. For a discussion of extraterritorial application of American law, see Lea Brilmayer and Charles Norchi, "Federal Extraterritoriality and Fifth Amendment Due Process," *Harvard Law Review* 105 (1992): 1217.

25. James L. Brierly, *The Law of Nations*, 4th ed. (Oxford: Clarendon Press, 1949), 48.

26. As the Permanent Court of International Justice held, "The question of whether a certain matter is or is not solely within the jurisdiction of a State is an essentially relative question; it depends on the development of international relations." *Tunis and Morocco Nationality Decrees*, 1923 PCIJ (ser. B) No. 4, at 24 (Feb. 7).

27. McDougal, Lasswell, and Chen, *Human Rights*, 211.

28. UN charter, art. 2(7).

driven custom. Because the lawmaking process is consensual, it is not accurate to describe the changes in states' domestic jurisdiction as an "erosion" of sovereignty. *Erosion* implies an external force at work; international law is wholly internal to the community of states, since it is made by the community and defines its very structure. It is more accurate, therefore, to describe sovereignty as evolving. I will now consider the question of whether, as a result of that evolution in the field of human rights, the state has been diminished as a political unit.

The Law of Human Rights: Normative and Institutional Trends

Before describing the process of strengthening the state, which I believe is the ultimate objective of current humanitarian efforts, it is important to note two broad areas of overlap between my position and what I have described as the conventional view.

The Growth of Human-Rights Law

The first point of agreement is purely normative; it is the belief that international law no longer permits states to defend violations of fundamental human rights as legitimate exercises of national sovereignty. While some leaders retain the rhetoric of nineteenth-century territorialism, the immense proliferation of institutions and norms dedicated to protecting human rights suggests that these claims do not reflect the current state of international law. Even those states that violate human-rights norms rarely assert a legal entitlement to do so; more often, they deny that the abuses occurred or claim that they were the work of rogue officials.[29]

---

29. As the United States government explained in a landmark case concerning the right against torture: "In exchanges between United States embassies and all foreign states with which the United States maintains relations, it has been the Department of State's general experience that no government has asserted a right to torture its own nationals. Where reports of such torture elicit some credence, a state usually responds by denial or, less frequently, by asserting that the conduct was unauthorized or constituted rough treatment short of torture. The Department's *Country Reports on Human Rights* . . . reports no assertion by any nation that torture is justified." Brief for the United States as *Amicus Curiae,* in *Filartiga*

These explanations, while often disingenuous, do not vitiate the status of the norm precisely because they are not counternormative explanations. By making every argument except that they are entitled to break the law, these states pay a backhanded compliment to the law's authority. This is not true for all rights. Discussions of the status of women, for example, often provoke claims of legal right to act counter to Western norms of gender equality. But such claims are noticeably absent in the case of torture, genocide, extrajudicial killing, disappearances, and other practices that appear on most short lists of core human rights.[30]

This lack of tolerance for human-rights violations was captured by the UN secretary-general in his 1991 *Report on the Organization*. Secretaries-general have traditionally avoided taking positions on divisive issues in order to preserve their status as mediators. Nevertheless, Javier Pérez de Cuéllar stated bluntly: "It is now increasingly felt that the principle of non-interference with the essential domestic jurisdiction of States cannot be regarded as a protective barrier behind which human rights could be massively or systematically violated with impunity."[31]

The Institutionalization of Human-Rights Protection

The second point of agreement between my position and the conventional view is institutional: in recent years, but particularly since 1989, issues of human rights have found their way into virtually every aspect of international decision making and significantly altered the range of policy options available to actors at the national and multilateral levels. Perhaps more so than the evident agreement on norms, this point is a direct challenge to traditional realism. It suggests that any international actor will now suffer a substantial loss of what might be called "legitimacy capital" by acting in blatant disregard of core human rights. There are six broad issue areas in which human-rights concerns have made tangible inroads.

---

v. Pena-Irala, 630 F.2d 876 (2d Cir. 1980), reprinted in *International Legal Materials* 19 (1980): 585, 598.

30. See, for example, the list appearing in the American Law Institute's *Restatement of the Law Third: The Foreign Relations Law of the United States*, section 702 (St. Paul: American Law Institute, 1986).

31. UN Doc. A/46/1, at 10, 1991.

1. EXPANDING JURISDICTION OF THE UN SECURITY COUNCIL

From 1945 to 1989, the five permanent members of the Council cast 279 vetoes, effectively paralyzing the United Nations' enforcement capabilities.[32]

The only exceptions in the area of human rights were the embargoes placed on Southern Rhodesia in 1966[33] and on South Africa in 1977.[34] From 1989 through 1993, only one resolution was vetoed. Admittedly, an ongoing threat of a Chinese veto is reflected in the drafting of such resolutions as 688, concerning the Iraqi Kurds and Shi'ites. In deference to Chinese concerns, Resolution 688 contains no explicit authorization for enforcement of the so-called no-fly zones in northern and southern Iraq.[35] Other cleavages may yet develop. But to date disagreements have been the exception. The Security Council is now making regular use of its powers under chapter VII of the charter, which not only allows it to use any sort of force necessary to restore the peace but also overrides article 2(7) of the UN charter. This article provides that the organization shall not interfere "in matters which are essentially within the domestic jurisdiction of any State."

The Gulf War, in which the Security Council first began exercising its long-frozen chapter VII powers, was a classic case of state aggression. It was precisely the sort of challenge to international peace that the drafters of the UN charter had in mind: a state's regular army moving across internationally accepted borders with the intention of annexing another sovereign state. The 1945 UN charter was first and foremost an attempt to guard against the hegemonic designs of future Hitlers. Chapter VII allows the Council to act not only against such open movement of troops but also against potential "threats to the peace." By its nature this phrase involves intangibles and invites speculation as to the cause of international conflict. It is susceptible to broad interpretation, allowing a Security Council otherwise free of internal dissension virtually unlimited discretion in mobilizing the collective-security apparatus.[36]

---

32. Boutros-Ghali, *Agenda for Peace,* para 14.
33. S. C. Res. 221 (1966); S. C. Res. 232 (1966).
34. S. C. Res. 418 (1977).
35. S. C. Res. 688 (1991).
36. Paul C. Szasz, "Centralized and Decentralized Law Enforcement: The Security Council and General Assembly Acting Under Chapters VII and VIII," in *Allocation of Law Enforcement Authority in the International System,* ed. Jost Delbrück (Berlin: Dunckert Humbolt, 1995).

In the wake of the Gulf War, the Security Council has identified a number of "threats to the peace" that are increasingly remote from classic cross-border aggression.[37] In the case of the Iraqi Kurds and Shi'ites, the Council identified the "repression of the Iraqi civilian population" as a threat to the peace, although the Council also made mention of the flow of Iraqi refugees into Turkey and elsewhere. In Somalia, as we have already seen, the Council focused solely on the internal situation, designating "the magnitude of the human tragedy caused by the conflict in Somalia" a threat to the peace.[38] And in the case of Haiti, the Security Council imposed an oil embargo after declaring the failure to reinstate elected president Jean-Bertrand Aristide a threat to the peace.[39]

The broadest construction of the Council's jurisdiction came in its reaction to the bombing of Pan Am flight 103 over Lockerbie, Scotland. The Council became involved in the matter after the United States and Britain demanded that Libya extradite two of its citizens allegedly responsible for the explosion. Libya refused to do so. Its claim was based on the Montreal Convention, a treaty concerned with attacks on civil aircraft to which all three states were party.[40] Libya argued (quite correctly) that under the Montreal Convention, it had the option of either extraditing the two suspects or trying them in Libyan national courts for the offenses charged. Libya declared that it was prepared to conduct a trial. The Security Council rejected this response and on 31 March 1992 passed a resolution declaring that Libya's failure to extradite the two constituted a threat to the peace.[41] It demanded immediate extradition and imposed a number of punitive measures on Libya for its failure to comply.

The Montreal Convention provides that in the event of a dispute over its application, the parties may have recourse to the International Court of Justice. Libya immediately filed claims against the United States and the United Kingdom, asserting that the Council had violated its rights under the convention by denying it the option of holding a trial. It asked

---

37. In January 1992, the heads of state and government of Security Council member states issued a joint declaration of principles. In it they stated: "The absence of war and military conflict amongst States does not in itself ensure international peace and security. The non-military sources of instability in the economic, social, humanitarian, and ecological fields have become threats to peace and security." UN Doc. S/23500, at 3, 1992.

38. S. C. Res. 794 (1992).

39. S. C. Res. 841 (1993).

40. "Convention for the Suppression of Unlawful Acts Against the Safety of Civil Aviation" (23 September 1971), 974 UNTS 177, 1971.

41. S. C. Res. 748 (1992).

the court in essence to enjoin the United States and the United Kingdom from enforcing the sanctions imposed by the Security Council. This was a claim of inestimable constitutional significance for the UN system. Libya was asking the court to declare ultra vires a resolution of the Security Council, a political body assumed to have plenary authority over all issues related to international peace and security. Many have seen this as an attempt to introduce the American practice of judicial review into the UN system.[42]

In an initial decision on provisional measures, the court rejected the Libyan claim.[43] It held that whatever rights Libya possessed under the Montreal Convention were trumped by its obligation to follow decisions of the Security Council. It cited article 103 of the UN charter, which provides that where charter obligations conflict with rights or obligations under any other international agreement, the charter obligations shall prevail.[44] The court did not address the question of whether a failure to extradite suspects can plausibly be construed as a threat to the peace. As this was merely a request for provisional measures, that issue may resurface when the full claims are heard. But the court's evident deference to the Council's decisions is perhaps just as important.

In essence the court affirmed that if the Council chooses to make the traditionally sovereign act of deciding whether to extradite one's own citizens a subject of a multilateral enforcement action, it faces no legal barriers to doing so. It is no wonder that the Council now seems prepared to designate any civil war with a sufficiently high level of carnage a threat to the peace: it has already done so in Somalia, Yugoslavia, and Liberia. Humanitarian crises, in other words, are now on a par with cross-border invasions in their ability to trigger the full panoply of UN enforcement measures. After the Libya decision, this inversion of traditional legal principles can be readily absorbed into the jurisprudence of UN peacemaking.

---

42. Thomas M. Franck, "The 'Powers of Appreciation': Who Is the Ultimate Guardian of UN Legality?" *American Journal of International Law* 86 (1992): 519; Christian Tomuschat, "The Lockerbie Case Before the ICJ," *Review of the International Commission of Jurists*, no. 48 (1992): 38; W. Michael Reisman, "The Constitutional Crisis in the United Nations," *American Journal of International Law* 87 (1993): 83.

43. *Case Concerning Questions of Interpretation and Application of the 1971 Montreal Convention Arising from the Aerial Incident at Lockerbie (Libya v. United States)*, 1992 ICJ Rep. 114.

44. Ibid., 126.

2. MEDIATION OF CIVIL WARS

The second area in which human-rights issues have been introduced into multilateral institutions is in UN brokering of cease-fires in civil wars. The UN charter's 1945 view of the world contains no explicit mention of civil conflict, and even the most creative interpretations of its text seem to yield no more than a capacity to negotiate an end to hostilities. But in recent years the United Nations has done much more. Its supervision of Namibia's independence from South Africa in 1989 seems a suitable starting point.[45]

In that mission the Security Council appeared to recognize that civil conflicts, including secessionist movements, often originate in the exclusion of certain groups from the national political process. To prevent fighting from resuming, the United Nations sought to ensure that the political process developed for an independent Namibia was a broadly inclusive one. Respect for human rights was deemed essential to facilitating mass political participation. Provisions for both democratic elections and judicially enforced human-rights guarantees were included in the new constitution drafted under UN supervision. The initial results were encouraging: more than 97 percent of registered Namibian voters cast ballots in the November 1989 election.

Since then the United Nations has become somewhat of a fixture in agreements to end internal conflicts, each of which has contained significant human-rights provisions. It exercised supervisory control over the Cambodian government in order to move that country toward a republican constitution and free elections;[46] it engaged in extensive human-rights monitoring in El Salvador, including recommending the purge of top army officers as part of a cease-fire accord between the government and the Frente Farabundo Martí para la Liberación Nacional (FMLN);[47] it monitored elections in Angola, although with limited initial success;[48] it agreed to monitor the disarming of combatants in the Mozambican civil war and to oversee a process of political restructuring, leading up to multiparty elections;[49] it monitored presidential elections in Nicaragua as part of a

45. National Democratic Institute for International Affairs, *Nation Building: The UN and Namibia* (Washington, D.C.: National Democratic Institute, 1990).

46. *Further Report of the Secretary-General Pursuant to Paragraph 7 of Resolution 860,* UN Doc. S/26649, 1993.

47. UN Doc. A/46/864 and S/23501 (Annex: Peace Agreement), 1992.

48. S. C. Res. 747 (1992); *Further Report of the Secretary-General on the United Nations Angola Verification Mission (UNAVEM II),* UN Doc. S/24145, 1992.

49. S. C. Res. 797 (1992), approving peace-keeping mission for Mozambique. See also

peace plan negotiated by the five Central American presidents;[50] and plans have been made to supervise an end to the Liberian civil war in partnership with a West African peacekeeping group, including monitoring a cease-fire, repatriating refugees, and monitoring elections.[51]

3. ELECTION MONITORING

The third area of involvement, the monitoring of national elections, is related to the second. Not all such missions come at the end of civil wars. The growth of election-monitoring missions has been remarkable: at the end of 1991 the United Nations had received five requests for electoral assistance; one year later thirty-one requests had been received, most of which had been acted upon in some fashion.[52] The result has been a new role for the United Nations as midwife to nascent democratic institutions, mostly located in developing countries.

Election monitoring stands out from the array of other human rights of concern to the United Nations because it implicates what is perhaps the core function of a sovereign political unit, the selection of leaders. The state-centered model of international law—perfected in the nineteenth century and still much in evidence today—had as one of its initial functions the protection of dynastic succession in the European monarchies. From this specific example of safeguarding autonomy in choosing forms of national government arose a legal principle applicable to all regime types. The leading treatise on international law at the turn of the century bluntly asserted that "The Law of Nations prescribes no rules as regards the kind of head a State may have. Every State is, naturally, independent regarding this point, possessing the faculty of adopting any Constitution according to its discretion."[53] Yet the United Nations has now established a permanent coordinator for monitoring activities and has consistently taken the position that the only form of government to which it will lend its verifying imprimatur is one chosen through free and fair

---

Report of the Secretary-General on the United Nations Operation in Mozambique, UN Doc. S/24892, 1992; UN Doc. S/24635 (Annex: General Peace Agreement for Mozambique), 1992.

50. Gregory H. Fox, "The Right to Political Participation in International Law," *Yale Journal of International Law* 17 (1992): 539, 579–83.

51. *Further Report of the Secretary-General on Liberia,* UN Doc. S/26200, at 2–3 (1993).

52. *Report of the Secretary-General, Enhancing the Effectiveness of the Principle of Periodic and Genuine Elections,* UN Doc. A/47/668, at 3 (1992).

53. Lasa Oppenheim, *International Law,* vol. 1 (London: Longmans, 1905), 403.

elections.[54] Slowly, the legitimacy of governments is coming to depend less on issues of power and more on their democratic pedigree.

4. THE LAW OF RECOGNITION

The fourth development is a slow shift in recognition practices to take more account of a new regime's or state's human-rights record. In the case of new states, traditional international law held that so long as an entity met certain functional criteria—such as stable borders, a definable population, and effective governmental control of the territory—the decision to recognize the state was entirely a political question for other states.[55] The decision to recognize a new regime was equally discretionary. International organizations such as the United Nations applied similarly pragmatic criteria for recognition, with the notable exceptions of Rhodesia, South Africa and, for many years, China.[56]

But after Haitian president Jean-Bertrand Aristide was ousted in a military coup in 1991, both the Organization of American States and the UN General Assembly resolved not to recognize the new military government, a decision based solely on its lack of democratic legitimacy.[57] The Maastricht Treaty on European Union restricts EU membership to democratic states that respect human rights.[58] The Organization of American States recently amended its charter to provide for the suspension from the General Assembly of member states whose democratically elected governments are overthrown by force.[59] Along similar lines, the Badinter Commission, convened by the European Community to decide whether the states of the former Yugoslavia merited recognition, concluded that commitments to representative government and protection of minority rights were essential prerequisites.[60]

54. UN General Assembly Resolution (hereafter G.A. Res.) 46/137 (1990).

55. Brownlie, *Principles of Public International Law,* 92–93.

56. Fox, "Right to Political Participation," 598–602.

57. MRE/RES.1/91, corr., at 2, OEA/ser.F/V.1 (3 October 1991), declaring that OAS would recognize delegates from the Aristide government "as the only legitimate representatives of Haiti." See also G.A. Res. 46/7 (1991), referring to the Aristide regime as "legitimate" and the coup as "illegal."

58. "Treaty on European Union," Title I(F), reprinted in *International Legal Materials* 31 (1992): 247, 256.

59. OAS charter, art. 8 bis; see OEA/Ser. P, AG/doc. 11 (XVI-E/92) rev. 1 (1992).

60. For example, see *Opinion No. 4 on International Recognition of the Socialist Republic of Bosnia-Hercegovina by the European Community and its Member States* (11 January 1992), reprinted in *International Legal Materials* 31 (1992): 1501.

These actions by multilateral bodies appear to have had some effect on states' bilateral recognition policies. The United States, in deciding whether to recognize former Soviet and Yugoslav republics, as well as the new government in Angola, has made at least a rhetorical commitment to requiring these new states and regimes to adopt democratic constitutions and legal protection for ethnic minorities as preconditions for recognition.[61]

5. International Lending Practices

The fifth area of change is in international lending practices, which are beginning to take account of debtor states' political institutions. The clearest example is the new European Bank for Reconstruction and Development, established to assist the former communist states of Eastern Europe. The bank's charter provides explicitly that its lending policies shall attempt to foster the growth of multiparty democracy.[62]

The World Bank, by contrast, operates under a charter that specifically proscribes interference in the political affairs of member states.[63] Nevertheless, the bank has recently begun to factor issues of "governance" into its lending decisions. There is apparently a conflict within the bank over the meaning of this concept: some stress efficiency, while others emphasize political accountability. If the 1991 pledging conference on Kenya is any guide, the bank has decided not to stress one factor to the exclusion of others but to insist that as part of a mix of reforms, in certain cases, recipient states must make their governments more popularly accountable. Individual states have been much more explicit in revamping their lending practices. At the Kenya Conference, the United States called on President Daniel Arap-Moi to permit the formation of opposition parties and withheld a substantial portion of a previously approved aid package in response to his failure to do so.[64] French president Mitterrand recently echoed this sentiment, telling Vietnamese leaders that aid from the West

61. "U.S. Recognition of Former Yugoslav Republics," *U.S. Department of State Dispatch* 3 (September 1992): 19; "U.S. Recognition of Angolan Government," *U.S. Department of State Dispatch* 4 (May 1992): 375.

62. "Agreement Establishing the European Bank for Reconstruction and Development," reprinted in *International Legal Materials* 29 (1990): 1077, 1084.

63. International Bank for Reconstruction and Development charter, art. IV(10).

64. Jane Perlez, "Stormy Relations for U.S. and Kenya," *New York Times,* 21 November 1991, A9; Perlez, "On Event of Talks With Aid Donors, Kenya Is Under Pressure to Democratize," *New York Times,* 25 November 1991, A9; Perlez, "U.S. Reveals Sum of Aid It Withheld from Kenya," *New York Times,* 1 December 1991, A10.

would be conditioned on democratization and improvements in human rights.[65]

6. YUGOSLAV WAR-CRIMES TRIBUNAL

The sixth development involves a single but seminal event: the decision of the UN Security Council on 22 February 1993 to establish a war-crimes tribunal for the former Yugoslavia.[66] The underlying premise of the Council's action is that there is sufficient agreement among states on a body of human rights and humanitarian principles that "international crimes" may be prosecuted in the name of the community of nations as a whole. This could not be said of the first war-crimes tribunal at Nuremberg. First, there was serious doubt as to whether the offenses charged against the Nazi leaders were firmly established in international law at the time they took place. Second, the tribunal suffered from the perception that it dispensed the justice of victors against the vanquished. Winston Churchill is said to have remarked when told of the proposed tribunal, "Remind me not to lose the next war."

Neither of these criticisms can be leveled at the Yugoslav tribunal. The human-rights norms that will form the basis for the prosecutions are now widely accepted, in particular the Four Geneva Conventions of 1949 and the Genocide Convention.[67] It is indeed difficult to imagine any of the warring parties claiming they were not bound by these norms; their legitimating power is simply too strong to be discarded. And, not surprisingly, each of the former Yugoslav republics involved in the conflict has accepted the Geneva Conventions and Genocide Convention as binding.[68]

The charge of dispensing victor's justice is similarly inappropriate. While one may certainly divine strategic advantages accruing to regional and global powers from a victory by one side or the other, it is fair to say that specific hegemonic goals are not driving the decision to prosecute war criminals. Of course all states stand to gain if the prosecutions lessen the chances of a broader Balkan war. But one should not regard such a desire for regional stability as equivalent to the mood of vengeance against

65. Associated Press, "Mitterrand, in Vietnam, Links Aid to Democracy," *New York Times*, 10 February 1993, A8.

66. S. C. Res. 808 (1993).

67. *Interim Report of the Commission of Experts Established Pursuant to Security Council Resolution 780*, UN Doc. S/25274, at 15 (Annex I), 1993.

68. *Report of the Committee of French Jurists*, UN Doc. S/25266, at 17, 1993.

Nazi Germany that prevailed after World War II. One need only contrast the genuine attempts at procedural fairness that mark the statute of the Yugoslav tribunal with the writings of normally sober-minded academics on the trial at Nuremburg.[69] One scholar, for example, writing in the *Harvard Law Review* in 1946, declared that "If ever there was a gang of malefactors who deserved extermination without the privilege of legal defense, it is the Nazi ringleaders."[70]

Strengthening the Sovereign State

What is the significance of these normative and institutional developments for the sovereign state? Has this growth in the scope of international law and in mechanisms overseeing its implementation taken human-rights issues "off the table" of exclusive domestic jurisdiction? The conventional view I have described would argue that the state has been weakened as a political unit. Many of its formerly exclusive prerogatives have been opened to scrutiny by international bodies. In many core areas of relation between government and citizen, regimes that transgress international norms may be subject to condemnation, sanction, or intervention. In extreme cases, such as OAS and General Assembly resolutions concerning the Haitian junta, a regime may be declared "illegal" in toto. If, as the World Court has suggested, the content of domestic jurisdiction shrinks in direct proportion to the expansion of binding international norms,[71] has the human-rights movement left the state with an increasingly emaciated core of functions it can call its own?

I believe this is not the case. The international community does not intend to assume (nor, given the weakness of international institutions, can it assume) permanent supervisory authority over governments' treatment of their own citizens. This is not to deny the reality of human-rights norms or the substantial efforts at their enforcement through

69. *The Statute of the International Tribunal* contains an impressive array of procedural protections for the accused. See *Report of the Secretary-General Pursuant to Paragraph 2 of Security Council Resolution 808* (1993), UN Doc. S/25704, 1993 (statute and official commentary on each article).

70. Sheldon Glueck, "The Nurenberg Trial and Aggressive War," *Harvard Law Review* 59 (1946): 396, 397–98.

71. *Tunis and Morocco Nationality Decrees,* 1923 PCIJ, at 24.

increasingly intrusive means. It is rather to argue that the international community has granted itself authority over the welfare of individuals for the more temporary purpose of remaking national institutions according to a liberal model. States organized on this model, it is assumed, will be stronger and less in need of attention by the international community. This is true because participation in the state's political life will be significantly broadened, thus creating among citizens a commitment to maintaining the institutions of government that make such participation possible.

This argument begins with the human-rights treaties themselves. These may be seen as social blueprints, in which the international community has crafted a model of relations between government and citizen, covering all important aspects of political life. States achieve compliance with the treaties when their political institutions come to resemble those described in the model. Apartheid South Africa, for example, was a pariah state; after all-race elections it is no longer so. Its shift in status came about after complete revision of its constitutional structure.

The international model, one must note, does not speak to every aspect of the political process. Human-rights treaties are phrased in broad, open-ended terms. As a result, significant national variations are permitted on issues not deemed to implicate questions of fundamental fairness; on these questions local political values may continue to govern. Where the treaties' core, nonderogable obligations are concerned, however, the dominant values are rather clearly those of a traditional liberal democracy. The treaties purport to guarantee political equality,[72] political liberty,[73] majoritarian elections, and, to the extent possible, the fostering of a tolerant civic culture.[74] These are the values that must mark political institutions seeking compliance with international norms.

For many years the ideological polarization of the Cold War precluded

72. All human-rights instruments prohibit discrimination on grounds such as gender, race, religion, ethnic group, etc. During the era of decolonization, the United Nations monitored elections and plebiscites in developing countries in which local groups sought to restrict the franchise on one or more of these grounds. The United Nations refused to conduct the votes under these circumstances. A more recent example is the insistence of both the European Community and the United States that the former Yugoslav republics accept international instruments on protection of minorities before they attained recognition.

73. This involves rights of political dissent, essential in a system in which decisions are taken by majority rule. The "International Covenant on Civil and Political Rights" protects the right to hold opinions (art. 19[1]); freedom of expression (art. 19[2]); the right to peaceful assembly (art. 21); and the freedom of association (art. 22).

74. See generally, Gabriel A. Almond and Sidney Verba, *The Civic Culture: Political*

agreement on whether human-rights norms embodied such liberal values, other values, or no values at all. The extensive practice of states and international organizations discussed above is evidence that such controversies have subsided. One particularly divisive issue was the legitimacy of the one-party state, with cleavages falling along predictable ideological lines. In late 1993, however, the UN Human Rights Committee became the last major human-rights tribunal to hold one-party states violative per se of the norm requiring "genuine" elections.[75] Regional schisms over human-rights issues, such as debate over the existence of distinct "Asian values," may represent more how diffuse and concerted the promotion of liberal democracy has become than the strength of resistance to such efforts by certain regimes.

The treaties' goal of fostering liberal transformations has in turn dictated the nature of the sovereign authority lodged in international institutions. The liberal communities envisioned by the treaties are assumed to be self-legitimizing and self-sustaining. The former as a result of the principle of popular sovereignty; the latter based on the hope that the new political systems will enjoy broad bases of participation and peaceful transitions of power. By providing such means for individuals to alter government policies that they find objectionable or even repressive, a liberal political culture relieves the international community of primary responsibility for the enforcement of human-rights norms. The locus of sovereign authority, in other words, is returned to the domestic level after an initial intervention. Barring a breakdown in the newly established political order, the assumption is that there it will stay. Even when a breakdown occurs, however, any intervention by international bodies will again serve the

---

Attitudes and Democracy in Five Nations (Princeton: Princeton University Press, 1963). UN voter education projects, conducted prior to most monitored elections, are the most obvious example of this goal at work. In the 1990 Haiti monitoring mission, for example, the secretary-general reported that the "first task" of UN monitors was "to help create a psychological climate conducive to the holding of democratic elections. To do this, permanent observers deployed throughout the country established numerous contacts with the local authorities, particularly the electoral and military authorities, and with all sectors of society." *First Report of the UN Observer Group for the Verification of the Elections in Haiti,* UN Doc. A/45/870, at 22 (Annex), 1990. The secretary-general stated bluntly that this education campaign was undertaken because "there is no democratic tradition in Haiti." Ibid., at 9. Similarly in Somalia, Boutros-Ghali reported to the Security Council that the UNOSOM II mission (United Nations Operation in Somalia) would assist Somalis in "recreating a Somali State based on democratic governance." *Report of the Secretary-General,* 19.

75. *Bwalya v. Zambia,* Communication No. 314/1988, reprinted in *Human Rights Law Journal* 14 (1993): 408.

limited purpose of creating conditions in which legitimate local authority may resume effective control.

International practice reflects this dynamic in a rather obvious fashion. The vast majority of efforts by international institutions to protect human rights has been targeted narrowly at what some scholars refer to as "illiberal" states; those whose treatment of their citizens does not conform in most respects to the Universal Declaration of Human Rights. By contrast, the standing of liberal states within the international community has not been significantly altered by the human-rights movement precisely because their internal structures are generally consistent with human-rights norms. Human-rights enforcement in these states is primarily a matter for domestic courts, administrative agencies, and other such institutions. The decisions of such liberal regimes are accorded substantial deference.

In a 1991 resolution promoting the establishment of democratic institutions, for example, the UN General Assembly declared that all states must "respect the decisions taken by other States, in accordance with the will of their people, in freely choosing and developing their electoral institutions."[76] Because their internal sovereign arrangements are acceptable, liberal states' external sovereignty remains fundamentally unaltered.

Illiberal states, on the other hand, have experienced significant changes in their external sovereignty. They are, in many ways, the beneficiaries of far fewer legal entitlements than are liberal states. But this is an interim condition. The evident goal is to remake their internal sovereign structures so that they resemble those of liberal states and, as a result, become self-sufficient in their policing of human-rights violations. Secretary-General Boutros-Ghali made this point recently in discussing election monitoring: "Although the United Nations is currently viewed as a primary source of electoral assistance, its role in this field should diminish over time as countries develop their own expertise and institutions to support the electoral process. A decline in demand for United Nations assistance would indicate that the Organization has fulfilled its role successfully and can focus on other important elements of the democratization process such as post-election follow-up and institutionalization."[77]

If the not-so-hidden agenda of human-rights law is civic-nation building, the human-rights regime would appear to complement rather than

---

76. G. A. Res. 46/137, operative paragraph 5 (1991).
77. *Report of the Secretary-General, Enhancing the Effectiveness of the Principle of Periodic and Genuine Elections*, UN Doc. A/47/668, at 20, 1992.

undermine the statist foundations of the Westphalian legal order. More specifically, it may be seen as reinforcing two trends or tendencies in the evolution of the international community that underline the privileged position of states as the community's defining constituent elements.

The first is the slow incorporation into the community of states formerly the territories of dissolved empires. Following the dismantling of the Austro-Hungarian and Ottoman Empires after World War I and the various colonial empires after World War II, the newly created states struggled with illogical borders, a patchwork of ethnic minorities, failure by former rulers to assist in transitions to independence, and other problems often leading to economic privation and civil war. Internationally, the result for these states was continued dependence and a perception of inferior status, despite the legal principle of state juridical equality (now codified in article 2[1] of the UN charter).

Human-rights law, as described above, may be seen as assisting in an ongoing process of moving these states from marginality to more effective membership in the international community. Its goal is not formal but functional equality. By addressing a chronic source of domestic instability—exclusionary political processes in which governments and citizens engage in destructive battles for power—human-rights law seeks to transform these states into vigorous and autonomous actors, capable of both formulating coherent national interests and articulating these interests in the full range of international forums.

The second, more recent trend is the international response to the rise of ethnic identity and solidarity as competitors to civic notions of citizenship. Despite the rampage of centrifugal forces that, in the post–Cold War era, have seemingly called into question the viability of the multiethnic state, international law has steadfastly resisted compromising its traditional refusal to equate the right to self-determination with an entitlement to independent statehood for all groups claiming coherence as a "people."[78] The state as a territory rather than the state as an ethnic nation continues to be the dominant norm. Human-rights law can be seen as assisting in the preservation of territorial statehood through attempts to establish (or reestablish) confidence in the legitimacy of multiethnic political communities.

It does so premised on the view that exclusionary political systems, particularly those in which ethnic minority groups are the victims of

---

78. See generally, Gregory H. Fox, "Self-Determination in the Post–Cold War Era: A New Internal Focus," *Michigan Journal of International Law* 16 (1995): 733.

human-rights abuses, may lead directly to calls for secession. The creation of inclusionary political processes, it is believed, works to diffuse secessionist claims. The notion of an "internal" right of self-determination—manifested in majoritarian elections and autonomy regimes for discrete minorities—is an expression of this impulse. Of course the international community's refusal to recognize even a limited right of secession need not be ascribed to such a lofty motive as promoting tolerance: states, not surprisingly, have an interest in remaining whole and are thus unlikely to support a norm that might someday lead to their own dismemberment. But the norm of territorial integrity is surely strengthened if the citizens of existing territorial states feel a stake in its continuation as such.

Conclusion

This chapter has described a normative model of a state. It is one in which citizens participate equally in a democratic process and whose essential liberties are not infringed by the majoritarian decision-making process that results. This model may succeed or it may fail, though clearly the number of liberal states has been increasing steadily. But under the model itself, which I have identified as an aspiration of the international community, liberal states will not have their jurisdiction to prescribe norms circumscribed in any significant way. Granted, the international community would retain residual authority to step in should the liberal model break down. But for the functioning liberal state, this is not sovereign authority in any meaningful sense. If the day-to-day process of governing is conducted within a liberal paradigm, the international law of human rights will matter very little. And paradoxically, the very irrelevance of that law will be the ultimate indicator of its success.

5

Clash of Principles
Self-Determination, State Sovereignty, and Ethnic Conflict

Kamal S. Shehadi

Transcending the nation-state, therefore, is a very ambiguous
topic, even a dangerous one for the future of the planet.
—Boutros Boutros-Ghali, speech at
the German Foreign Policy Association, Bonn,
January 1993

The clash of two principles, self-determination and state sovereignty, in
the late twentieth century is dangerous "for the future of the planet." It
has caused more than headaches to academics and lawyers who have had
to interpret and sometimes balance these principles. It has caused ethnic
conflicts between communal groups armed with one of these principles.
Most contemporary ethnic conflicts are conflicts between opposing views
on who has the right to exercise self-determination or how to exercise it,
including who has the right to exclusive or absolute sovereign statehood
over any given territory.

Ethnic self-determination conflicts are challenging the traditional understanding of both self-determination and state sovereignty. Where violent,
protracted ethnic conflict has been terminated, either the institutions of state
sovereignty have been remodeled to accommodate the contending groups'
different conceptions of state sovereignty and ethnic self-determination
(as has happened in Nigeria, Spain, Ethiopia, and South Africa), or a self-
determination claim has been crushed by an opposing state (as happened

with the Armenians after World War I, the Kurds in Iran after World War II, the East Timorese in 1975, and many others), or the central state has been defeated and its sovereignty destroyed and replaced, as happened in Ethiopia with the emergence of Eritrea in 1991, the former Yugoslavia, and the former Soviet Union. The resolution of most ethnic conflicts and the prevention of future ones requires a redefinition of the principles and institutions of state sovereignty and self-determination.

This chapter shows why such a redefinition is needed and how the two principles can be reconciled in the concept of shared sovereignty. The redefinition is needed, it is argued, because the clash of the two principles of state sovereignty and self-determination is at the root of most ethnic conflicts. To reconcile the two principles in theory and in practice, one has "to suggest acceptable guidelines for the operation of the principle of self-determination which, for obvious reasons, may not accede to the demands of every parochial sentiment but which must also avoid an uncritical affirmation of the supremacy of the 'sovereign' State."[1]

Ethnic self-determination is perhaps the most powerful force shaping the strategic environment of the 1990s. It has speeded up the collapse of the Soviet Union, Czechoslovakia, Ethiopia, and Yugoslavia, and it has helped replace totalitarian and authoritarian regimes with democratizing regimes. It has ignited and sustained civil wars in Azerbaijan, Burma (Myanmar), Georgia, Moldova, Sri Lanka, Sudan, Turkey, and the former Yugoslavia. It threatens to tear apart many countries, including Ethiopia and Russia; to fuel more ethnic conflicts and irredentist claims similar to the ones in Nagorno-Karabakh, the former Yugoslavia, and throughout Africa; and possibly to cause regional wars in the Balkans, the Middle East, and the Caucasus.

Uncontrolled and unchecked, ethnic self-determination conflicts will continue to challenge the international system. The first, and more direct and urgent, challenge is to international peace and security. In the words of Boutros-Ghali, "Rather than the 100 or 200 countries, you may have at the end of the century 400 countries, and we will not be able to achieve any kind of economic development, not to mention more disputes on boundaries."[2]

1. Lee C. Buchheit, *Secession: The Legitimacy of Self-Determination* (New Haven: Yale University Press, 1978), 7.

2. Evelyn Leopold, "UN Chief Laments Split of World into Powerless Mini-States," *Times* (London), 21 September 1992, 12.

Some conflicts over self-determination constitute a threat to international security and, therefore, require international intervention. Ethnic self-determination conflicts present a second challenge to the principle of state sovereignty and consequently to the existing international order, since the former is the basis of the latter.[3] British foreign secretary Douglas Hurd perhaps summarized the thinking of many of his counterparts when he expressed concern about the dangers to the sovereign state from "problems of minorities and . . . different perceptions of national identity."[4] It should be clear, however, that although self-determination itself does not pose a direct threat to the existing international order, the continued absence of a collective and consistent international response to the proliferation of claims to ethnic self-determination will destroy the international legal principle of state sovereignty that is the basis of the international order.

A Question of Principles

State sovereignty and self-determination are sometimes seen as contradictory principles of international relations. Few would disagree with Alfred Cobban's summary that "the history of self-determination is a history of the making of nations and the breaking of states."[5] Equally clear is that the history of state sovereignty has been a history of state building and the breaking of ethnic nations. Sometimes, as in the Western European experience, the breaking of ethnic loyalties and other primordial allegiances preceded the construction of a civic (territorially based) nationalism.[6] More commonly, the creation of sovereign states has exacerbated ethnic conflict and resulted in the domination by one ethnic group over many

3. Hedley Bull showed how state sovereignty—and the exchange of its recognition by states—is the basis of an international order. See *The Anarchical Society: A Study of Order in World Politics* (London: Macmillan, 1977), 8–9, 16–20, 36, 70. This is the theme of the article by Amitai Etzioni, "The Evils of Self-Determination," *Foreign Policy* 89 (Winter 1992–93): 21–35. For a fuller discussion of the strategic implications of self-determination and the strategies to control them, see Kamal S. Shehadi, *Ethnic Self-Determination and the Break Up of States* (London: Brassey's for the International Institute for Strategic Studies, 1993).

4. Speech to the Atlantic College, 15 February 1993. Transcript provided by the Foreign and Commonwealth Office, London.

5. Alfred Cobban, *The Nation-State and National Self-Determination,* rev. ed. (London: Collins, 1969), 42–43.

6. Anthony D. Smith, *The Ethnic Origins of Nations* (Oxford: Basil Blackwell, 1986), 136–37.

others.[7] Ethnic groups compete for the domination of a state because "it is the very process of the formation of a sovereign civil state that, among other things, stimulates elements of parochialism, communalism, racialism, and so on, because it introduces into society a valuable new prize over which to fight and a frightening new force with which to contend."[8]

While the principle of self-determination continues to inspire communal groups to seek greater self-government, even independence, state sovereignty strengthens the ability of states—and the communal groups that dominate them—to oppose the exercise of self-determination. This clash of principles provides the backdrop for many of the ongoing ethnic conflicts, hence the need to reconcile these two principles. This chapter suggests possible ways to achieve a reconciliation while promoting international peace and stability.

Sovereignty is an attribute of modern states.[9] Absolute state sovereignty is a product of the process of state building that took place in Europe and later spread to the rest of the world. Parallel to the state's two faces are the two faces of sovereignty. The internal aspect of sovereignty is the assertion of "supremacy over all other authorities within that territory and population."[10] The external aspect of sovereignty that entitles political entities to participate in international relations is twofold: it is in part constitutional and practical independence,[11] and in part " 'the totality of international rights and duties recognized by international law' as residing in an independent territorial unit—the State."[12]

The institution of state sovereignty has evolved since it was codified in

7. Walker Connor, "Nation-Building or Nation-Destroying?" *World Politics* 24 (April 1972): 319–55.

8. Clifford Geertz, "The Integrative Revolution: Primordial Sentiments and Civil Politics in the New States," in *Old Societies and New States: The Quest for Modernity in Asia and Africa,* ed. Clifford Geertz (New York: Free Press, 1963), 120.

9. Gianfranco Poggi, *The Development of the Modern State: A Sociological Introduction* (Stanford: Stanford University Press, 1978), 54, 87–92. On the formation of states, see Tilly, *Coercion, Capital, and European States.*

10. Bull, *Anarchical Society,* 8. Stephen D. Krasner defines it as the "final authority" in "Sovereignty: An Institutional Perspective," in *The Elusive State: International and Comparative Perspectives,* ed. James A. Caporaso (Newbury Park, Calif.: Sage Publications, 1989), 89. Friedrich Kratochwil calls it—more accurately—an "internal hierarchy," with the state at the top. See "Of Systems, Boundaries, and Territoriality: An Inquiry into the Formation of the State System," *World Politics* 39 (October 1986): 35.

11. Robert H. Jackson, *Quasi-States: Sovereignty, International Relations, and the Third World* (Cambridge: Cambridge University Press, 1990), 32. Hurst Hannum, *Autonomy, Sovereignty, and Self-Determination* (Philadelphia: University of Pennsylvania Press, 1990), 15.

12. James Crawford, *The Creation of States in International Law* (Oxford: Clarendon Press, 1979), 26. Crawford draws his definition from an International Court of Justice report.

the Treaties of Osnabrück and Münster, which laid the basis for the Peace of Westphalia. "The shift from the medieval to the modern international system," writes John G. Ruggie, is "the most important contextual change in international politics in this *millennium*."[13] In the medieval era, as Daniel Philpott has shown in chapter 1, there were various layers of "sovereignty" resulting from as many layers of suzerainty: a given territory afforded a number of competing lords over it, each in a relation of vassalage (subordination) or overlordship (superordination) to the other, but all sharing a common body of laws, religion, and custom. There was no distinction between the internal and external realms, but a complex system of overlapping hierarchies. In the shift to the modern era, a shift that occurred as a result of centuries of warfare and competition, but also as a result of military, technical, and economic changes, the state emerged as the absolute sovereign over a territory in a world system of territorial states. "The distinctive feature of the modern system of rule is that it has differentiated its subject collectivity into territorially defined, fixed, and mutually exclusive enclaves of legitimate dominion."[14]

The path to the modern absolutist state went through the stage of absolute monarchy. "Cette conception [of absolute monarchy] par laquelle des théoriciens extrêmes ont cru servir l'autorité royale l'a tuée, mais n'est point morte avec elle, au contraire elle a pris son essor au service d'une autorité nouvelle."[15] The institution of state sovereignty has evolved continuously since the emergence of the absolutist state, under pressure from increasing economic, social, and political interdependence at the international level, but also from new or reemerging ethnic nationalisms at the domestic level.[16]

Self-determination is taken to mean that a people determine their future.[17] This straightforward definition masks the complexity of deciding

13. John Gerard Ruggie, "Continuity and Transformation in the World Polity: Toward a Neorealist Synthesis," *World Politics* 35 (January 1983): 273.

14. John Gerard Ruggie, "Territoriality and Beyond: Problematizing Modernity in International Relations," *International Organization* 47 (Winter 1993): 151.

15. "The concept [of absolute sovereignty] by which extremist theoreticians believed they were serving royal authority killed it, but did not die with it. On the contrary, [the concept] expanded rapidly in the service of a new authority." Bertrand de Jouvenel, *De la souveraineté: À la recherche du bien politique* (Paris: Librairie de Médicis, 1955), 216.

16. For a comprehensive overview of the challenges to the sovereign state, see Joseph A. Camilleri and Jim Falk, *The End of Sovereignty? The Politics of a Shrinking and Fragmented World* (Aldershot: Edward Elgar Publishing, 1992).

17. For an excellent introduction to self-determination, see Morton H. Halperin and David J. Scheffer, with Patricia L. Small, *Self-Determination in the New World Order* (Washington, D.C.:

who the people are and what is the future they wish to determine. The answers to these questions have changed radically over time. Beneath the historical evolution of the two concepts, people and future, there are unchanging aspects upon which rests the definition of self-determination. First, it is a dynamic process, not a definitive state. Self-determination is exercised continuously without even temporary interruptions. Second, self-determination has two dimensions: an internal one that regulates relations between rulers and ruled within the community,[18] and an external one that regulates relations between the people and the outside world.[19] The internal dimension makes the people—the citizens—the source of state sovereignty and thus requires a democratic form of government. Ever since the French and American Revolutions, the "Divine Right of Kings" has been replaced with the "Divine Right of the People."[20] The external dimension of self-determination makes the community a distinct political entity entitled to shape its ties with other political entities, be they sovereign states, minority groups, or international organizations. Sovereign statehood is only one of many forms these ties can take.

The definition of who is entitled to claim self-determination and how self-determination can be exercised has changed since the principle first emerged in the eighteenth century. Initially, in both cases, there seems to have been no problem in identifying the people. The U.S. Declaration of Independence speaks of "one people," and the French Déclaration des droits de l'homme et du citoyen refers to the *peuple français*. The American Revolution aimed at establishing both internal and external self-determination in the form of democracy and independent statehood, respectively. The French Revolution, at least in its initial phases, aimed at tearing down an absolutist monarchy and establishing representative government.

The ideal of self-determination quickly spread to Latin America and the rest of Europe, sparking wars of national liberation that ultimately led to the emergence of new states. In this second wave, the people were identified

---

Carnegie Endowment, 1992). For the best overview of the legal dimension of self-determination under the UN system, see Hector Gros Espiell, *The Right to Self-Determination: Implementation of United Nations Resolutions* (New York: United Nations, 1980).

18. Michla Pomerance, *Self-Determination in Law and Practice* (Boston: Martinus Nijhoff, 1982), 1. Hannum, *Autonomy, Sovereignty, and Self-Determination*, 30. Buchheit, *Secession*, 14 and 16. The use of *internal* and *external* should not be confused with *domestic* and *foreign*, respectively. It is only in certain cases that the boundaries of the internal and the domestic, and those of the external and the foreign, coincide.

19. Buchheit, *Secession*, 14–15.

20. Cobban, *Nation-State and National Self-Determination*, 40.

by "popular proto-nationalisms," or by "feelings of collective belonging which already existed and which could operate, as it were, potentially on the macro-political scale."[21] These nationalist movements sought and obtained the creation of sovereign states, often with the support of a foreign power. In Latin America, decolonization created border conflicts between the new states. They responded to the challenge by eventually adopting the principle of *uti possidetis,* which meant that established colonial frontiers were accepted as permanent. This principle served as the basis for a collective policy to avoid setting off all-out regional war.

During World War I, Woodrow Wilson promoted self-determination as "an imperative principle of action, which statesmen will henceforth ignore at their peril."[22] To President Wilson self-determination meant: "No people must be forced under sovereignty under which it does not wish to live. No territory must change hands except for the purpose of securing those who inhabit it a fair chance of life and liberty."[23] There were at least two perceived strategic interests in promoting the principle of self-determination. The Allies hoped to secure the support of oppressed nationalities for the war effort and encourage them to rise against the multinational empires with whom they were at war. Furthermore, President Wilson thought that coupling popular sovereignty with national independence was a formula for a peaceful and harmonious world. But as he found out, translating the principle into practical policy was very problematic.[24] There was no way to define a priori what was a nation and therefore who was entitled to exercise the right to self-determination. In addition, the European powers opposed the application of the principle in many instances because of strategic and economic interests.

The covenant of the League of Nations did not mention self-determination but it set up three mechanisms, ostensibly to promote it: internationally supervised plebiscites, League of Nations mandates, and international protection of national minorities.[25] The League did not concern itself at all

21. E. J. Hobsbawm, *Nations and Nationalism Since 1870* (Cambridge: Cambridge University Press, 1990), 46–79.

22. Quoted in Cobban, *Nation-State and National Self-Determination,* 53.

23. Message from President Wilson to Russia, 9 June 1917. Reprinted in *Official Statements of War Aims and Peace Proposals, December 1916 to November 1918,* ed. James B. Scott, 104–5. Quoted in Halperin, Scheffer, and Small, *Self-Determination in New World Order,* 17.

24. On the problems of applying the principle of self-determination, see Cobban, *Nation-State and National Self-Determination,* 57–117.

25. Lawrence T. Farley, *Plebiscites and Sovereignty: The Crisis of Political Illegitimacy* (Boulder, Colo.: Westview, 1986).

with promoting democratic systems of government beyond the occasional supervision of plebiscites. It only regulated the external aspect of self-determination that was managed by the Allies in the postwar settlements arrived at in Versailles and in subsequent meetings. But these settlements proved very temporary. Nationalism and irredentism reared their ugly heads and came to dominate much of the history of the interwar period.[26]

The charter of the United Nations began to redefine the principle of self-determination. Self-determination became one of the purposes of the United Nations, as this organization was mandated with promoting self-government in, and the independence of, non-self-governing territories. It elevated the "principle" to a "right" of self-determination through various resolutions.[27] Some even argued that the right to self-determination was a "peremptory right."[28]

According to UN practice and public international law, the right to self-determination in the period of decolonization was to apply only to territorial entities, and it was to take mostly the form of sovereign statehood. It did not supersede the right of governments to preserve the sovereignty and territorial integrity of the states they governed. Sovereign states thus were entitled to use force to quell any attempt at secession. They were also entitled to request and receive outside help, while the secessionists were not. Some, however, argued that international support to self-determination movements, if they were fighting colonialism, was legally acceptable.[29] In the 1960 war for Katangan independence and secession from the Congo, and in the 1967 war for Biafran independence and secession from Nigeria, the sovereign state benefited from UN support. A few years later, UN secretary-general U Thant defended the UN policy: "You will recall that the United Nations spent over $500 million in the Congo primarily to prevent the secession of Katanga from the Congo. As an international

26. Hobsbawm, *Nations and Nationalism*, 143.

27. Hannum, *Autonomy, Sovereignty, and Self-Determination*, 33. See also G.A. Res. 1514, "Declaration on Colonial Countries," 1960; and G.A. Res. 2625, "Declaration on Friendly Relations," 1970. In *The Encyclopedia of the United Nations and International Relations*, ed. Edmund Jan Osmanczyk (New York: Taylor and Francis, 1990), 419, 459–61, respectively.

28. Espiell, *Right to Self-Determination*, 11.

29. Richard A. Falk, "Janus Tormented: The International Law of Internal War," in *International Aspects of Civil Strife*, ed. James N. Rosenau (Princeton: Princeton University Press, 1964), 185–248; Rosalyn Higgins, "Internal War and International Law," in *The Future of the International Legal Order*, vol. 3, *Conflict Management*, ed. Cyril E. Black and Richard A. Falk (Princeton: Princeton University Press, 1971), 81–121.

organization, the United Nations has never accepted and does not accept and I do not believe will ever accept the principle of secession of a part of its Member State."[30]

East Pakistan's secession and independence from Pakistan in 1970–71 to form Bangladesh is the exception that confirms the rule enunciated by U Thant. The secession was recognized internationally because, with the help of the Indian military, it had become a fait accompli and because the UN Security Council realized that doing otherwise would endanger international peace and security with the resumption of the Indo-Pakistani war.[31]

The United Nations did not resolve the debates over who is entitled to self-determination and how to exercise it. Even at the height of decolonization, the Western powers never accepted the restriction of self-determination to colonies and trust territories.[32] In particular, they—the Federal Republic of Germany especially—always insisted on its applicability to the peoples of the Soviet Union and the Soviet bloc. Furthermore, UN General Assembly Resolution 2625 broadened the definition of who is entitled to self-determination. It enunciated criteria that imply that, under certain conditions, secession may be permissible: "Nothing in the foregoing paragraphs shall be construed as authorizing or encouraging any action which would dismember or impair, totally or in part, the territorial integrity or political unity of sovereign and independent states conducting themselves in compliance with the principle of equal rights and self-determination of peoples as described above and thus possessed of a government representing the whole possible belonging to the territory without distinction as to race, creed, or colour."[33]

The West was able to make further inroads in expanding the definition of what constitutes a people entitled to self-determination. Beginning with the Covenant on Civil and Political Rights, self-determination was recognized as a human right.[34] By elevating it to a human right, self-determination became a peremptory norm of international relations.

---

30. UN secretary-general U Thant's press conference on 9 January 1970. *UN Monthly Chronicle*, February 1970. Quoted in Buchheit, *Secession*, 87.

31. Halperin, Scheffer, and Small, *Self-Determination in New World Order*, 15.

32. Interviews with legal experts attached to Western states' missions to the United Nations, fall 1992.

33. G.A. Res. 2625, in Osmanczyk, *Encyclopedia*, 461.

34. Louis Henkin argues that even though self-determination rights are collective rights, they were included in the covenant because governments recognized that "these rights [of self-determination] inured to individuals and were the foundation of all other rights." *The*

Article 1 of the covenant states that "All peoples have the right to self-determination. By virtue of that right they freely determine their political status and freely pursue their economic, social, and cultural development."[35] One interpretation of this article argues that peoples of independent and sovereign states are entitled to exercise self-determination.[36] It has also been argued that "national peoples, federated in a sovereign state and enjoying a distinct constitutional status, enjoy the right of external self-determination. This includes the right to independence, which the central sovereign, if a party to the Covenant, is bound to honor."[37] This interpretation, however, is not widely accepted and the right to self-determination does not justify secession from a federal state.[38]

The UN system attempts to reconcile the two principles of self-determination and state sovereignty in a straightforward manner. Territorial entities that have not achieved independence are entitled to claim the right to self-determination and achieve sovereign statehood. Once a state acquires the status of an independent sovereign state, however, no communal group within it can legitimately claim the right to self-determination for itself if this claim entails changing established international frontiers.

The reconciliation of self-determination and state sovereignty was carried out more consistently by the Conference on Security and Cooperation in Europe (CSCE). The Helsinki Final Act (1975) restated and linked explicitly the internal and external dimensions of self-determination.[39] This was done at the insistence of the Western nations, in particular the Federal Republic of Germany, over the opposition of the Soviet bloc nations.[40] The Final Act also restated the principles of the inviolability of borders, the sovereign equality of participating states and their territorial integrity, and the peaceful settlement of disputes. By lumping all these principles together, the CSCE did not just create enough confusion to make the compromise palatable to all parties. It also agreed that

---

International Bill of Rights: The Covenant on Civil and Political Rights, ed. Louis Henkin (New York: Columbia University Press, 1981), 18. For the text of the covenant, see 377–98.

35. Henkin, *International Bill of Rights*, 378.

36. Antonio Cassese, "The Self-Determination of Peoples," in Henkin, *International Bill of Rights*, 94.

37. Cassese, "Self-Determination of Peoples," 101.

38. Interview with legal experts attached to UN missions.

39. Principle VIII, "Helsinki Final Act" (1975), in Osmanczyk, *Encyclopedia*, 370–72.

40. Victor-Yves Ghebali, "Le droit des peuples à disposer d'eux-mêmes en Europe," *Arès* 13 (2), 91–94.

self-determination had to be reconciled with international peace and security, thus limiting the legitimate ways in which it could be pursued without diminishing its legitimacy as a peremptory norm of international relations.

In 1990, another step was taken along this road. CSCE's Copenhagen Conference on the Human Dimension issued a "Concluding Document" that reaffirms the CSCE's commitment to human rights; specifies criteria for free and fair elections, pluralistic democracy, and the rule of law; and develops the rights of persons belonging to national minorities. Some of the latter rights are in the nature of collective rights. Their definition implicitly redefines state sovereignty. For example, persons belonging to national minorities are allowed to "establish and maintain unimpeded contacts among themselves within their country as well as contacts across frontiers with citizens of other States with whom they share a common ethnic or national origin, cultural heritage, or religious beliefs."[41]

State sovereignty, in this case, cannot be invoked to cut such ties. What heretofore had been a prerogative of sovereign states has now become an internationally guaranteed right for persons belonging to national minorities. The creation of a CSCE high commissioner to whom national minorities can appeal directly is yet another change in the traditional understanding of state sovereignty that heretofore had kept international relations the preserve of independent states.

The UN and CSCE definition of self-determination notwithstanding, the dominant interpretation of self-determination today does not allow for a reconciliation of that principle with the traditional principle of absolute state sovereignty. Self-determination has given way to ethnic-national self-determination. Leaders of ethnic communities within internationally recognized states are claiming the right to self-determination for their ethnic groups, and they are successfully mobilizing significant support for it. From Radovan Karadzic, the Bosnian Serb leader in Bosnia-Herzegovina, to Djohar Dudaev, the Chechen leader in the Russian Federation, to Ibrahim Rugova, the Albanian leader in Kosovo, Serbia, the claim to self-determination has been made and is being made effectively in spite of the UN and CSCE interpretation of that principle. The claim to self-determination, which is sometimes caused by an abuse of sovereignty, collides with the principle of sovereignty. The collision leads to conflicts over sovereignty.

41. "Concluding Document," *World Affairs* 153 (Summer 1990): 28–39.

Conflicts over Sovereignty

At the root of many ethnic conflicts are irreconcilable, or seemingly irreconcilable, claims to sovereignty. Conflicts over sovereignty are either about who is entitled to claim the right to self-determination in a given territory and population, or they are about how self-determination is to be exercised within a state. These conflicts also vary according to the power base of the movement claiming self-determination and the state(s) opposing it, particularly whether it is intrastate or transstate.[42] Conflicts over sovereignty and self-determination create a need for the redefinition of both principles.

Conflicts over who is entitled to assert sovereignty over a given territory and population are conflicts over who is entitled to claim the right of self-determination. This type of conflict tends to be the most violent. Belligerents see the other side—people and leadership—as a threat to their own existence that has to be eliminated, hence the ferocity of combatants toward civilians. They see no room for cooperation: if one side accepts the other side's claim to self-determination, it fears its own claim will be invalidated. There is a reason for this zero-sum perspective: in an international system of exclusive territorial sovereignty, only one state can claim sovereignty over a territory and population.

Conflicts over who is entitled to self-determination do not present a theoretical challenge that can undermine the principle of state sovereignty because, after all, that is precisely what the adversaries are after. To the winner goes the claim to exclusive sovereignty over the disputed territory. In most cases, however, a settlement of the conflict requires power sharing or territorial agreements that change the nature of the conflict from a zero-sum conflict to a positive-sum conflict. Such agreements entail a redefinition of state sovereignty away from exclusive (or absolute) state sovereignty and toward the sharing of sovereignty between the state and the communal groups in the form of power sharing or territorial arrangements.[43]

The second type of conflicts over sovereignty are conflicts over the method by which a separate ethnic, religious, or linguistic group can

---

42. Halperin, Scheffer, and Small have suggested six categories of self-determination: anticolonial, substate, transstate, dispersed peoples, indigenous, and representative. See *Self-Determination in New World Order*, 49–52. These categories are not very useful analytically.

43. Shehadi, *Ethnic Self-Determination*, 59–72.

exercise self-determination (even if the word itself is not used by any of the parties involved). These conflicts are internal (civil) wars, yet they are just as likely to warrant international intervention as are the first type of conflicts (as we will see in the following section). There are different ways to exercise the right to self-determination. All of them involve a redefinition of the sovereignty of the central state, except when independence is sought, in which case the ethnic, religious, or linguistic group demands the total rejection of the central state.

Demands for self-determination have been myriad. The list includes minority rights (mainly cultural) within an existing state; consociational democracy or another form of ethnic power-sharing arrangement granting a certain degree of autonomy to the various communities (e.g., to Afars in Djibouti); representative democracy within an existing state (e.g., for Karens and Rohyingas in Burma); cultural autonomy, including religious and linguistic (as the Hungarians demanded in Rumania); territorial autonomy, both geographic and economic (e.g., for Albanians in Macedonia and for some of the North Caucasus republics of the Russian Federation); a federal unit in a federal state (as the Kurds demanded in Iraq); an independent state in a confederation of states (as the Bosnian Serbs demanded in Bosnia-Herzegovina); and independent statehood (such as that demanded by Eritrea, "Somaliland," and "Dnestr Republic").

Establishing the domain of self-determination in each particular case is not a straightforward process because declared goals are not always the real ones. Furthermore, there are usually many factions or parties with different views on how to exercise self-determination, and the goals often change over time. In any case, conflicts over how to exercise self-determination undermine the state's absolute sovereignty, and their solution requires a redefinition of that state's sovereignty to account for the changes in the political architecture of the state. A stable and peaceful resolution of such conflicts necessitates a move away from absolute state sovereignty to shared sovereignty.

Self-determination conflicts also vary according to the power base of the movement claiming self-determination and that of the state (or states) opposing it. The movement claiming it may have its power base in one country (intrastate) or in a number of countries (transstate). Transstate support may come directly from the government of a neighboring country, as support for the Workers' Party of Kurdistan came from Iran and Syria, or as support for the Rwanda Patriotic Front came from Uganda. Support may also come from the people, as when Iraqi Kurds supported the Workers' Party of Kurdistan before Turkey invaded Northern Iraq, or it may come from refugee camps set up across the border of the target state. The latter case occurred with the Palestinians in Lebanon and with the Karens in Thailand. A transstate power base, unlike an intrastate power base, contains the potential of transforming an internal conflict into an international one, opening up the possibility of international intervention under the umbrella of the United Nations.[44]

The state opposing self-determination movements may also benefit from international support, in which case there are real dangers of escalation into a regional war. Armenia has tried to mobilize Russian support for its conflict with Azerbaijan on the basis of its signing of the Commonwealth of Independent States Treaty. Similarly Azerbaijan, at one point, tried to draw Turkey—which, along with Russia, is a coguarantor of the Nakhichevan enclave sandwiched between Armenia and Turkey—into the fighting. If these alliances had materialized, the Nagorno-Karabakh conflict would have engulfed the whole region. Fortunately, both Russia and Turkey were cautious enough in their alliance policy not to let themselves be dragged into a war by proxy. But the potential of that happening elsewhere is very real.

The transnational dimension of self-determination conflicts makes it necessary to seek international, often regional, solutions to them. Foreign parties are just as influential as local ones in the negotiations, since they often provide the material support (arms and financing) that sustains the conflict. The need to redefine the principle of state sovereignty is not simply an academic exercise, as the spread of ethnic conflicts shows. The process of redefining institutions based upon absolute state sovereignty is already under way. This process, if not managed wisely, will have even more serious negative consequences on international security than it has heretofore.

Ethnic Self-Determination and International Security

Ethnic self-determination is a threat to state sovereignty and, consequently, to the existing international order. The threat is less from the proliferation

---

44. Halperin, Scheffer, and Small, *Self-Determination in New World Order*, 15.

of claims to self-determination than it is from conflicting international—in particular, Western—responses to those claims. There is indeed a threat to international security from individual self-determination conflicts. The consequences of self-determination need to be analyzed at two levels, the systemic and the international.

Systemic Consequences of Self-Determination

Self-determination has not yet changed the way units of the international system relate to each other. However, it has changed the number of the units. The structure of the international system, which is based on state sovereignty, has been damaged. It has not been damaged fatally, but there is increasing confusion about the meaning of state sovereignty. The international order has survived waves of self-determination (or state creation), and it can probably survive the post–Cold War wave. This latest wave, like the preceding ones, reinforces the system inasmuch as many of those seeking self-determination want recognition as sovereign states. As for conflicts over how to exercise self-determination, they often result in limiting the sovereignty of a state yet still fall short of endangering the state as the organizing principle of international relations.

The increase in the number of units of the system is not threatening in and of itself, even though cooperation and economic development are made more difficult. What is threatening to the international order, however, is a process of fragmentation that does not follow internationally accepted rules and norms. It is not the number of units but how they are created that should be of concern. If the process unfolds according to international rules and norms, the international system is reinforced. If it does not, either because there is no agreement on the rules or because no rules exist, the process of fragmentation is likely to be violent and a threat to international order. The Western community's response to the breakup of Yugoslavia is a case in point.

The vagueness of the two principles of self-determination and state sovereignty and the difficulty in reconciling them created confusion first and disagreement later among the Western allies over what policy to follow with respect to Yugoslavia in the summer of 1991. When disagreement turned into division over the policy of recognition, the European Community looked ineffective. Instead of adopting a common policy regarding Yugoslavia and regarding the secession of Croatia and Slovenia, the European countries adopted independent and conflicting policies.

These policies contributed to the hardening of the combatants' positions.[45] There is no doubt that the EC's failure to respond in a concerted fashion to the breakup of Yugoslavia was a contributing factor to the civil war and to the prevailing impression that the international order had broken down.[46]

International Security Consequences of Self-Determination

Cases of self-determination have implications for international security. There are four categories of consequences that can trigger international intervention:

1. Conflict in a strategically important country: There is a justified concern that the demands for self-determination in the Russian Federation and Ukraine will bring about either a nationalist, antidemocratic backlash or the collapse of state institutions followed by the outbreak of many civil wars. The problem is compounded by the fact that Russia and Ukraine have nuclear weapons that, if either scenario materializes, will constitute a major security threat. There are limits, however, to what the international community can do to avoid the breakup of the Russian Federation, Ukraine, China, or India, all nuclear powers and all, to varying degrees, vulnerable to being reshaped by the forces of ethnic self-determination.

2. Escalation of conflicts into regional wars: Self-determination conflicts can escalate into regional wars by drawing into the conflict the regional powers. The Somali-Ethiopian war over the Ogaden region is such a case. In the Western Sahara, Morocco and Algeria fought a war by proxy, with Algeria backing the Polisario. Throughout the last few years, the war between the Burmese government and the Karen rebels has escalated into the occasional confrontation between the Thai and the Burmese military. There is a fear that Serb actions in the province of Kosovo could draw Albania into a war with Serbia, or that the Armenian-Azeri conflict over the Nagorno-Karabakh enclave's right to self-determination could drag Turkey, Russia, or Iran into the conflict. This fear is

---

45. Interview with Hans van den Broek (EC commissioner for External Political Relations), *Financial Times*, 8 March 1993.

46. In interviews conducted at the United Nations in fall 1992 with diplomats from the Security Council member states, most would use concurrently the two terms *new world order* and *new world disorder*.

often overstated, especially by those parties hoping to garner international support for their cause. Regional powers are much more reluctant to intervene in civil wars, even if they have domestic political reasons to do so. Even in the case of intervention, regional powers often limit their ambitions and cooperate tacitly to avoid a regional conflict.[47]

3. The spread of conflicts: Self-determination claims spread through the "demonstration effect." If one group succeeds in establishing its claim to the right of self-determination by force against a central government, others will be encouraged. The Abkhaz and Ossetian separatism in Georgia, the Russian and Gagauz separatism in Moldova, and the separatism in the North Caucasus region of the Russian Federation have all fueled each other. Self-determination claims can also spread by "contagion." Militias infiltrate the borders of neighboring countries, stockpile weapons, and set up bases from which to launch cross-border attacks, often with the consent of the host government. This introduces an element of insecurity and anarchy in an area that hitherto had been at peace. Contagion brought the war from Sri Lanka to the state of Tamil Nadu in India, and from Burma to Bangladesh. It could also bring the Balkan conflict to Macedonia and pit ethnic Albanians against ethnic Macedonians.

4. Spillover of conflicts: Conflicts can spill over borders if they cause, as they often do, massive population movements. The fighting between the Iraqi government and the Iraqi Kurds spilled over into Turkey; the fighting between Rohyingas and the Burmese military has caused the movement of more than two hundred thousand refugees into Bangladesh; the fighting in Sudan led to refugees flowing into Ethiopia. In some cases (such as the India-Pakistan war of 1971 and the Iraqi-Kurdish war of 1991) the UN Security Council deemed the situation a threat to international peace and security and, on that basis, intervened.

The wave of self-determination conflicts threatens both the international order and international peace. The clash between self-determination and state sovereignty cannot be ignored much longer, nor can the various conflicts born from it be treated with the same old medicine: supporting the state's war-making capabilities to ensure its victory over those claiming the right to self-determination.

47. Examples of regional power tacit cooperation: India and Sri Lanka; Israel and Syria in Lebanon; Morocco and Algeria in the Western Sahara conflict since 1988.

Conclusion: Reconciling Self-Determination and State Sovereignty

The great powers will have to develop cooperative policies to deal with the security consequences of self-determination if they wish to preserve the existing international order. The starting point for such a cooperative approach is to reach an agreement on a common interpretation of the principles of self-determination and state sovereignty. This interpretation has to be consistent with the requirements of international security: avoiding the breakup of a strategically important state, controlling escalation, containing the spread of conflicts, and dealing with the spillover effects of self-determination conflicts.

Sometimes, however, the redrawing of boundaries is necessary to end the conflict. It should be remembered that the first wave of state creation in the nineteenth century that followed the end of the Napoleonic wars began with the Concert of Europe's carving of Greece out of the Ottoman Empire. Then, as in many subsequent ethnic wars, the great powers recognized that a redrawing of boundaries was necessary for the stability of the international order.[48]

But in many, if not most, ethnic conflicts, partition is not—or cannot be—an option. Solutions need to be developed that reconcile the demands of the belligerents, which always amount to either state sovereignty or self-determination. Unfortunately, the reconciliation of these two principles today prevails only in the corridors of the United Nations and in the language of diplomats, while in the killing fields and war rooms of ethnic groups, it is rejected as irrelevant either because it does not satisfy the ambitions of would-be state builders or because it does not address the real fears and concerns of a community. The clash of the two principles has, unfortunately, a violent and destructive side to it in the realm of international law and interethnic relations.

The principle of absolute state sovereignty has to be made more flexible if the international community is to reach agreement on a new definition of the balance between sovereignty and self-determination. The international institution of absolute sovereignty is already under attack from the global economic developments that limit the state's ability to

---

48. See Kamal S. Shehadi, "Great Powers, International Institutions, and the Creation of National States: A Comparative Study of the Concert of Europe, the League of Nations, and the United Nations" (Ph.D. diss., Columbia University, 1995).

control the domestic economy. In the economic realm, states have learned to share sovereignty with other states, international organizations, and amorphous international markets. A similar process of adaptation has to take place at the political level to make it easier for ethnic minorities to accept the internationally recognized boundaries and forego secession. Where ethnic minorities take up arms to achieve a certain level of self-determination short of independence, territorial and political arrangements have to be made to allow for the effective sharing of sovereignty between ethnic groups and between those groups and the state of which they are citizens.

A cooperative approach can ensure that self-determination does not destroy the institution of state sovereignty and that there is a consensus on the goals and methods of international interventions. But the institution of state sovereignty has to be made more flexible if it is to resist the challenges of self-determination.

6

Shared Sovereignty, Enhanced Security

Lessons from the Yugoslav War

James Gow

In the post–Cold War world, there can be no doubt that something has changed. This is attested not only in the content of academic and political discussion, but in practice, in cases such as the Kurdish region of northern Iraq, Bosnia and Herzegovina, Somalia, and, in a different context, Libya.[1] Understanding of the key concept of sovereignty has clearly moved: as yet

This chapter has evolved from two papers that I presented at the two conferences leading to this volume. Since that time, one of these papers was developed into "Serbian Nationalism and the Hisssssing Sssssnake: Which Nation? Whose Sovereignty?" *Slavonic and East European Review* 73 (July 1994): 456–77. Parts of this chapter draw on that study. In addition, this chapter draws on work for the Harry Frank Guggenheim "Nationalism" project and the workshop "International Society After the Cold War: Sovereignty and Self-Determination," sponsored by the Ford Foundation at the London School of Economics, where a presentation of the legitimation-of-sovereignty theme in this chapter was made. In addition, I am grateful for the assistance of Spyros Econimides at the LSE; Sir John Coles, permanent undersecretary at the Foreign and Commonwealth Office, London; and my colleagues Jan Willem Honig and Christopher Dandeker.

1. See, for example, the following discussions: Paul Fifoot, "Functions and Powers, and Inventions: UN Action in Respect of Human Rights and Humanitarian Intervention," in *To*

it is not clear where to. Often the content of contemporary thought on sovereignty and other key concepts is not entirely new; interpretations may recall theoretical work from earlier periods. What is new, however, is the relevance of these ideas to security crises at the end of the twentieth century and, concomitantly, their bearing on policy and practice in international relations.

In June 1992, the changing nature of international-security problems and of the central concept of sovereignty was reflected in the UN secretary-general's report *An Agenda for Peace*. In it, Boutros Boutros-Ghali emphasized the need to improve activities such as preventive diplomacy, peacemaking, peacekeeping, and the reconstruction of peace after wars (civil or international). He also called for increased attention to the problems of economic despair, social injustice, and political oppression. He continued:

> The foundation-stone of this work is and must remain the State. Respect for its fundamental sovereignty and integrity are crucial to any common international progress. The time of absolute sovereignty, however, has passed; its theory was never matched by reality. It is the task of the leaders of states today to understand this and to find a balance between the needs of good internal governance and the requirements of an ever more interdependent world. Commerce, communications and environmental matters transcend administrative borders; but inside these borders is where individuals carry out the first order of their economic, political and social lives.[2]

The secretary-general's words reveal increasing appreciation of the fact that international security depends on the internal political development of states. This is especially the case in the postcommunist countries of Europe, where the position of national minorities is commonly (and increasingly perceived to be) a security concern both within and between states.

The end of the Cold War provided a new set of challenges to international

---

Loose the Bands of Wickedness: International Intervention in Defence of Human Rights, ed. Nigel Rodley (London: Brassey's, 1992); Jarat Chopra and T. G. Weiss, "Sovereignty Is No Longer Sacrosanct: Codifying Humanitarian Intervention," *Ethics and International Affairs* 6 (1992): 95–117; Christopher Greenwood, "Is There a Right to Humanitarian Intervention?" *The World Today* 49 (May 1993): 5; and "Human Rights and External Intervention," Ditchley Conference Report No. D93/8, The Ditchley Foundation, 1993.

2. Boutros-Ghali, *Agenda for Peace*, para. 17.

order, resulting in the third wave of state formation in the twentieth century and increasing UN membership from 50 in 1945 to 185 in 1995. Three communist federations, Yugoslavia, the Soviet Union, and Czechoslovakia, gave way to new states formed from the erstwhile federal elements. In turn, many of these new states were themselves subject to disintegrationist pressures. The new situations in the former communist world drew attention to the position of weak states in other parts of the world where substate groups, sometimes supported politically and militarily by neighboring kin-states, raised critical questions concerning statehood. This process of challenge and formation was accompanied by violent unrest and war—most prominently in the former Yugoslavia. The events in Yugoslavia and elsewhere have pushed concepts inherent in the "hissing snake"[3]—sovereignty, statehood, self-determination, and security—onto the international agenda, both for students of international society and for policy makers and practitioners in national governments and international bodies such as the Organization for Security and Cooperation in Europe (OSCE) or the United Nations.[4]

A better understanding of what these concepts entail is crucial to resolution of Europe's postcommunist conflicts and has ramifications around the world. Until it has been established who is entitled to do what and in what circumstances, the representatives of the international community will find both dealing with the breakup of states and making judgments on the question of external—particularly humanitarian—intervention in internal crises and conflicts confusing, painful, and crippling. One of the major problems manifest in the international handling of the disintegration of Yugoslavia was the absence of established international standards for dealing with the challenges involved, and indeed a general lack of understanding of concepts at the heart of debates.

The aim of this chapter is to consider the Yugoslav war of dissolution

3. For an explanation of the hissing-snake image, see Gow, "Hissssing Sssssnake," where the clash of the four Ss noted here (sovereignty, self-determination, statehood, and security), as well as the four Ss of Serbian nationalism (*samo sloga srbina spasava*, "only unity saves the Serbs"), are used in an attempt to provide a prism for understanding the issues at stake in the Yugoslav war of dissolution. Discussion of these issues also appears in James Gow, *Triumph of the Lack of Will: International Diplomacy and the Yugoslav War* (New York: Columbia University Press, 1977), chap. 4, and is reflected in the present text.

4. The designation OSCE (Organization for Security and Cooperation in Europe), which came into being formally on 1 January 1995, is used throughout to refer to its immediate ancestor, the Conference on Security and Cooperation in Europe (CSCE), which was responsible for the Helsinki Final Act of 1975.

for two purposes. The first is to illustrate the continuing importance of sovereignty (complemented by statehood and self-determination in a vital troika) and the ways in which it is disputed at the end of the twentieth century. The second purpose is to identify the critical evolution in practice and, gradually, in principle, of conventional interpretations of the concept in international affairs, recognizing that in the 1990s, while sovereignty remains absolute, the unitary quality long ascribed to it is proving to be divisible and capable of being shared, both within the state and internationally, creating, potentially, a "compound international sovereignty regime."

It should be stressed that however much sovereignty may prove to be divisible through the apportionment of the exercise of sovereign rights, each portion, while potentially insufficient in practice, remains necessarily absolute in theory. This process, as yet incomplete and largely unrecognized as such, has major implications for international security. The divisibility of sovereignty and its reapportioning constitute the legitimation of sovereignty. The legitimation of sovereignty, including general acceptance of new understandings of it, in both practical and conceptual terms, is essential to internal and international peace and security. Shared sovereignty can mean enhanced security.[5]

Sovereignty, Statehood, and Self-Determination

States are the necessary components of an international system, and the principle by which they are ordered is that of sovereignty. Sovereignty is one of the concepts that falls into a category of ideas in which a great part of the value is that they are "essentially contested."[6] In practical use, sovereignty has a number of purposes, as Alan James has pointed out.[7] The major ones are rhetoric, power, competences, and status.[8]

---

5. This idea underpins a variety of ideas for creating security in Northern Ireland through models of "co-sovereignty." See Brendan O'Leary et al., *Northern Ireland: Sharing Authority* (London: Institute for Public Policy Research, 1993), 127–32.

6. Similar notions are liberty and justice. See W. B. Gallie, *Philosophy and the Historical Understanding* (London: Chatto and Windus, 1964), chap. 8.

7. Alan James, "Sovereignty in Eastern Europe," *Millennium: Journal of International Studies* 20 (Spring 1991): 81–89.

8. James, "Sovereignty in Eastern Europe," 81.

The first of these refers simply to the resonance that use of the word can have on an audience, irrespective of any real meaning attached to it. The second connotes a state's ability, actual or implicit, to get its way in international dealings, whether preventing something from being done to it, or influencing another state to take a particular course of action. The third implies a legal right of jurisdiction in a particular sphere, whether that sphere be territorial or an abstraction of political, economic, or legal activity. These three aspects of sovereignty feed into the fourth and are symbiotically nourished by it: it is because sovereignty carries with it a particular status that is much played on and much sought after. It is the qualification, in conventional thought on international relations, for membership in the society of states. As Alan James, among others, has described it, the qualities of sovereignty, from the international perspective, are as follows: it is a "legal, absolute and unitary quality."[9] However, the traditional view of sovereignty as "unitary," or "indivisible," allows for abuse of state power, preventing external involvement in matters that are deemed to be covered by domestic jurisdiction.[10]

In practice, as Robert Jackson has argued with reference to the developing world, as others have argued generally, and as will be discussed below with reference to postcommunist states in Europe,[11] the quality of sovereignty associated with any particular state may vary, meaning that the content of sovereignty will change from one state to another. Certainly the meaning and content of sovereignty will often change according to the need of a particular government at a particular time. It is a plastic term, allowing a government to justify almost any action, whether assertive or contrite, in terms of exercising its sovereign rights. Essentially, this means

9. Alan James, *Sovereign Statehood: The Basis of International Society* (London: George Allen and Unwin, 1986), 39.

10. On the apparent absolute protection provided by conventional understandings of sovereignty in international politics and law, as encapsulated in the UN charter, see Nigel Rodley, "Collective Intervention to Protect Human Rights and Civilian Populations: The Legal Framework," in Rodley, *To Loose the Bands of Wickedness*.

The degree to which the world has changed is notable: when the original version of what became this analysis was presented in April 1992, the suggestion that sovereignty was divisible met with considerable opposition. As the paper and the project of which it was part evolved, in some quarters the original opposition had given way to musing on whether the "conventional" idea of sovereignty might be a straw man.

11. Robert H. Jackson, *Quasi-States: Sovereignty, International Relations, and the Third World* (Cambridge: Cambridge University Press, 1990). See also Barry Buzan, *People, States and Fear: An Agenda for International Security Studies in the Post–Cold War Era* (Hemel Hempstead: Harvester-Wheatsheaf, 1991), 67–69.

it has decided for itself what to do. It is the "power of action without being bounded unto others."[12] While often taken to be a fundamentally legal concept in international relations,[13] sovereignty is, in reality, both legal and political. Indeed, it is ultimately a political concept because, as I shall emphasize below, the basic meaning of sovereignty is the political supremacy to make law (even though, in modern practice, the makers of law themselves are likely to be subject to legal restraint).

The origin of the sovereignty system lies in the Treaty of Westphalia of 1648, and although sovereignty may be susceptible to different interpretations, its general importance and formal content have remained constant: that is, the key to the Westphalian system was mutual recognition between sovereigns. This has remained the case, despite the manifold variety in and changes to the exercise of sovereign rights and duties. The content of sovereignty changed in one essential way as the system of which it was the guiding principle was extended. Whereas the Westphalian agreement had been made between sovereigns who were individuals (monarchs), this prescriptive mode of sovereignty had been generally supplanted by a popular one in Europe by the twentieth century. This meant that the exercise of sovereign rights was no longer the prerogative of a single personality but that of the representatives of the state's governing institutions. Increasingly, the degree to which power holders are seen to embody the will and interests of the people of a particular state has become a factor in their being accepted and granted recognition as representatives of the sovereign by others in international society.[14]

The rise of the importance of the principle of self-determination alongside the shift from prescriptive to popular sovereignty went hand in hand with the rise of modern nationalism.[15] Associated especially with the shift from monarchical to republican rule in France, the idea of the nation-state

12. Gordon Pocock, "Nation, Community, Devolution, and Sovereignty," *Political Quarterly* 61 (July–September 1990): 323.

13. For this reason, many international lawyers, in particular Americans, assume sovereignty to be not only a legal concept, but to refer to a "constitution," because in the United States the Constitution is held to be invested with sovereignty—although in reality, domestic sovereignty is shared between the executive and legislative branches of government and the judiciary and, of course, the people. The case for purely legal conceptions of sovereignty is made, for example, by Gregory H. Fox in Chapter 4 of this book. Fox draws on Brownlie, *Principles of Public International Law*, 4th ed., 1990.

14. See James Mayall, *Nationalism and International Society* (Cambridge: Cambridge University Press, 1990), 28.

15. See Alfred Cobban, *The Nation-State and National Self-Determination* (London: Collins. 1969).

developed. The essence of this idea is that those of what Anthony D. Smith terms the *"ethnie"*[16] (the ethnic community,[17] sharing a collective name, a myth of common ancestry, social solidarity, and certain elements of culture, often language and religion) should have the right to decide on their own government. By analogy with the freedom of individuals, nations were taken, paraphrasing John Stuart Mill, to be free to pursue their own good in their own way, so long as they did not deprive others of theirs or impede their efforts to obtain it.[18]

The critical difference between an ethnic group defined by a separate culture, of which more than eight thousand have been identified,[19] and an ethnic community that may be regarded as a nation is the degree to which the group is politically dynamic. More precisely, the distinction between an ethnic community qua ethnic community and a nation is its relationship to statehood and, by implication, to sovereignty. Nations either form a sovereign state, or have or seek a constitutional stake in one, or are politically engaged in trying to form one, or define themselves vis-à-vis one.

Thus, historically, Gypsies have never formed a national, or nationalist homeland; rather, they have been an ethnic community (usually despised) in whichever of the countries they were to be found. In contrast, another historically dispersed group, the Jews, had a politically dynamic character, leading to the formation of an independent state. Nationalism, therefore, is simply that phenomenon in which the sentiment of common, usually ethnic, identity is used to mobilize political sentiment. Any ethnic group can form a nationalist movement once it seeks to assert, or defend, itself politically as a community. The political action of one nationalist program forces others to address their own identity.[20] One group's claim for political status challenges the status of other groups in a quest for political supremacy.

The UN system confirmed the preeminence of the sovereign state as the primary unit of international relations. Articles 2(4) and 2(7) of the UN charter determine legally, and often politically and practically, the conduct

16. Anthony D. Smith, *National Identity* (London: Penguin, 1991); and Anthony D. Smith, "The Ethnic Sources of Nationalism," *Survival* 35 (Spring 1993): 49–50.

17. Benedict Anderson, *Imagined Communities*, rev. ed. (London: Verso, 1991), 6. Anderson argues that these are imagined communities for the reason, among others, that the members "will never know most of their fellow members, meet them, or even hear of them, yet in the minds of each lives the image of their communion."

18. John Stuart Mill, *On Liberty* (Harmondsworth: Penguin, 1974), 60.

19. Ernest Gellner, *Nations and Nationalism* (Oxford: Blackwell, 1983), 43–52.

20. Slavenka Drakulic, "Overcome by Nationhood," *Time* (International), 20 January 1992, 52.

of international relations. Conventionally, it has been these paragraphs that have confirmed the sanctity of the state and its right to be free from interference in its internal affairs. Article 2(4) proscribes "the threat or use of force against the territorial integrity or political independence of any state," while 2(7) establishes the concept of "domestic jurisdiction": "Nothing contained in the present Charter shall authorize the United Nations to intervene in matters which are essentially within the domestic jurisdiction of any state."

In addition, among its key principles, stated in article 1, the charter established the role of the Security Council in dealing with matters of international peace and security and "respect for the principle of equal rights and self-determination of peoples."

To some extent, the UN charter was drafted in response to the second wave of nationalist pressure for the formation of new states in the twentieth century (the first having followed World War I, as identified above), although it perhaps also fostered the phenomenon. The second wave was characterized by what has been termed "anticolonialist nationalism."[21] In this phase, "nationalist leaders more often than not mobilized diverse groups who shared a hostility to colonial rule rather than a pre-colonial group sentiment or identity of interest."[22] The physical product of this process was a large number of new states, many of which were in crucial respects weak.[23]

The new states inherited the territorial configurations of former colonial units. Ineluctably, in all those cases where "diverse groups" sharing only a common opposition to colonial rule emerged as residents of a single state, the right of various substate groups to continue the process of self-determination was, in effect, curtailed in an attempt to "freeze the political map."[24] In short, the concept of national self-determination was confined to "anti-colonial self-determination."

In Africa members of the Organization of African Unity opted in 1963 against challenges to the border regime established under colonialism and in favor of the state-sovereignty system. Despite the almost complete absence of congruence between ethnic communities and state borders, OAU members voted to preserve colonial boundaries, reasoning that any attempt to redraw frontiers would create more problems than it would

21. Mayall, *Nationalism and International Society,* 47.
22. Mayall, *Nationalism and International Society,* 49.
23. See Jackson, *Quasi-States.*
24. Mayall, *Nationalism and International Society,* 56.

solve.[25] With the single exception of the secession of Bangladesh from Pakistan, until the collapse of the communist federations at the beginning of the 1990s led to a wave of new state formation, no group or territory claiming to exercise a right to self-determination beyond the anticolonial context achieved international recognition of its claim to sovereignty and statehood.

Sovereignty and Self-Determination: Implications of the Yugoslav Dissolution

In the two years leading up to the declarations of independence by Slovenia and Croatia, and in the wake of those declarations, different understandings of who held what rights were in conflict with the rights to sovereignty and self-determination.[26] These conflicting conceptions were addressed in the European Community's Conference on Yugoslavia, held first in The Hague and later in Brussels. In particular, they were considered by a legal advisory and arbitration commission established during the conference and led by the president of the French Constitutional Court, Robert Badinter. It was their interpretation of constitutional and international legal matters that provided the framework for the council of the European Community to act politically to settle these questions, at least partially.

Despite the consideration that has been devoted to establishing what it means and who possesses it, in the final analysis, sovereignty means only one thing: the sovereign, whoever or whatever it might be in particular circumstances, is the inalienable ultimate authority. The sovereign, simply put, has the right not to be overruled.[27] Self-determination is the right accorded to "all peoples" in, among other places, the International Covenant on Civil and Political Rights (1966) to "determine their political status and freely pursue their economic, social and cultural development." Although it is a general right that is usually assumed to include

---

25. Mayall, *Nationalism and International Society,* 56.

26. These issues are discussed more fully in James Gow, *Legitimacy and the Military: The Yugoslav Crisis* (London: Pinter; New York: St. Martin's Press, 1992). The present analysis is adapted from Gow, "Hissssing Ssssnake."

27. See Michael Akehurst, *A Modern Introduction to International Law* (London: George Allen and Unwin, 1970).

the right to statehood for all communities that seek to rule themselves, in practice, its application has been more limited.[28] It has remained, however, an evocative and effective symbol.

At the heart of the constitutional-political dispute, although not a part of it, as such, was the meaning given to the word *nation*. Divergent interpretations of *nation* rendered radically different outcomes in terms of the compound concepts of national self-determination and national sovereignty. Nation refers to people who are, with small exceptions, born together into a particular community. Nation may, therefore, refer to all the people born within the territorial boundaries of a political community in which they have citizenship rights. It is in this sense that American presidents often address "the nation." Nation may also, however, allude to all the people born within a particular ethno-national group (which might be defined by genetic, linguistic, cultural, religious, and so forth, characteristics) irrespective of the territorially defined political communities in which they find themselves.[29]

The declarations of independence by Slovenia and Croatia were based in claims to sovereignty and the inalienable right to national self-determination for the republics and their populations. These were directly opposed by a Serbian claim to the sovereignty of the Serbs as an ethno-national people, wherever they were to be found, with the fundamental and inalienable right to national self-determination. Both claims were made on the basis of the Yugoslav constitution.

The right to self-determination, up to and including the right to secession, was granted in the preamble to the Yugoslav constitution.[30] Each republic was a "nation-state" formation that was endowed with sovereignty.[31] The general problem of defining the right holder—that is, which nation was repository of these inalienable rights—was compounded in the Yugoslav case. *Narodno samoopredeljenje* ("national self-determination" in Serbo-Croat) intensified the terminological tension.

28. In his *Agenda for Peace,* UN secretary-general Boutros Boutros-Ghali noted the unending fragmentation that could occur if every "national" group claimed the right to form a state.

29. Tomaz Mastnak, "Is the Nation-State Really Obsolete?" *Times Literary Supplement* (London), 7 August 1992, 11. Mastnak points out the interchangeable use of *nation* and *state* in some instances.

30. Ustav Socijalističke Federativne Republike Jugoslavije (Constitution of the Socialist Federal Republic of Yugoslavia, with amendments), Službeni List SFRJ (Yugoslav Official Gazette), Belgrade, 1991, p. 9.

31. "The Socialist Republic is a state, founded on the sovereignty of the nation . . ." Ibid., art. 3, p. 23.

In Serbo-Croat, *narod* means both "people" and "nation." In both senses, it can refer to the ethno-national group or to the inhabitants of a state. The difficulty here is amplified with reference to the global organization, the United Nations, which can be rendered as either Ujedinjeni Narodi or Ujedinjenje Nacije. In other words, in some cases a separate word may be used to refer to nation-as-state.[32] This implies that in Serbian minds, the term *narodno samoopredeljenje* was taken (both really and, where appropriate, disingenuously) to refer to the Serbian people wherever they were.

The ambiguity over national self-determination in the Yugoslav context has peculiar features. These, however, are particulars that only add emphasis; they do not render the Yugoslav example itself unique. Outside that context, the issue has generally been more clearly defined. Indeed, the general understanding received from previous periods (particularly decolonization) in which self-determination and sovereignty were key questions informed the Badinter Commission as it considered the Yugoslav case.

The commission effectively rejected the Serbian claim to sovereignty for the ethno-nation in its official opinions. It deemed sovereignty to rest with territorial units, that is, the republics. It was less categoric when the Serbian camp sought clarification about the right to self-determination of the Serbs in Croatia and in Bosnia and Herzegovina. It did not express the opinion that a right to self-determination was not available to the Serbs in Croatia and in Bosnia and Herzegovina.[33] Rather, the commission implied that there might possibly be a second level at which self-determination operated. In this case, self-determination could be regarded as a principle that extended from the protection of individual human rights and involved the possibility of individuals claiming membership of an ethnic, religious, linguistic, or other group. Groups of this type would be entitled to respectful treatment by states under the imperative norms of international law (*jus cogens*).[34]

The commission's opinions were based largely on traditional international law and convention, although to some extent there was innovation appropriate to the Yugoslav problem. Whereas in theory self-determination might be interpreted as applying at the lowest level to individuals, it is

32. Both *narod* and *nacija* could be used in both senses in all Serbo-Croat variants. However, this example is offered to highlight the confusions and ambiguities involved.

33. See Marc Weller, "The International Response to the Dissolution of the Socialist Federal Republic of Yugoslavia," *American Journal of International Law* 86 (July 1992): 591.

34. I am grateful to Ben Kingsbury for this point and others, which benefited from his international lawyer's perspective.

essentially a collective right. In practice, application of the right has been restricted to specific circumstances, and only with regard to predetermined territorial units, mostly in the course of decolonization.[35] Badinter made clear that the principle of *uti possidetis*, originally established in the context of decolonization, pertained to Yugoslavia. This meant that in the absence of peaceful agreement to alter frontiers that were changing status, "the former boundaries acquire the character of boundaries protected by international law."[36]

According to this opinion, the protection in international law of their boundaries was extended to the emerging states. A number of legally non-binding international documents, including the Helsinki Final Act, upheld the importance of preserving international frontiers unless change is peacefully negotiated. Most important, however, it was backed by reference to the UN charter. In effect, the commission judged that the republics were entitled to the protection and provisions of article 2 of the UN charter concerning the territorial integrity and political independence of states.[37]

The following is a summary of the arbitration commission's opinions on what is implied by the terms *sovereignty* and *self-determination*. The former applies to territorial units, as does self-determination, up to and including statehood. However, self-determination may also apply to other national groups (self-defining ethnic, religious, genetic, cultural, linguistic, and so forth), as an expression of their members' individual human rights. This does not include the right to form a state, although it entails the right to status, including levels of autonomy—political and cultural prerogatives and powers, perhaps of self-governance, operable within the boundaries of a state.

The blending of elements of international law (*uti possidetis juris*) with the provisions of the Yugoslav constitution offered clarification of the issues at stake. Sovereignty and statehood were both linked to territory; national self-determination was linked to them in cases where *nation*

35. The entities that have had claims to statehood granted have fallen into the following cases: mandated, trust, and other territories treated as non-self-governing under chap. IX of the UN charter; distinct political-geographical entities subject to *carence de souveraineté* (decay of sovereignty—the only successful case here is Bangladesh); territories whose parties agree to a plebiscite; formerly independent entities reasserting their independence; and, following the demise of the communist federations in Yugoslavia, the Soviet Union, and Czechoslovakia, federating republics from a dissolved state.

36. Avis no. 3, 11 January 1992.

37. See Nigel Rodley, "Collective Intervention to Protect Human Rights and Civilian Populations," 14–15.

referred to the people living within the boundaries of a defined territorial unit. Sovereignty, statehood, and national self-determination were not necessarily linked and were not juridically to be combined where *nation* alluded to the members of an ethno-national community that formed part of one or more states, or to territorial units with the potential to become states.

While none of this ruled out completely the possibility of statehood for an ethno-national group seeking to exercise a right to self-determination, it meant that there would be a bias against this happening. The emphasis would remain on preserving existing states. In the Yugoslav context, this meant that once the Vance-Owen plan (which would have preserved a single Bosnian state on the basis of ten provinces) had been abandoned in May 1993, it was replaced by discussions on the basis for an internal division of the country that would create a Union of Republics with sovereignty granted to each of the three ethnically defined republics that would form the union.[38]

That notion was eventually superseded by a dual arrangement between two entities (the Muslim-Croat Federation of Bosnia-Herzegovina and the Republika Srpska) in the Bosnian peace settlement, agreed at Dayton, Ohio, in November 1995 and signed in Paris on 14 December 1995.[39] Although, crucially, the quality of sovereignty was not attributed to the entities, this did not, of course, prevent fears that the agreement sowed the seeds for possible dissolution of the country at some stage in the future. To avoid this, a further implication emerged with regard to the security of the new states: security for the state was related to legitimation in both internal and international dimensions.

The Legitimation of Sovereignty: Building Peace from Below and Within

In a case in which one group, perhaps illegally, refuses to accept a particular situation, then it is, in effect, carrying out a sovereign act in the sense identified earlier: if sovereignty is to mean anything, it means the inalienable right

38. See Graham Messervey-Whiting, *Peacebrokering: The Politico-Military Interface* (London: Brassey's for the Centre for Defence Studies, 1994).

39. See "General Framework Agreement for Peace in Bosnia and Herzegovina," peace conference at Dayton, Ohio, 21 November 1995.

not to do what someone else wants. In the context of the dissolution of the Socialist Federative Republic of Yugoslavia, this has a clear manifestation.

Although the dissolution of Yugoslavia is too complex to consider the war in Croatia and in Bosnia and Herzegovina as a Serb rebellion against independence, it is undeniable that the war was in part a product of the genuine feelings of Serbs living in Croatia and in Bosnia and Herzegovina. The reality that Serbia and the Serbs outside its borders provoked the other republics into declaring their independence and initiated the war cannot be overlooked. Nor can the reality that without the acceptance of the Croatian and Bosnian states by the Serbs living within them, there remains a problem. The question raised by situations of this kind is fundamentally one of legitimation: how can those responsible for governance within the boundaries of a state, and those in the international community looking to create a more stable and secure international environment, make arrangements that allow the international legal legitimacy and sovereignty of the state to coincide with political conditions within the state? The following section will consider international aspects of legitimate sovereignty, while the present segment will consider the internal dimensions of shared sovereignty and legitimation.

Legitimacy is frequently used to confer approval on something, that is, to convey a sense of rightfulness. Apart from this general and subjective use ("it is legitimate" means "I approve of it"), legitimacy is used in two very different ways in the disciplines of law and politics. In legal terms legitimate means that the action or entity in question has legal validity or authority. In politics, legitimacy refers to the social compact between groups involved in power relationships, usually rulers and the ruled in a given context (although not exclusively).[40] Although there are many arguments on the nature of the compact (the degree to which there is free consensus, for example), the concept is only really useful when reduced to the basic relationships involved: Why can a smaller group act in certain ways and why does a larger group accept the situation?

Socio-political legitimacy is important at three levels: authorities, regime, and political community.[41] It comes into focus in times of crisis.[42]

40. I have dealt with the question of legitimacy at greater length in *Legitimacy and the Military*, 14–21.

41. These terms, which may be equated with the government, the political structures, and the state or country itself, are borrowed from David Easton, *A Systems Analysis of Political Life* (New York: John Wiley, 1965), 177.

42. For the classic discussion of legitimacy crises, see Jürgen Habermas, *Legitimation Crisis* (London: Heinemann, 1970).

In critical times, the ability of an organism to recover its equilibrium is a measure of its legitimacy. A critical challenge to legitimacy at the governmental level is not so serious as a challenge at the community level where the very existence of a political community, such as the old Yugoslav state, is brought into question. To the extent that—in spite of the niceties of political or legal philosophy—sovereignty ultimately lies with the people, as Locke realized even in the context of absolute monarchies, the people are sovereign. In political reality, if not in international law, rejection of a political community by one group within it represents both the loss of legitimacy and the loss of sovereignty within that political community. It is also a manifestation of the political sovereignty of the rejectionist group.

Few states in the former communist part of Europe are ethnically homogeneous, nor are numerous states in other parts of the globe. Moreover, while the communists professed to transcend ethnic identities so that both majority and minority national groups would disappear, this did not happen. For the most part, the communist regimes managed only to suppress national problems and, even, to fuel their reassertion by turning to nationalist appeals to generate regime support as the communist grip weakened.[43] In reality, ethnic homogeneity is inconceivable in most places around the world unless it is accompanied by unacceptable corollaries. Therefore, accommodation between majorities and minorities will be necessary if states are to be stable with no clashes of sovereignty or self-determination claims.

The parameters for the potential accommodation of sovereignty and self-determination clashes were partly indicated by the Badinter Commission and the Council of the European Community. This involved the possible decoupling of self-determination from the notions of sovereignty and statehood. The potential decoupling appeared first in the findings alluded to earlier, in which the implication was that self-determination could operate for groups within states but not at the expense of states. Self-determination, including self-governance, was possible within the confines of the recognized and existing state, but it could not mean the achievement of statehood.

The commission and the council went further when it was decided to invite applications from those Yugoslav republics wishing to be recognized as having independent international personalities. At that time, the

---

43. See George Schöpflin, *Politics in Eastern Europe* (Oxford: Blackwell, 1993), especially 66–68.

EC Council asked the arbitration commission to establish the conditions that would have to be satisfied if new states in Eastern Europe were to be recognized diplomatically by the EC.[44] There were five conditions, chief among which were respect for international agreements on the rights of minorities and the inviolability of borders.[45] There were two major implications of this action: first, that the understanding needed to be developed that aspects of sovereignty might be shared within a compound; and second, that the traditional version of sovereignty entailing absolute and unitary characteristics, particularly with regard to the notion of domestic jurisdiction, might no longer fully apply. In both cases the essential point was the need to validate, or legitimate, the exercise of sovereign rights.

As in the former Yugoslavia and its successor states, and as James Mayall has pointed out, sovereignty, even if it is not conventionally regarded as divisible, is susceptible to challenge not only in whole, but in part.[46] However, the conceptual problem presented by the indivisibility of sovereignty is not new in itself. It was already being addressed in the sixteenth century with regard to the question of the sovereign within states, after Jean Bodin had made the first inquiry into the conditions of sovereignty.[47] He had found that it was an absolute and indivisible quality. However, the repressive nature of absolute monarchy in certain European countries—notably his own, France—was encouraged by this analysis. While Bodin himself appears to have had a relatively liberal disposition and, in fact, placed countless qualifications on the manner in which power was exercised by the sovereign, the idea of absolutism nonetheless held strongly.

Sovereignty must, of course, refer to something absolute,[48] an inalienable ultimate authority. It is less clear, though, how that absolute power can be validated or controlled. For those concerned with international security, this is the critical question. Sovereignty is the trump card in politics, whether

44. "Guidelines on the Recognition of New States in Eastern Europe and in the Soviet Union," adopted by the EC Council on 16 December 1991.

45. See Foreign Affairs Committee, *Central and Eastern Europe: Problems of the Post-Communist Era* (first report), vol. 1 (London: Her Majesty's Stationery Office, February 1992), p. xxi.

46. Mayall, *Nationalism and International Society,* 42.

47. Jean Bodin, *On Sovereignty,* ed. Julian H. Franklin (Cambridge: Cambridge University Press, 1992).

48. See, for example, Akehurst, *A Modern Introduction to International Law.* According to Adéhar Esmein, sovereignty concerns "the existence in a society of men superior to individual wills which recognizes no force superior or concurrent in the sphere where it acts. This superior authority is called sovereignty." Cited by Hymen Ezra Cohen, *Recent Theories of Sovereignty* (Chicago: University of Chicago Press, 1937), 15.

domestic or international. It is a constant: although the incumbents of sovereignty, or its apportionment, may change, its nature does not. Portions of sovereignty may be given away by a state to an international body, as has occurred with the member states of the European Union, but sovereignty itself remains the same—it has merely been redistributed. Moreover, in the final analysis, although sovereignty is often regarded as a legal concept, as discussed earlier, it is hard to avoid the reality that "theories of sovereignty are theories of politics, of power."[49] It is ultimately a political phenomenon.

Laws are determined by lawmakers, and lawmakers are politicians. Politics concerns the resolution of conflicts, whether actual or latent, real or imagined, through the authoritative allocation of resources and values—who gets what, when, where, and why.[50] Laws regulate the processes of resolution and allocation, but they can ultimately be supervened by sovereign political authority determining new legal parameters, or overriding old ones. In the reality of modern constitutional, pluralist, legally based and democratic systems, this means that, although the political remains supreme, sovereignty is shared.

The constitutional arrangements of numerous states since Bodin's time have demonstrated that sovereignty is not indivisible. An important example is the United States, where the division of powers within the state creates a "compound" sovereignty.[51] This division of powers squares the circle created by the idea of ultimate authority in an indivisible sovereign. While sovereignty by its nature must be absolute, it need not be unitary. The answer to the following vital question is found in the separation of powers and the division of sovereignty: If there is no higher rule-making power to validate and enforce the state's own rules, how can the avoidance of abuses of absolute power be guaranteed?

Each portion of divided sovereignty is absolute in its sphere, but incomplete, as it represents only one part of what constitutes the sovereign. As summarized concisely by David Beetham, "The absence of any higher legal authority than the state, to which state power is subject, can be remedied by a separation of powers whereby one part of the state is made accountable to another for its respect of the law."[52] In order to rectify

---

49. Cohen, *Recent Theories of Sovereignty*, 3.

50. This is a synthetic definition of politics. For the various sources from which it is drawn, see Gow, *Legitimacy and the Military*, 14.

51. Julian H. Franklin, introduction to Bodin, *On Sovereignty*, xvii.

52. David Beetham, *The Legitimation of Power* (Atlantic Highlands, N.J.: Humanities Press International, 1991), 123.

the discrepancy between the ultimate power implied by sovereignty and the absence of any higher authority to prevent abuse, the powers must be separated in the different institutions of a constitutional order, and these powers must have a "firm anchoring within society."[53]

Conceptually, in recent history this has entailed a regime in which it has been incumbent on governments to accommodate the desires of groups within the country for autonomy in spheres that have not challenged statehood, including self-governance. At the same time, the claims of groups within states to independence, or to association with a neighboring state, have been preemptively rejected. This arrangement has been conceptually a way of squaring the circle of the international imperative of maintaining order among states and the inviolability of borders, on the one hand, and on the other of recognizing the reality of nonconformity between ethno-nations and nations as states in postcommunist Europe and elsewhere. The solution has been judged to lie in provision of autonomy for ethnic groups within states. This type of solution, in many variations, has proved a sometimes useful model in the past, while retaining great potential for extension and further development.[54]

To a notable extent, this prescription was put into practice by the new Ukrainian state.[55] Ukraine, in a move to assure its integrity and survival as a nation-state, granted all people living in the country at the time of independence full and unconditional citizenship and created bodies with responsibility for dealing with the status of more than one hundred minority groups living in the country. Ukraine sought to establish accommodation with all minority groups in Ukraine, working out agreements on varying degrees of autonomy. In particular, this strategy was successful in heading off a movement toward independence in the Crimean region. Crimea was granted full autonomy in all spheres, with the exception of being able to establish independent armed forces and foreign policy. Although Ukraine's initial success could not be guaranteed in the long term, this represented a good start. It also provided a model for security policy in postcommunist Europe and beyond.

The kind of security practice offered by Ukraine and suggested in the Yugoslav context by the international community means a new dispensation

53. Beetham, *Legitimation of Power*, 125.
54. Hurst Hannum, *Autonomy, Sovereignty, and Self-Determination* (Philadelphia: University of Pennsylvania Press, 1990), looks at nine major and a number of minor cases.
55. See James Gow, "Independent Ukraine: The Politics of Security," *International Relations* 11 (December 1992): 253–67.

in state sovereignty with a view to enhancing security. Sovereignty is being reapportioned at the expense both of the collective rights of groups within states and of the rights of the international community to intervene in some way on behalf of those groups. This process of development has begun, but it is not yet clear where it will finish. Yet several indications have already been given in international arenas of the ways in which this kind of change is developing.

Sovereignty and Security: Building from Above and Outside

International security issues are intrinsically linked to the changes in state sovereignty currently under way. If there is to be international peace, it must be built both from above and from below. The international community has become increasingly involved, during the first half of the 1990s, in affairs previously judged to rest exclusively in the domain of internal affairs of states. Increasingly, it was thought to be in a state's interest to accept an international stake in these matters because to do so would enhance security. More significantly, there were rapid developments with regard to the protection offered to states by the claim to sovereignty and conventional readings of the UN charter. As international cooperation within the UN Security Council grew rapidly in the early 1990s, it became ever more evident that situations that could be judged to pose a threat to international peace and security could also reveal a greater practical propensity to breach the barriers provided by conventional understandings of sovereignty, while gradually alerting the world to long-forgotten commitments in the UN charter.[56] In effect, this meant sharing certain portions of state sovereignty that concerned matters of international peace and security.

The radical evolution of the interpretations of a threat to international peace and security and of sovereignty owes much to the initial optimism

---

56. The framers of the UN charter clearly seem to have understood the issues of sovereignty and security in a way that is consistent with the innovations on conventional understanding in the 1990s. See Age Eknes, "The United Nations and Intra-State Conflicts," in *Subduing Sovereignty: Sovereignty and the Right to Intervene,* ed. Marianne Heiberg (London: Pinter, 1994), 99.

raised by the prospect of a "new world order." This prospect resulted from the international cooperation shown in the handling of the Iraq-Kuwait War. The articulation of a new world order had a particularly emotional appeal because it included justice as one of its core qualities,[57] implying that the new world would be a better one. In practice, while the unprecedented international cooperation upheld the sovereignty of Kuwait in the war against Iraq, a new era and a new approach to questions of sovereignty followed in the aftermath.

The first step in a five-year period of revolutionary transformation was in response to pressure on Western governments. Evoked by the optimism engendered by the new world order, Operation Provide Comfort was launched to protect Kurds in northern Iraq who were being pursued and persecuted by Iraqi forces. This humanitarian intervention, although limited, clearly signaled that it was no longer impossible for there to be external interference, including even the insertion of armed forces, in the internal affairs of an individual state. Even though the Kurdish question and the international response to it was a function of specific circumstances, it fueled debate that is still ongoing. The debate centers on the character of external intervention in a state's internal affairs, definition of the conditions that would make this possible or justified, and the degree to which a state's internal problems could constitute a threat to international peace and security.

Evolution in practice (and more slowly in thinking) highlighted one small, but paramount, instance of states conceding part of their sovereignty to the international community, one that is unparalleled and beyond question, but that has generally been forgotten. That is the abdication of sovereignty made in the sphere of international peace and security by all states signing the UN charter, where in the last clause of article 2(7) and in chapter VII, the limit of state sovereignty is imposed at the point at which the UN Security Council determines a threat to international peace and security under chapter VII. This is complemented by article 25, in which states agree to be bound by the Security Council when it takes action with regard to the maintenance of international peace and security.

Although article 2 generally sets down the independence, integrity, and freedom from external meddling in internal affairs that is due to states, and in chapter VII, article 51 grants the inherent right to self-defense,

---

57. See the speeches by President George Bush to Congress, 11 September 1990, and at Air University, Maxwell Air Force Base, 13 April 1991.

both of these cease to apply in specific circumstances. These are when the UN Security Council has determined a "threat to international peace and security". In 2(7), the last clause sets out the limit of the principle of non-interference: "This principle shall not prejudice the application of enforcement measures under Chapter VII." Similarly, article 51, which establishes the "inherent right to individual and collective self-defense," also has the caveat that this is so only until the Security Council has "determined a threat to international peace and security" in order to take enforcement measures, whether military (article 42) or nonmilitary (article 41).

What this means is that sovereignty in the sphere of matters of international peace and security lies with the UN Security Council. It decides what constitutes the kind of threat to international peace and security that warrants suspension of a state's otherwise inherent rights. Conventionally, this has been taken to be applicable only in cases of an act of aggression by one state against another, although in the cases of Rhodesia (1966), especially, and of South Africa (1977), this was not strictly the case, as internal policies were in question (in the South African case, there was also an external dimension). What happened following the end of the Cold War, beginning with the Kurdish situation in northern Iraq, was that interpretation of what could be regarded as constituting a threat to international peace and security was significantly altered.

It became clear that there was no longer a single, more or less fixed, definition understood by all. Instead, the concept of a threat to international peace and security had become elastic and applicable in a variety of circumstances, all of which challenged traditional views of sovereignty. In January 1992, the heads of government and state of the members of the UN Security Council issued a declaration making this clear: "The absence of war and military conflict amongst States does not in itself ensure international peace and security. The non-military sources of instability in the economic, social, humanitarian and ecological fields have become threats to peace and security."[58]

In line with this, chapter VII resolutions were passed by the Security Council with regard to the extradition of suspected terrorists from Libya (Resolution 748, 1992); the restoration of peace and security within a country, Somalia (Resolution 733, 1992); and arms supplies and involvement in war, specifically regarding the former Yugoslavia (Resolutions 713, 1991; 757, 770, 781, 1992; 808, 816, 820, 836, 1993). Of all of these, per-

58. UN Doc. S/23500, 1992.

haps the most radical was Resolution 808, which established an International Criminal Tribunal for War Crimes in former Yugoslavia as an ad hoc body under the Security Council, giving it complete legal and political authority—an embodiment of a proto-international sovereign.

The Security Council resolutions on Bosnia and Herzegovina, Libya and Somalia, as well as later ones on Rwanda and Haiti, were radical departures in terms of sovereignty in international relations. In particular, with reference to Somalia and Libya, previously unthinkable definitions of a threat to international peace and security were given. However, although it became clear that the delineation of chapter VII situations could be far broader than had conventionally been the case, there was no indication of what the limits were to the expanding understanding of what could entail a threat to international peace and security.

Alongside changes in the interpretation of threats to international peace and security, and of sovereignty in the international system, there was a growing role for the international community in building security within states in order to enhance international security. Ideally, states would subject themselves to measures of external involvement in internal affairs. A relatively small, though psychologically vast, first step in this direction was taken in a 1987 treaty between the member states of the Council of Europe. This established a body, with a view to preventing abuses, that would have a right of intrusive inspection of all locations in signatory states where people were deprived of their liberty. Where fault was found, first private recommendation and then, failing that, public disclosure could be used to obtain suitable adjustments. If more states were willing to subject themselves to such measures of external involvement, a more general shift toward human values, especially with regard to minorities, would radically alter both the internal and external politics of many countries, and international peace and security would be positively affected.

Explicit recognition of this came in the Moscow Document of the Organization for Security and Cooperation in Europe, which abolished the possibility of referring to the principle of nonintervention in "human dimension" cases: "The commitments undertaken in the field of the human dimension of OSCE are matters of direct and legitimate concern to all participating states and do not belong exclusively to the internal affairs of the state concerned."[59]

This was conceived as a moral premise. It reflects, however, the reality

59. Moscow Document of the OSCE, October 1991.

that the moral and political health of societies is a determinant of stability and international security. It forms part of a series of initiatives within the OSCE to make progress in collective regulation of human-rights matters, particularly with regard to minorities. The Moscow Human Dimension Mechanism and the preceding Vienna Human Dimension Mechanism provided a number of limited ways in which human-rights doubts about a particular state could be addressed. The most extensive of these, agreed in Moscow, was the possibility that any state, with the support of at least nine others from the fifty-four-strong membership, could activate a mechanism whereby a commission of experts could be formed to investigate cases in which a particular state was suspected of failing to meet its commitments under the human dimension of the OSCE.

Finally, and perhaps most critically, at its July 1992 Helsinki Summit, the OSCE decided to create a high commissioner on national minorities.[60] This happened in response to events in parts of both the former Yugoslavia and the former Soviet Union. Conflicts there, which might have been ameliorated by preventive prior engagement, had reached armed hostility before external bodies could formally address them. The OSCE action was, therefore, in direct response to the wave of nationalism creating security crises in postcommunist Europe. The role of the high commissioner was essentially restricted to being part of an "early warning mechanism." Cases in which violence had already erupted were not generally part of the remit, although the only specific exclusion was for "national minority issues in situations involving organized acts of terrorism."[61]

The real task of the high commissioner is to identify potentially violent national or ethnic disputes, to seek to remedy them, and finally, when the prospect of open armed hostility is close, to issue a statement of early warning to the council of the OSCE. In its short period of activity in this area, the OSCE has been associated, along with the European Union (previously the European Community), the Council of Europe, and the International Court of Justice, with seeking to deal with a number of problems.[62] One

---

60. See Rachel Brett, *The Challenges of Change: Report of the Helsinki Follow-Up Meeting of the Conference on Security and Cooperation in Europe (OSCE)* (Essex: Human Rights Centre, University of Essex, 1992).

61. Organization for Security and Cooperation in Europe, *Official Verbatim Records, 9 and 10 July 1992/Helsinki Summit 1992 of the Heads of State or Government of the Participating States of the OSCE* (Helsinki: The Conference, 1992), II.5b.

62. Konrad J. Huber, "The CSCE and Ethnic Conflict in the East," *RFE/RL Research Report* 2 (30 July 1993): 32–34.

relatively successful example is the problem of Hungary, Slovakia, the Hungarians in Slovakia, and a dam close to the border between the two countries that, if built, would damage the livelihood of ethnic Hungarian farmers. There remain, however, questions requiring resolution with regard to the status of the Hungarians in Slovakia.

The cases mentioned above emphasize that at the end of the twentieth century, security problems seem less likely to be concerned with a rapid invasion from a neighboring country than with the quest of groups for identity, self-determination, and freedom from fear and uncertainty. This is especially the case in Eastern Europe and the former Soviet Union, where the gap that has emerged between political and economic expectations and their fulfillment—the no-man's-land between communism and liberal democracy—has bred frustration. International attention has been necessarily and increasingly focused on security below the level of the state as a means of ensuring security at the level of the state. This has particularly been the case with regard to problems of national minorities.

The steps that have already been taken in addressing the questions of national minorities, nations, sovereignty, statehood, self-determination, and security are only the first stage. The aim is the formation of an overall strategy for creating what might be called ethnic security. This will deal with manipulation of fears by old authoritarians, or nationalist newcomers, and work toward an international political norm with regard to the position of minorities within the borders of states.

In this respect, of note are the conditions set by the European Community Conference on Yugoslavia for the diplomatic recognition of the independence of republics that were formerly part of that country and of the Soviet Union.[63] Although in practice their strict application was not adhered to for reasons of realpolitik, these introduced a further innovation: it was acceptable for other states to express an interest in the internal affairs of a state through the collective setting of conditions governing internal political, legal, and constitutional provisions. This undermined the Westphalian-inspired practice of "Don't interfere in my business and I'll leave you to yours," particularly with regard to demands that provision for minorities be made as a condition for mutual recognition of sovereignty. International acceptance, then, could result from the adoption of practices in the sphere

---

63. As Hugh Miall, *New Conflicts in Europe: Prevention and Resolution* (Oxford: Oxford Research Group, 1992), 10, points out, the European Community's focus on minorities in the recognition process "represented outside pressure" for the observance of OSCE standards.

of human and political rights that could be expected to reinforce the process of legitimation within states.

In cases such as Bosnia and Herzegovina, it was unlikely that an environment conducive to positive intercommunal relations could emerge, or reemerge, without help from the outside world. To this end, following the peace settlement at the end of 1995, the international community made a major commitment to the reconstruction and rehabilitation of Bosnia, through the creation of a large civil-affairs program and the appointment of former Swedish prime minister Carl Bildt to head it. The possibilities for states further to share sovereignty with international bodies continued to be under investigation. The UN role in the peace settlement in Cambodia and the holding of elections there offered one framework, with the United Nations taking on certain aspects of Cambodian sovereignty. Other examples in which there were developments of this kind, albeit in extremely limited senses, were mentioned above.

In sum, in terms of both peace enforcement under chapter VII of the UN charter and peace building, there have been notable shifts in the sovereignty paradigm. It is necessary that for a (not too long) period, there will be further reflection and reassessment of the nature of sovereignty in the international system and its relationship to security questions. This will mean, among other things, recognition that in specific areas, certain states—and in one particular domain, all signatory states to the UN charter—have found it vital and in their interest to transcend the narrow (and somewhat erroneous) interpretation of state sovereignty as being absolute and indivisible in terms of the international system. Within the scope of chapter VII of the UN charter, each state's sovereignty is already split with the UN Security Council. It is possible that the future will bring broader definitions of what constitutes a threat to international peace and security. However, this represents the more negative side of the problem: measures taken once a problem has emerged. There is, perhaps, a greater requirement to evolve positive measures that can contribute to the avoidance of critical situations and the building of security.

In this regard, the emphasis is on identifying ways in which sovereignty can be shared between different communities within states, yet not create greater insecurity because one group feels threatened by another group's claims of rights and, crucially, not bring the territorial status quo in the international system into question. It is increasingly clear that "states should be encouraged, under specific circumstances, to surrender a certain amount of sovereignty to ethno-national minorities within the state's territorial borders in the name of security."[64] It is also fairly evident that minority communities within states are unlikely to have confidence in any arrangement unless there is some international dimension providing a minimum guarantee. This will mean the concomitant surrender of portions of sovereignty to international bodies, not only of a particular state, but of states in general. This in turn implies much for the understanding of sovereignty and security in the international security system.

The alternative to sovereignty shared internally and internationally may be ugly: either persistent intercommunal violence or the one-sided process of violent "ethnic cleansing" carried out primarily, but not exclusively, by Serbian forces in Croatia and Bosnia-Herzegovina, using the instruments of terror and massacre. This alternative is not compatible either with the nascent development of liberal-democratic systems or with the creation of a secure environment.

On the contrary, the establishment of liberal-democratic regimes would entail acceptance of concessions to minorities and self-limitation by the majority. It would also mean commitment to the state by the minority, once adequate provision for their status had been made. International agents would be essential to this process if there were to be progress. It is this still developing situation that requires the question of sovereignty to be addressed, with a view to permitting greater external intrusion in the internal affairs of states (something that would, paradoxically, enhance the real sovereignty of the state). This would have ramifications for all states, although they would be more significant for weaker states facing sovereignty and self-determination challenges.

In a sense, these weaker states are states because they are recognized by other states as such. However, Robert Jackson's label "quasi-states" could be applied to a good number of them in the decade after the collapse of the Berlin Wall.[65] Jackson denotes two types of sovereignty: negative and positive.[66] Following Sir Isaiah Berlin's distinction between negative and positive liberty (with regard to the individual), Jackson treats the two types as follows: negative sovereignty connotes the right of a state not to be subject to the interference of outside power, much as was elaborated above with reference to article 2 of the UN charter. Positive sovereignty, however, is analogous to the freedom to do things; it is a question of capability. The

---

64. Daniel Enger, Robert Pendley, Charles Ball, "Pending a Decision on the Main Issue: Dilemmas of European Security," *Arms Control: Contemporary Security Policy* 14 (December 1993): 433.

65. Jackson, *Quasi-States*.

66. Ibid., 26–31.

basic distinction, therefore, is between "freedom from" and "freedom to."

This conception extends to statehood: all states, under international norms, are endowed with formal sovereignty. At this level, they may be no more than "quasi-states," states in form but not in content. Certain states, in contrast (notably the advanced industrial ones), have "empirical statehood," that is, not only the form of a state but the capability to function in a number of ways, including the exertion of external influence.

Jackson's focus was the Third World. Yet his classification readily applies to the states that emerged from the collapse of the conglomerate communist federations. In some cases, there may be true quasi-states; in others, the state may be somewhere in between, but still bearing many of the characteristics of quasi-states. These are weak states. As Jackson points out, it is an attribute of weak, quasi-states that either the authorities treat sections of their population badly, or that sections of the population challenge the state, calling into question its very statehood. In these situations, the "freedom from" element of negative sovereignty, until the end of the Cold War (with the exception of the Republic of South Africa, which was subject to UN sanctions for twenty-five years) gave regimes a more or less free hand to be oppressive, to abuse human rights, and even, in the case of Cambodia (Kampuchea), to commit genocide.

Until the end of the Cold War, the international community and its agents did not understand themselves to have the right to involve themselves within states, under then-existing interpretations of the meaning of sovereignty in international relations, because the state was guaranteed undivided and absolute freedom from interference. This understanding of sovereignty automatically carried with it an absolute "freedom to" within state borders. In the first part of the 1990s, in spite of the many horrific events within the borders of sovereign states and the hesitant responses of world opinion,[67] significant changes in the approach to sovereignty have palpably curtailed the absolute freedom of state action.

Conclusion

International acceptance of absolute sovereignty in the internal sphere can no longer be taken for granted. Discussion on sovereignty within states

67. Guy Hermet, "The Human Rights Challenge to Sovereignty," in *Life, Death, and Aid: The Médecins Sans Frontières' Report on World Crisis Intervention,* ed. François Jean (London:

and on the sovereignty of states in the international system became the linchpin for a reevaluation of international security in the first part of the 1990s. The direction of the changes that occurred was toward the recognition that, just as within states, so at the international level, sovereignty cannot be allowed to be indivisible if abuses of it are not to be tolerated. Something equivalent to the constitutional separation of powers within states in order to validate and control power holders may be in the process of evolving, although it is, as yet, clearly not codified. Developments could include the formal incorporation of particular communities within a state in the constitutional order (on either a territorial or nonterritorial basis), or the presence of an external actor in an internal constitutional order. Whatever the developments are, they certainly will mean that states will have to subscribe to international norms on the accommodation of various communities within their territorial limits.

Nothing of this kind will be easy to attain, and whatever materializes will surely take time. If achieved, however, it would both place a limit on the potential for a state to abuse its sovereignty and promote greater international security. It would also go some way toward accommodating the change being forced on the international system after the Cold War by creating new conceptual, normative, and legal frameworks in which to deal with conflicts over sovereignty, self-determination, ethnic and state security, and statehood. A better understanding of the implications of these words-with-two-meanings, including an awareness of their existence, is required before the trouble that arises from their ambiguity can be addressed. The repercussions of differing understandings are clear in the former Yugoslavia.

That war cast some light on the importance and changed understanding of sovereignty in the post–Cold War world. The international legal sovereignty of the state may be pitched against the violent ethno-national political claim to sovereignty of a particular group, especially if that group is backed by a kin state. In such cases, the only solutions can be those in which the divisibility of sovereignty is recognized and a mechanism is found for sharing it through possession of parts of a compound whole, creating a division of sovereignty not only within the state but between the state and international bodies. The result will be that divisibility, or sharing, paradoxically, will strengthen the state and its security.

Routledge, 1993), 133. Hermet points out realistically that where international action occurs, there is usually some other motivation of "a political kind."

The reinterpretation of sovereignty in this way is essential to the promotion of security and settlement of conflicts. This is reflected in the shift in the 1990s toward acceptance that through sharing (at least temporarily) of sovereignty with international bodies, the sovereignty inherent in a state throughout its territory may be partitioned and parceled into new territorial packages. Each of these may form part of a "compound sovereignty" throughout the state's territory, shared both within the state and with an external agent. Ultimately, the new distribution of sovereignty could provide the mechanism for peaceful political changes or the redefinition of frontiers through the mutual consent of the constituent communities within this "compound sovereignty." The hypothesis behind thinking of this kind is simple: shared sovereignty leads to enhanced security.

7

Conservation, Development, and State Sovereignty

Japan and the Tropical Forests of Southeast Asia

Miranda A. Schreurs

The United Nations Conference on Environment and Development (UNCED), held in Rio de Janeiro in 1992, was the largest summit ever convened. Close to 175 nations sent delegates to what has been called the Earth Summit. The purpose of the summit, held twenty years after the first such conference in Stockholm, was to find common ground among states on approaches to transboundary and global environmental problems. The meeting symbolized an uneasy yet growing acceptance of the notion that problems like global warming, desertification, species loss, and ocean pollution cannot be solved by any one nation alone. It was another step in a process Lynton Caldwell suggests is leading to a "merging of sovereignty."[1]

When the UNCED came to a close, environmentalists could claim some substantial victories. More than 150 nations signed two international

---

1. Lynton Caldwell, *International Environmental Diplomacy: Emergence and Dimensions* (Durham: Duke University Press, 1990), 22.

treaties, one on climate change, the other on biodiveristy. Agenda 21, a six-hundred-page guideline for future national and international action for the environment and development, was adopted. In addition, general agreement was reached on the establishment of a Global Environment Facility to be administered by the World Bank, the United Nations Environment Programme, and the United Nations Development Programme, its purpose being to fund global environmental programs and projects. Finally, as an indirect result of the conference, international attention to the environment soared. People became more aware of the many environmental and ecological threats facing our planet, and this became a force behind policy change at the local, national, and international levels.

The UNCED failed, however, in reaching more than the most basic level of agreement on the control of greenhouse gases and the protection of forests. Particularly problematic were attempts to reach an international agreement on the protection of tropical forests; these attempts ended in what one observer called "an almost unmitigated disaster."[2] Led by Malaysia and India, the Group of 77 (a coalition of developing countries within the UN system) remained opposed to the establishment of a forest convention. In the words of Malaysia's chief negotiator at UNCED, Wen Lian Ting, "Forests are clearly a sovereign resource—not like atmosphere and oceans, which are global commons. . . . We cannot allow forests to be taken up in global forums."[3] By the end of the UNCED, a nonbinding set of forest principles was all that states could agree upon.

The central issues of contention are summarized well in a 1987 exchange of letters between a young British boy and the Malaysian prime minister, Mahathir Bin Mohamad. In his letter, the boy wrote, "I am 10 years old and when I am older I hope to study animals in the tropical rain forests. But if you let the lumber companies carry on, there will not be any left. And millions of animals will die." The Malaysian prime minister responded, "The timber industry helps hundreds of thousands of poor people in Malaysia. Are they supposed to remain poor because you want to study tropical animals? . . . When the British ruled Malaysia they burnt millions of acres of Malaysian forests so that they could plant rubber."[4]

2. Stanley P. Johnson, *The Earth Summit: The United Nations Conference on Environment and Development (UNCED)* (London; Boston: Graham and Trotman/Martinus Nijhoff, 1993), 23.

3. Quoted in the *New York Times*, 12 June 1992, A10.

4. Letters quoted in translation in the *Nihon Keizai Shimbun*, 18 August 1989. Copies of the original letters were also shared with me in an interview with a Japanese trading company's global environmental officer.

Many issues are either directly embedded in or closely related to this exchange. As the young boy suggested, forest conservation is a matter of ecological preservation and intergenerational equity. Mounting scientific evidence of rapid tropical deforestation has raised international concern about the fate of the rain forests and the loss of biological diversity. The rain forests play an important ecological role as home to countless animal and plant species; some experts estimate that as many as 90 percent of all living species are in the rain forests.[5] The loss of species deprives future generations of biological diversity. Reforestation of tropical areas, moreover, has proven difficult because of the limited nutrient base of the tropical forest soils. Most of the nutrients are held in the forest canopy; this means that when tropical forests are cut down, the nutrients go with them.[6] Large-scale tropical deforestation is probably irreversible.

Another related argument focuses on the role of forests in the global carbon cycle. Forests are believed to be an important carbon sink and, therefore, they play an important role in capturing carbon dioxide, a greenhouse gas. The burning of forests releases stored carbon into the atmosphere, and the felling of forests reduces the size of the forest sink. In the 1980s, forest preservation and reforestation became important components of the policy solutions that were offered as means for combating climate change.[7]

Finally, rapid development raises ethical questions involving the impact of development on indigenous peoples and their traditional way of life. Logging in remote regions often drives indigenous peoples from their homes or deprives them of the forest that provides them with food and fuel.[8] Claims of sovereignty have slowed efforts to establish regimes for protecting global biodiversity and preventing global climate change.[9]

---

5. The question of biodiversity loss and its implications is discussed in Edward O. Wilson, "Threats to Biodiversity," in *Managing Planet Earth: Readings from Scientific American* (New York: W. H. Freeman, 1990), 49–59.

6. Wilson, "Threats to Biodiversity," 59.

7. See, for instance, the German Bundestag, *Protecting the Earth: A Status Report with Recommendations for a New Energy Policy*, vol. 2 (Bonn: The German Bundestag, 1991).

8. The question of ethics and the environment has stimulated considerable debate. See Henry Shue, "The Unavoidability of Justice," in *The International Politics of the Environment*, ed. Andrew Hurrell and Benedict Kingsbury (Oxford: Clarendon Press, 1992), 373–97; and Edith Brown Weiss, *In Fairness to Future Generations: International Law, Common Patrimony, and Intergenerational Equity* (Dobbs Ferry, N.Y.: Transnational Publishers, 1989).

9. For a discussion of the relationship among regimes, sovereignty, and democracy, see Kal Raustiala, "Democracy, Sovereignty, and the Slow Pace of International Negotiations," *International Environmental Affairs* 8, no. 1 (1996): 3–15.

Claims of sovereignty have also been used to justify deforestation that has threatened indigenous peoples.

Yet, there is also a development prerogative. In debating questions about environment, development, and sovereignty, one cannot overlook the inequities in the distribution of wealth that exist between the North and the South, and between former colonizers and colonies. For former colonies, sovereignty is a particularly sensitive issue. Ken Conca suggests that one reason sovereignty has become so central to the ecology debate is that in the early 1970s, at the time of the first United Nations Conference on the Human Environment (the Stockholm Conference), Emory Lovin's notion of a world with a limited capacity for growth instilled a fear in developing countries that environmental regulation would restrict their ability to develop.[10]

Many Southeast Asian states only achieved independence in the post–World War II period. For these countries there are strong historical reasons why any kind of encroachment upon their sovereignty is strongly challenged. For former colonies like Malaysia, Indonesia, and India, the use of natural resources to alleviate poverty and promote economic growth is viewed as a right that was enjoyed by the advanced industrialized states and therefore should also be available to developing countries today. Clearly, the issue is complex. The debate over the fate of the rain forests pits short-term developmental concerns and the alleviation of poverty against long-term environmental preservation needs and the rights of indigenous peoples.

This chapter explores issues of sovereignty and the environment by exploring the struggle to determine the fate of tropical forests of Southeast Asia.[11] It finds that at least for this kind of international environmental issue—one that affects directly resources that lie within state boundaries—sovereignty can be a powerful obstacle to cooperative environmental protection arrangements. This chapter argues, however, that despite countries' frequent use of sovereignty claims to oppose international environmental-

10. Ken Conca, "Environmental Protection, International Norms, and State Sovereignty: The Case of the Brazilian Amazon," in *Beyond Westphalia? State Sovereignty and International Intervention*, ed. Gene M. Lyons and Michael Mastanduno (Baltimore: Johns Hopkins University Press, 1995), 147–69.

11. For discussions of sovereignty and forest preservation in the case of the Brazilian Amazon, see Conca, "Environmental Protection"; and Andrew Hurrell, "Brazil and the International Politics of Amazonian Deforestation," in Hurrell and Kingsbury, *International Politics of the Environment*, 398–429.

regime formation, growing international and grassroots pressures are producing changes in environmental values, institutions, and policy. The formation of new networks linking indigenous peoples and international
nongovernmental organizations has broadened the scope of political
debate beyond the confines of state borders to include what James Rosenau
refers to as "non-state," "non-sovereign" actors.[12] As a result of the activities of these networks of actors, new environmental norms are being
established in economic, social, and political institutions, and this in turn
is leading to policy changes at the domestic level. In both development-
oriented countries like Malaysia and consumer states like Japan, a more
globally oriented view of the environment is taking root, albeit slowly.

Because tropical-rain-forest preservation has become an issue of preserving biological diversity, protecting human rights, and maintaining
intergenerational equity, tropical forests are increasingly being viewed as
part of the global commons. This has multiple, if at times conflicting,
implications for sovereignty. On the one hand, sovereignty is being challenged by groups that have found means to go outside of the state to
apply pressure upon it. They have done this by pressuring consumers of
tropical-timber products to alter their practices and decrease their demand
for timber coming from unsustainably managed forests.

On the other hand, as forests take on an increasingly global importance,
developing states are finding that claims of sovereignty can work to their
advantage in winning concessions from advanced industrialized states on
financial and technological transfer issues. In using sovereignty as a negotiating tool, developing countries are challenging countries in the North
to help them find the means to achieve sustainable development while
protecting the environment.

While no international forest convention exists and many environmentalists fear that action taken to date is insufficient, the internationalization
of forestry politics has provided developing states with a powerful international negotiating tool in the principle of sovereignty. At the same time,
however, the internationalization of forestry politics is forcing developing
states to pay greater attention to environmental preservation as they pursue economic development, in the process narrowing the scope of policy
alternatives that are available to them.

12. James Rosenau, *Turbulence in World Politics* (Princeton: Princeton University Press,
1990). See also Charles Hermann, review of *Turbulence in World Politics*, by James Rosenau,
American Political Science Review 85 (1991): 1081–83.

International Environmental Protection and State Sovereignty

The environmental problems of an age of industrial expansion, growing economic interdependence, and rapid population growth pose a serious challenge to traditional state-centric approaches to environmental-policy formation. Many critics claim that it is in fact state sovereignty that poses one of the most serious obstacles to international environmental protection.

At a conference held in Boston in 1993, Mostafa Tolba, the director-general of the United Nations Environment Programme, warned his audience that something had to be done if the environment was to be protected. Challenging a system in which sovereign interests take priority over environmental conservation, Tolba warned of a need for change. "The reality is that we live in a semi-sovereign world—a dangerous world, a world in which the potential for conflict over our environmental issues grows every year. If we are to avoid those conflicts, then the reality of semi-sovereignty must be confronted. . . . Like it or not, countries' internal policies, even the most routine of daily activities, do have significant transboundary impacts and that being the case, no country is free to do completely as it chooses."[13]

The concept of restricting state sovereignty to promote environmental protection is relatively new in history. Only in the last century, and particularly since the 1970s, have steps been taken to establish cooperative arrangements for environmental protection at the international level. The United Nations Conference on the Human Environment (the Stockholm Conference) in 1972 marked a turning point, from a time when the prevailing view was that environmental problems and disputes should be settled at the local level to a new view—that this was also a national government responsibility.

A decade after the Stockholm Conference, Mostafa Tolba remarked that "environmental perceptions" were still "evolving."[14] It became increasingly apparent that despite the creation of new environmental regulations and institutions at the domestic level in many countries, a certain class of

13. Mostafa Tolba, "Impact of Environmental Treaties on International Relations," in *Global Environmental Accords: Implications for Technology, Industry, and International Relations* (symposium proceedings, Massachusetts Institute of Technology, 24–25 September 1992), 19–24.
14. Mostafa Tolba, ed., *Evolving Environmental Perceptions: From Stockholm to Nairobi* (London: Butterworths, 1988).

environmental issues required international cooperation if they were to be solved. Simple as the idea may now sound that local pollution and environmental degradation can have global ramifications, this was a relatively new idea at the political level, one with important implications for sovereignty. Traditionally, the balance between environmental protection and natural-resource exploitation on the one hand and economic development on the other were matters left to individual states.[15] Increasingly, however, they are becoming issues of international politics.

Robert Keohane has argued that technically, when states enter international agreements they are not undermining, but rather reinforcing their formal sovereignty. In some cases international agreements may even strengthen the state as a sovereign actor, by enhancing its legitimacy.[16] Ken Conca argues that through participation in international agreements, a state may even gain "authority, legitimacy, and control," because international agreements codify environmental regulation as a responsibility of the state.[17]

In entering such an agreement, however, a state's operational sovereignty or its legal freedom of action is indeed being reduced. States choose whether or not to enter into agreements, but by doing so they are narrowing their scope of permissible activities.[18] It is this loss of operational sovereignty that is perceived as the real threat to developing states in many international environmental treaty negotiations.

This tension between sovereignty and the prerogative to protect the environment is embedded in the declarations produced both by the 1972 Stockholm Conference and the 1992 UNCED (the Rio Conference). Principle 21 of the Stockholm Declaration and Principle 2 of the Rio Declaration read: "States have the sovereign right to exploit their own resources pursuant to their own environmental policies, and the responsibility to ensure that activities within their jurisdiction and control do not cause damage to the environment of other states or of areas beyond the limits of national jurisdiction."[19]

15. For a historical overview of the formation of international environmental agreements, see Caldwell, *International Environmental Diplomacy.*

16. See Robert O. Keohane, "Sovereignty, Interdependence, and International Institutions," in *Ideas and Ideals: Essays in Honor of Stanley Hoffmann,* ed. Linda Miller and Michael Smith (Boulder, Colo.: Westview, 1993), 91–107; and Ken Conca, "Rethinking the Ecology-Sovereignty Debate," *Millenium: Journal of International Studies* 23 (1994): 701–11.

17. Conca, "Rethinking the Ecology-Sovereignty Debate," 701–11.

18. Keohane, "Sovereignty, Interdependence, and International Institutions," 91–92.

19. For a reprint of the 1972 declaration, see Mostafa Tolba, ed., *Evolving Environmental*

This principle recognizes sovereignty at the same time that it seeks to restrict it. It suggests both the strength and the inadequacies of the jurisprudential notion of sovereignty within the international system. These tensions were also manifested in the process leading up to the formation of the Forest Principles during the UNCED.

Sovereignty, Development, and the Preservation of Forests

The Forest Principles emerged when efforts to form a world forest treaty failed. The idea of a world forest treaty was first proposed in 1990 by the Food and Agriculture Organization of the United Nations, at a time when global environmental issues were high on the agendas of many countries. The idea was endorsed at the Houston Summit of the G7, where it was agreed that negotiations should move forward rapidly so that a treaty would be ready for signing at the UNCED in Rio de Janeiro. Initial discussions on a text began in the first UNCED preparatory committee meeting.

By the second preparatory committee meeting in 1991, however, negotiations had broken down. At the meeting, Malaysia steadfastly refused the idea of a forest treaty, claiming that since forests were sovereign, an international treaty was inappropriate. India was also vocal in its opposition, expressing similar concerns over sovereignty and adding its suspicions that the United States was pushing the idea of a forest treaty because of its reluctance to reduce its own greenhouse gas emissions.

Faced with an impasse, the UNCED secretariat had to lower its expectations and work instead toward a nonbinding Authoritative Statement of Forest Principles. Even this proved difficult, and long battles ensued over the wording of the text.

A clear divide emerged in the negotiations between the industrialized Northern consumers, who wanted to establish a future date for negotia-

---

Perceptions, 3–11. An unabridged version of Agenda 21, adopted at the UNCED, can be found in Daniel Sitarz, ed., *Agenda 21: The Earth Summit Strategy to Save Our Planet* (Boulder, Colo.: Earth Press, 1993). A similar point about the tensions between sovereignty and environmental protection prerogatives is made by Karen Litfin in "Eco-regimes: Playing Tug of War with the Nation-State," *The State and Social Power in Global Environmental Politics*, ed. Ronnie Lipschutz and Ken Conca (New York: Columbia University Press, 1993), 108.

tions on a binding forest treaty, and the developing Southern producers, who feared the impact of strict environmental regulations on their logging operations. The South, led by Malaysia and India, demanded that the forestry principles clearly specify their sovereign right to develop their woodlands. To a large extent, the difficulty in achieving agreement on a forest treaty was related to broader North-South issues. The South was keenly aware that the North accounts for only a relatively small share of the world's population but uses the bulk of the world's natural resources. Burdened by heavy debts and expanding populations, many developing states resented Northern conservation pressures.

Malaysia, which is in a stronger position than are many other developing states due to its relatively low debt burden, led the Southern states in objecting to Northern conservation pressures and instead called upon the North to recognize the need for development. Malaysia is one of several developing states that has used claims of "sovereignty" over natural resources to push the international community to pay greater attention to North-South inequities.

In the negotiations, Malaysia also resisted the idea of including language in the text that would open the way for negotiations for a forest treaty in the future. It argued that there was little need for such a treaty if a set of forest principles was established and objected that a treaty might interfere with a nation's sovereign right to exploit its forests.

Nevertheless, in the end, compromise of a sort was obtained, reflecting the growing ambiguity surrounding the notion of sovereignty over natural resources that lie within the territorial boundaries of a state. While the Forest Principles incorporated strong protection of individual national sovereignty, they also promoted forest conservation. Principle 2(a) reads: "States have the sovereign and inalienable right to utilize, manage and develop their forests in accordance with their development needs and level of socio-economic development and on the basis of national policies consistent with sustainable development and legislation, including the conversion of such areas for other uses within the overall socio-economic development plan based on rational land-use policies."[20]

The following section of Principle 2, however, calls on states to manage forests sustainably "to meet the social, economic, ecological, cultural and spiritual human needs of present and future generations." These are identified as needs for forest products and services, including wood and

---

20. Johnson, *Earth Summit*, 105.

wood products, water, food, employment, recreation as well as habitats for wildlife, landscape diversity, and carbon sinks and reservoirs.[21]

Whereas in the past states had a clearly recognized right to use resources within their territories as they liked, this is now being qualified by statements that demand consideration of intergenerational equity and protection of cultures. The meaning of *sovereignty* as it pertains to natural resources is being challenged by a more global perspective on the environment.

The Rain Forests of Southeast Asia

It is useful to take a brief look at the history of the debate over tropical deforestation in Southeast Asia and particularly in Malaysia, a leader among developing states using sovereignty as an argument against the formation of an international forestry agreement. According to a recent United Nations Food and Agriculture Organization report, there was an estimated 3.4 billion hectares of forest in 1990, of which about half was tropical forest. From 1981 to 1990, approximately 15.4 million hectares of tropical forests was lost every year. Brazil has by far the largest amount of rain forest, accounting for approximately 40 percent of the world's total. Southeast Asia and Oceania are also rich in rain-forest coverage. Indonesia has the world's second largest rain forest, approximately 10 percent to 13 percent of the global total. Papua New Guinea, Malaysia, and Myanmar are other states in the region with large tracts.[22]

The main causes of tropical deforestation in Southeast Asia are agricultural pressures, demand for fuelwood and fodder, and commercial logging. In many Southeast Asian countries, poverty and rapid population growth exacerbate these pressures. Conversion of forested area to agricultural land or to plantations occurs through both state-sponsored programs and traditional slash-and-burn agriculture. Commercial logging also accounts for a major share of the deforestation in many of these states. In Malaysia, it is the main reason behind the rapid deforestation of the states of Sarawak and Sabah.

21. Ibid.
22. The World Resources Institute, *World Resources, 1994–1995* (New York: Oxford University Press, 1994). For a more detailed analysis of the history of deforestation in Southeast Asia, see Philip Hurst, *Rainforest Politics: Ecological Destruction in South-East Asia* (London: Zed Books, 1990).

Tropical deforestation has affected many countries of Southeast Asia. In the 1960s and early 1970s, the Philippines was the major supplier of tropical logs in Southeast Asia, and much of its exports went to Japan. Little was done to conserve tropical forests, however, until under former president Corazon Aquino, a decision was reached that deforestation was so widespread that the export of tropical timber should be banned altogether.[23]

As a result of growing resource nationalism in the Philippines during the 1970s (the country initiated a policy that required timber producers to process logs before exporting them), Indonesia, with Japanese investment capital, began to replace it as the largest supplier of tropical timber. In 1979 Indonesia followed the path of the Philippines and announced its own plans to terminate raw-log exports by 1985, although this policy was reversed in 1992.[24] In the meantime, the largely undeveloped Malaysian states of Sarawak and Sabah became the largest suppliers of timber in Southeast Asia.

As of 1991, although Malaysia had only about 2 percent of the world's tropical forests, according to the International Tropical Timber Organization (ITTO) it supplied approximately 90 percent of the world's unprocessed tropical-hardwood logs.[25] Because of bans on the export of unprocessed logs in most Malaysian states on the peninsula, almost all of the raw-log exports are from the states of Sabah and Sarawak on the island of Borneo.[26] From 1970 to 1993, production of logs in Sarawak jumped from 4.7 million cubic meters to 16.5 million cubic meters.[27] Forestry exports accounted for nearly one-third of all export earnings in Sarawak.

A 1989 ITTO survey listed Japan, France, Italy, Spain, Portugal, the former West Germany, and the former Soviet Union as the biggest importers of tropical timber. According to 1990 Organization for Economic Cooperation

23. *Asahi Shimbun,* 15 February 1991, 2.

24. Yoshifusa Kitabatake, "What Can Be Learned from Domestic and International Aspects of Japan's Forest Resource Utilization?" *Natural Resources Journal* 32 (Fall 1992): 855–81.

25. *Asahi Shimbun,* 9 March 1991, 8.

26. Yōichi Kuroda and François Nectoux, *Nettairin Hakai to Nihon no Mokuzai Bōeki* (Tokyo: Tsukiji Publishers, 1989), 76. An English version of this report was published under the title *Timber from the South Seas* (Gland, Switzerland: World Wide Fund for Nature, International, 1989).

27. Nihon Bengoshi Rengōkai Kōgai Taisaku Kankyō Hozen Iinkai (Japan Lawyers' Association's Pollution Countermeasures and Environmental Protection Committee), eds., *Nihon no Kōgai Yushutsu to Kankyō Hakai* (Tokyo: Nihon Hyōronsha, 1991); and Michael Vatikiotis, "Clearcut Mandate," *Far Eastern Economic Review,* 28 October 1993, 54–55.

and Development (OECD) data, Japan was by far the largest, importing 123 million cubic meters, or approximately 32 percent of the total amount of tropical wood exported from developing countries, as compared with 28 percent for all other OECD countries combined.[28]

Rapid economic growth in Japan in the 1970s and 1980s, and the protected status of the country's domestic forests, led Japanese companies overseas in search of cheap lumber. Most of Japan's tropical-wood imports come from nearby Southeast Asian nations. According to the Japan Association of Wood Importers, Japanese imports of tropical timber from the South Seas amounted to 11 million cubic meters in 1990. Over 90 percent of this came from Sabah and Sarawak.[29]

The Internationalization of Grassroots Protest

The Malaysian states of Sabah and Sarawak provide a good example of how forest preservation developed into an international concern. These states became a part of Malaysia in 1963 and account for about one-third of the island of Borneo, the other two-thirds belonging to Indonesia. The population of Borneo includes about two hundred indigenous tribes, collectively known as the Dayak and including the Iban, the Penan, and the Kadazan.[30] In Sarawak, in 1980 approximately 44 percent of the population was Dayak.[31] Until the middle of this century, the Dayak lived largely isolated from modern civilization. *Adat,* an indigenous customary law, dictated the use of the environment among groups involved in slash-and-burn agriculture.[32] The Penan are the last nomadic forest peoples in Borneo.

The first major legal encroachment on indigenous land came in 1953, with the enactment of a British Colonial Government Ordinance. Under this ordinance, the rights of indigenous peoples were limited to a part of the forests, and logging was allowed only under government permit or

28. *Nihon Keizai Shimbun,* 23 September 1991, 9; and Organization for Economic Cooperation and Development (hereafter OECD), *Environmental Performance Reviews: Japan* (Paris: OECD, 1994), 170.
29. *Asahi Shimbun,* 15 February 1991, 2.
30. See the chapters on Malaysia in Hurst, *Rainforest Politics,* 46–126.
31. Nihon Bengoshi Rengōkai, *Nihon no Kōgai Yushutsu,* 13.
32. Kitabatake, "What Can Be Learned," 860–62.

license. Subsequent changes to these laws have further curtailed the free-dom of indigenous peoples to live in and make use of the forests. The practical result of changes in land codes has been to make it easier for companies to gain title to land for timber production and more difficult for indigenous peoples to continue traditional ways of life. Timber con-cessions are frequently handed out in this region as a means of strength-ening political allegiances. Accusations of corruption abound, since concessions are often given to politicians and their families, who receive a percentage of the value of timber that is sold.[33] By 1984, 60 percent of Sarawak's total forest area was under logging license.[34]

Initially, protest of state-supported logging was small in scale and lim-ited to a handful of indigenous groups. Beginning in the 1980s, with their means of securing a livelihood and their ancestral burial sites destroyed by felling, indigenous peoples began to protest the destruction of forests and the failure of logging companies to provide them with adequate com-pensation. In 1981, for instance, members of the Kenyah tribe were arrested for threatening to burn a logging camp after the logging company ignored their numerous petitions asking the company to enter into nego-tiations over compensation for their longhouses.[35]

A Japanese company that won a bid to build the Batang Ai dam was also a target of criticism. Completed in 1985, the dam required the flood-ing of 8,500 hectares of forested land and the relocation of three thousand Iban people. Opposition grew as the Iban came to recognize what the building of the dam would mean for them. In protests, ignition keys to thirty large vehicles were confiscated by a group of Iban, and a Japanese worker was killed. At the official opening of the dam, police broke up a group of protesting Iban demanding the 10 million Malaysian dollars that were still due them as compensation.[36]

The best-known protest activities occurred when a coordinated effort was launched by three ethnic groups to blockade logging roads in the spring of 1987 and then again in 1988 and 1989. By this time, international nongovernmental organizations (NGOs) were lending support to the efforts of indigenous groups. Two thousand Penan, Kayan, and Kelabit

---

33. Hurst, *Rainforest Politics,* 103–5.

34. Kitabatake, "What Can Be Learned," 879.

35. Nihon Bengoshi Rengōkai, *Nihon no Kōgai Yushutsu,* 18; Hurst, *Rainforest Politics,* 117.

36. Hurst, *Rainforest Politics,* 93; Richard Forrest, "Japanese Economic Assistance and the Environment: The Need for Reform," National Wildlife Federation, rev. ed., November 1989, 35–36.

blockaded twelve logging roads in an effort to win recognition that logging activities were threatening "ourselves, our future generations, our land, our crops, our properties."[37] One of the occupied roads was built with Japanese official development assistance (ODA) as part of a forest-development project in Limbang.[38]

The Malaysian government did not take the protestors' challenge to its authority lightly. The first blockade stayed in place until October 1987, when the government amended its forest law, making the blockading of logging roads a criminal offense punishable by up to two years in prison and a fine of six thousand Malaysian dollars.[39] After this law was passed, protesters were arrested when they participated in road-blocking activities.[40] The law also severely restricted the ability of international NGOs to lend direct support to indigenous groups in Malaysia.

In the short term, the Penan, Kayan, and Kelabit gained little from their protests. In the long term, however, the strong reaction of the Malaysian state may have backfired. Passage of the law served to intensify concern abroad about what rapid deforestation meant for indigenous people and the environment. It also meant that because international NGOs were now effectively closed out of Malaysia due to restrictive visa rules and fears of imprisonment, these international groups increasingly focused their attention on the role of foreign governments and companies in tropical deforestation. In other words, they found an indirect means to apply pressure on Malaysia by targeting the demand side of the problem. In doing this, NGOs found a means to circumvent the Malaysian government's sovereignty claims by applying pressures on consumer nations to refuse to import products from unsustainably managed forests.

Targeting Consumer States

Japan, as the world's largest tropical-timber importer, became a central target of NGO criticism. As the major importers of Malaysian timber, Japanese companies wielded considerable influence over forestry management in

37. Quoted in Hurst, *Rainforest Politics,* 119.
38. Forrest, "Japanese Economic Assistance," 31–33.
39. Nihon Bengoshi Rengōkai, *Nihon no Kōgai Yushutsu,* 18–19.
40. Forrest, "Japanese Economic Assistance," 31–33.

Malaysia. Japanese trading companies, for instance, provided much of the credit needed by Malaysian logging companies in exchange for the right of first refusal on the timber harvested. Since quality concern ran high in these trading companies, there were few fixed contracts with logging operations. Rather, the lumber was cut and floated down the river to await a buyer. If the price was not right or the quality not high enough, it was left there to rot.[41] Japanese ODA was also criticized for being closely tied to lumbering operations in Malaysia.[42]

As the environmental movement picked up steam, numerous critical reports of Japan's role in tropical deforestation in Southeast Asia began to appear. One report that gained considerable attention was a book by Yōichi Kuroda and François Nectoux entitled *Timber from the South Seas.* This book, which was published in both Japanese and English, documented the extent of Japan's involvement in tropical deforestation in Southeast Asia and attacked Japanese trading companies for their investments in lumbering operations in the Philippines, Indonesia, Malaysia, and Papua New Guinea. The report charged that the majority of Japanese imports were not of value-added products, that is, of processed lumber, as was the case with the United States and Western Europe, but rather of cheap, unprocessed logs. This meant that most of the profits from logging ended up in the hands of Japanese processing companies rather than in the timber-producing state. Moreover, the report charged, most of the wood was used as a disposable material by the construction industry, for concrete molds.[43]

Unlike environmental groups in the United States and Western Europe, environmental groups in Asia are small, with memberships that often do not exceed a few dozen to a few hundred people. This is particularly true for Japan's internationally oriented environmental groups, most of which only appeared on the scene in the mid- to late 1980s. Thus there was little domestic policing by environmental groups of Japan's international logging practices.

In the 1980s, however, several NGOs concerned with tropical deforestation and linked to international groups emerged on the scene. Friends

41. Hurst, *Rainforest Politics,* 108.
42. Forrest, "Japanese Economic Assistance."
43. Kuroda and Nectoux, *Nettairin Hakai to Nihon no Mokuzai Bōeki.* According to an NGO report published in 1992, 84 percent of tropical logs imported into Japan were turned into plywood, and the construction industry used about half of this. *International Environment Reporter* (Washington, D.C.: Bureau of National Affairs), 2 December 1992.

of the Earth, which has fought tropical deforestation internationally, was one of the first to set up an office in Tokyo. In 1987 the Japan Tropical Action Network (JATAN) was formed. In 1989 the Rainforest Foundation Japan was established, and in 1990 the Sarawak Campaign Committee was founded. While these and a handful of other groups involved in forestry issues are still very small in size, they have played an important role in raising awareness in Japan of the country's role in tropical deforestation. These groups also began to form international networks. At the end of October 1988, for example, JATAN and other Japanese environmentalists participated in a campaign coordinated across twenty countries to protest tropical deforestation and to show support for Kayan tribal people, scheduled to go on trial for their role in blockading timber roads.[44] In 1991, a League of Legal Experts for a Tropical Forest Protection Law was established by Malaysian and Japanese lawyers.[45]

In the fall of 1989, the Japanese government hosted the Tokyo Conference on Global Environmental Protection. Unaccustomed to sitting at the table with NGOs, the government refused to allow environmental activists from Asia, Africa, or South America to participate. JATAN, the Japan International Volunteer Center, Greenpeace Japan, and the Japanese Consumers' League reacted by holding their own international conference on the rain forests. That three-day conference, held at Tokyo's Hosei University, included twenty-eight representatives of environmental groups and indigenous peoples from fourteen countries, including Malaysia and Brazil. Khor Kok Peng, research director of the Consumers' Association of Penang, Malaysia, and an active supporter of tribal people who resist logging companies in the rain forests of Malaysia, sharply criticized the official Tokyo conference: "In the name of aid, the ecology of the Third World countries is being destroyed. . . . The official meeting should not be a PR exercise . . . it should not be a whitewash to hide the fact that Japan is the number one destroyer of the environment in the Third World."[46]

These developments had considerable impact in Japan because the Japanese government picked up the environment as a foreign-policy issue

44. David Swinbanks, "Protests in Japan About Trade in Tropical Forest Timber," *Nature* 336 (10 November 1988): 100.

45. *Asahi Shimbun*, 13 December 1991, 3.

46. Michael Cross, "Tokyo Nods Its Head Toward the Environment," *New Scientist*, 16 September 1989, 24. This meeting gained widespread international attention. See, for instance, coverage of the People's Forum in "Charging Japan with Crimes Against the Earth," *Business Week*, 9 October 1989, 108–12.

in the late 1980s. International interest in tropical deforestation began to grow just at a time when, out of a variety of foreign-relations concerns, the Japanese government became especially interested in expanding its presence in the fields of development assistance and global environmental protection. Japan needed to address the role it played in tropical deforestation if it was to shed its image as an environmental spoiler and take on the image of an environmental leader.

Signs of Greening of Policies and Institutions in Japan and Malaysia

There have been several consequences to the internationalization of the rain-forest preservation movement. It has focused considerable negative attention on Malaysia and other Southeast Asian states that have used the principle of sovereignty to justify rapid deforestation, and it has led to campaigns to change forestry policies from outside the state through economic pressures. The movement also has redirected attention to the responsibility of consumer states in promoting deforestation, as well as their responsibility to assist developing states in finding ways to protect forests while promoting growth. Finally, the movement has led to a certain greening of relevant international institutions, such as the International Tropical Timber Agreement. Each of these developments will be discussed in more detail below.

In the 1980s, neither Malaysia nor Japan showed much real interest in tropical-forest conservation. For Malaysia, logging was an integral part of a plan for national economic growth. For Japan, the forests of Southeast Asia supplied a booming construction industry with lumber.

By the end of the 1980s, however, important changes became evident in Japan, and these have had important implications for Malaysia and other Southeast Asian states. In response to criticism that Japanese ODA has contributed to tropical-rain-forest loss, ODA policies are being revised. A new ODA charter lists environmental preservation as a guiding principle in all Japanese lending. Specific projects for rain-forest renewal have also been initiated with Japanese ODA funds. In August 1991, for example, the Japan International Cooperation Agency began a project that involved reforestation with both quick-growing species and slow-maturing lauan.[47]

Industries that have been targeted by NGOs because of their link to tropical deforestation have also started to alter their policies, although the pace of change is slow. As a result of movement efforts, by 1991 over 60 percent of Dutch local governments and at least 130 local governments in Germany had banned the use or required a reduction in the use of tropical hardwoods in public construction. The European Parliament debated a bill to stop imports of tropical woods.[48] Austria began to label tropical timber and tropical-timber products,[49] and a similar but smaller effort was launched in a district of Tokyo in response to a women's cooperative's demand that the city stop using tropical hardwoods in public-works projects.[50]

As a result of these kinds of pressures, in June 1991 the Japan Plywood Industry Association announced plans to reduce dependence on plywood produced from tropical broadleafs and replace it with plywood produced from coniferous trees.[51] A few months later, the Japan Wood Importing Association produced its own set of guidelines, which aim at promoting lumber imports from sustainably managed forests.[52]

Similarly, after a full-page advertisement purchased by the Rainforest Action Network in the *New York Times* targeted the chief executive officer of Mitsubishi, along with the president of the World Bank, former U.S. president George Bush, and several other company presidents, Mitsubishi tried to improve its image.[53] In December 1990, the company announced that it was opening an environmental-affairs department and that its first environmental project would be a tropical-rain-forest reforestation study. In light of criticisms that reforestation efforts in the tropics have relied heavily on fast-growing species rather than using native species that may take up to one hundred years to mature, the company proposed that new reforestation methods be explored. It pledged U.S. $1.5 million for a four-year study to create a native rain-forest ecosystem in Malaysia that might take one hundred years to mature.[54] Still, this was viewed by environ-

47. *Mainichi Shimbun*, 3 August 1991, 22.

48. Sarawak Kyanpeen Iinkai (Sarawak Campaign Committee) brochure, "Save the Sarawak, Save Our World," 1991. See also *Asahi Shimbun*, 3 December 1991, 3.

49. *International Environment Reporter*, 2 December 1992.

50. *Asahi Shimbun*, 13 December 1991, 3.

51. *Nikan Kōgyō Shimbun*, 1 June 1991, 9.

52. *Tokyo Yomiuri Chōkan*, 4 December 1991, 2.

53. *New York Times*, 8 August 1989, B7.

54. Mitsubishi Corporation, "Mitsubishi Corporation Establishes Environmental Affairs Department," *MC Now* 1 (February 1991): 1.

mentalists as little more than a public-relations move. In 1993, the Rainforest Action Network purchased another full-page advertisement calling for a boycott of Mitsubishi as "the world's worst destroyer of rainforests."[55] In threatening boycotts worldwide, NGOs had discovered a powerful means to press for change in the tropical-forestry management practices of multinational corporations. NGOs have continued to pressure Japanese multinationals to adopt sustainable forestry policies.

Some changes are evident in Malaysia as well. Because of intense negative international publicity and economic concerns, including tourism, Malaysia and neighboring Indonesia have demonstrated increased interest in conservation. Some efforts have been made, for example, to curtail illegal logging, although this may be more for economic reasons than conservation ones. As is discussed more fully below, Malaysia also has banned exports of unprocessed logs from some regions. It is also noteworthy that in the summer of 1994, Malaysia and Indonesia announced plans to establish one of the world's largest wildlife sanctuaries in forested areas of Sarawak and West Kalimantan on the island of Borneo, which the two states share between them.[56]

Interestingly, in the post-UNCED period, it was Malaysia and Canada—both major producers of timber—that jointly organized the first meeting of an Intergovernmental Working Group on Global Forests to facilitate dialogue on approaches to the management and sustainable development of the world's forests.

Conservation and the ITTA

International criticism and growing conservation norms in Japan have combined to push conservation issues higher onto the agenda of the International Tropical Timber Agreement (ITTA), the primary international institution regulating trade in tropical timber. The idea of a tropical-timber commodity agreement to regulate trade in timber was first proposed to the United Nations Conference on Trade and Development (UNCTAD) by Japan in 1977. The ITTA was established by the UNCTAD in 1983 (and ratified in 1985) for a ten-year period in order to manage and

---

55. *New York Times,* 10 May 1993, A13.

56. "Joint Wildlife Sanctuary Planned with Indonesia," *Comtex International Intelligence Reports,* 28 July 1994.

enforce regulations in international tropical-timber trade.

In the lengthy negotiations leading up to the treaty's formation, there were strong pressures from some European states to include environmental-protection measures in its text. These states demanded that the treaty also promote sustainable logging and preservation of genetic material. Thus, when the ITTO was finally established as part of the agreement in 1986, it was given the dual, if seemingly contradictory, mandate of promoting trade in tropical timber while encouraging the sustainable use of tropical forests and the conservation of their genetic resources.[57]

Nevertheless, forest preservation initially played a minor role in the activities of the ITTO. Some argue that this was a result of the international body's organization. The ITTO represents twenty-three producing and twenty-six consuming countries plus the European Union. Voting rights within the ITTO were established so that producing and consuming country blocs would have equal representation. Within these blocs, each country received votes equal to its proportion of tropical-timber production or consumption. As a result of this weighted voting, Japan, the world's largest consumer of tropical timbers, became the most powerful member within this UN body. Japan holds 33 percent of voting rights in the organization. After Japan provided start-up costs, it was also decided that the ITTO should be headquartered in Japan. Malaysia was given preference for the influential post of first executive director within the organization.[58] Many environmentalists argued that because of this voting system, the dice were loaded in favor of production and consumption rather than conservation.[59] This may in fact have been the case so long as Japan, the organization's most powerful member, showed little real interest in tropical-forest preservation.

It is still premature to talk of the greening of the ITTO. Still, forestry preservation has become a more important element of the organization, particularly because of the growing political importance of the environment as an issue within Japan. In the late 1980s, concerned with its international image and seeking areas in which it could exert leadership in a post–Cold War era, Japan began to play a larger role in both the environmental and development areas.[60] This has led to some important changes in the ITTO.

57. Marcus Colchester, "The ITTO, Kill or Cure for the Rainforests?" *The Ecologist,* September–October 1990, 166.

58. Colchester, "ITTO," 166–67.

59. See, for instance, comments made by a Friends of the Earth representative quoted in *International Environmental Reporter,* 18 November 1992, 741.

60. Miranda Schreurs, "Policy Laggard or Policy Leader: Global Environmental Policy

As a result of mounting international concern over deforestation, in 1989, at the invitation of the Malaysian government and with Japan's support, the ITTO commissioned three surveys of logging practices in Sarawak. The surveys found that logging was excessive and that at the existing pace, forest resources would be completely gone by the year 2000. The report recommended a 30 percent reduction in exports, from the 1991 planned exports of 14 million cubic meters to 9.2 million cubic meters.[61] Later that year, the state government of Sarawak agreed to reduce its log production over a two-year period to the 9.2 million cubic meters recommended in the report.[62] Also in line with the ITTO recommendation, in the spring of 1991 Japanese tropical-timber importers reached an agreement with the Sarawak state government to reduce imports of tropical timber by 15 percent of planned 1991 levels.[63] In 1992, the federal government in Malaysia announced that exports of unprocessed logs from the state of Sabah would be banned effective January 1993.[64]

At a June 1991 meeting of the ITTO in Ecuador, the Japanese government proposed the adoption of three principles: (1) trade in tropical timber should be monitored, and import of timber exceeding estimated demand should be controlled, as a way of preventing stockpiling in consuming states; (2) consuming states should work to reuse tropical lumber (presumably this was a reference to the practice in Japan of using tropical lumber for concrete molds and then discarding it after a single use); (3) consuming states should work to diversify their tropical-timber products and produce more value-added products.

These principles, which were formulated by the Ministry of Foreign Affairs, the Environment Agency, and the Forestry Agency in Japan, were tantamount to a formal recognition that Japanese companies had played a role in promoting unsustainable forestry practices in Malaysia and elsewhere.[65]

During negotiations in 1993 to extend the ITTA for another decade, it was apparent that wide differences in opinion still existed between tropical-timber-producing and -consuming states about a future course of

---

Making Under the Liberal Democratic Party," *Journal of Pacific Asia* 2 (1995): 3–34.

61. Information compiled from *Asahi Shimbun,* 15 February 1991, 2; and *Nihon Keizai Shimbun,* 23 September 1991, 9.

62. *Mainichi Shimbun,* 4 December 1991, 3.

63. *Asahi Shimbun,* 9 March 1991, 13.

64. Medea Intaafeisu, ed., *Chikyū Kankyō Joho Shimbun Kiji Deeta Beesu, 1996* (Tokyo: Daiyamondo Sha, 1996), 76.

65. *Tokyo Yomiuri Chōkan,* 4 December 1991, 2.

action. It was also clear, however, that the debate was being changed from one that focused exclusively on sovereignty issues to one that explored means of achieving sustainable forestry management with Northern assistance.

In the negotiations, producing states remained eager to avoid stricter guidelines on logging and timber trade that were being pushed by some Northern countries. They called instead for the establishment of a treaty that would also regulate timber produced in nontropical countries. They argued that any other kind of agreement would discriminate against developing states, subjecting them to stricter environmental standards than timber producers in the Northern hemisphere. In a reversal of roles, consuming states in the North resisted the extension of the treaty to include boreal forests, presumably because of concerns over sovereignty, and instead advocated the introduction of stronger environmental regulations domestically. As a compromise, at the end of the negotiations, the consuming states pledged to respect conservation guidelines for their own forests, although this was not written into the body of the text. And as a concession to the demands of the developing countries and in recognition of the global-scale efforts required to protect the world's tropical rain forests, it was decided that a fund should be established to help developing countries meet a target that was established within the organization to achieve sustainable management of tropical forests by the year 2000.[66]

Conclusion

The case of the tropical rain forests of Southeast Asia suggests that achieving international agreement on environmental-protection priorities remains a difficult, and often illusive challenge in a world system that is still defined by the principle of sovereignty. Sovereignty has been embraced by states that seek rapid economic development. In Southeast Asia, where rapid economic growth is only now allowing some states to emerge from their dependence on international official development assistance and World Bank loans, sovereignty remains a powerful symbol. Malaysia, in particular, seeks to protect its economic-development rights and considers itself

66. Compiled from reports appearing in the *International Environment Reporter*, 2 December 1992; 30 June, 20 October 1993; 26 January, 9 February 1994.

a spokesman for other developing states. Priorities lie with economic development and equity between the North and the South. Thus, Malaysia and many other developing states that share its views have resisted conservation pressures that do not take into consideration rights to economic development. It is for this reason that developing states pushed hard in negotiations for a revised International Tropical Timber Agreement that would include the establishment of a fund to help them achieve sustainable-forest management by 2000. This is also why those countries have strongly challenged bans on tropical-timber products that have begun to emerge in various European states. Finally, this is why developing states with tropical rain forests have resisted the formation of a tropical-forest protection agreement and pushed for the extension of the ITTA to govern the management of boreal forests as well as tropical forests.

Nevertheless, the case of the tropical rain forests in Southeast Asia suggests that state sovereignty is indeed under challenge. Despite efforts to define forests as sovereign, questions of intergenerational equity, biodiversity loss, climate change, and the rights of indigenous peoples have made forests a global concern. New international norms are emerging that demand that resources be protected for future generations. Tropical-forest protection has become a human-rights concern because of the plight of indigenous peoples threatened by the encroachment of logging companies. Forest protection is now widely viewed as critical to the protection of biodiversity and important in efforts to combat global climate change.

The emergence of international networks of environmental activists and scientists has helped to turn tropical-forest protection into an international political issue and a domestic political issue in Japan and other consumer states. These networks have used the media and other communication networks to heighten international awareness about the rapid rate at which the forests of Southeast Asia are being lost and to press for changes in logging practices in these rain forests. Importantly, these groups have focused their attention not just on the role of logging companies in developing states but also on the industries that consume and trade in tropical timbers.

In a world of growing interdependency, environmental politics are becoming increasingly internationalized. As a result, traditional notions of sovereignty as they pertain to natural-resource use are being challenged and redefined. Sovereignty over natural resources is still universally asserted, and at times claims of sovereignty over a resource that is of international interest has proved an effective tool for developing states seeking to apply leverage on Northern states for development assistance. At the same time, however, growing recognition of the global importance of many natural resources is challenging the ability of states to use sovereignty as a justification for environmentally unsustainable activities. As a result of international grassroots activities and international bargaining, states are under considerable pressure to restrict activities that may cause long-term environmental damage. The principle of sovereignty as it pertains to natural-resource use and the environment is being challenged and slowly redefined.

Contributors

GREGORY H. FOX is adjunct professor of law at New York University School of Law. He was a research fellow at the Max Planck Institute for Comparative Public and International Law in Heidelberg, Germany, in 1995–96. Previously, he served as a law clerk to the Hon. Alan H. Nevas of the United States District Court, District of Connecticut, and as an attorney with Hale and Dorr in Boston. He is the author of several articles dealing with democracy, self-determination, and security issues in international law. He was an SSRC-MacArthur Foundation fellow in international peace and security in 1990–92.

JAMES GOW is reader in war studies at King's College London and research associate in the Centre for Defence Studies, University of London. He is the author of *Legitimacy and the Military: The Yugoslav Crisis* (London: Pinter, 1992), *Triumph of the Lack of Will: International Diplomacy and the Yugoslav War of Dissolution* (New York: Columbia University Press, 1977), and of numerous articles on the Yugoslav war and on Central and Eastern European security issues. In addition, he was an expert adviser to the Office of the Prosecutor at the International Criminal Tribunal for Yugoslavia in The Hague, and in October 1995 he was the first witness to give evidence there.

SOHAIL H. HASHMI is assistant professor of international relations at Mount Holyoke College. He is the author of several articles on Islamic ethics and on law relating to international relations; he is currently completing a book on the Islamic ethics of war and peace. He was an SSRC-MacArthur Foundation fellow in international peace and security in 1990–92.

BEATRICE HEUSER is senior lecturer in war studies at King's College London. She is the author of books on Western Cold War policies, on nuclear strategy, and on European security since 1945. She is currently working on books dealing with strategy and political culture, and with the transatlantic relationship. She was an SSRC-MacArthur Foundation fellow in international peace and security in 1989–91.

DANIEL PHILPOTT is assistant professor of political science at the University of California, Santa Barbara. His publications include articles on self-determination and on the history of sovereignty. He is currently completing a book on revolutions in norms of sovereignty. He has been a fellow at the Olin Institute for Strategic Studies at Harvard University, and at the Princeton Center for International Studies.

MIRANDA A. SCHREURS is assistant professor of government and politics at the University of Maryland, College Park. Her specialization is in comparative environmental policy making regarding global environmental problems in Japan and Germany. She is the coeditor of *International Environmental Protection* (Cambridge: Cambridge University Press, forthcoming in 1997). She was an SSRC-MacArthur Foundation fellow in international peace and security from 1991 to 1993 and a Fulbright fellow in 1990.

KAMAL S. SHEHADI is research director at the Lebanese Center for Policy Studies in Beirut, where he is responsible for research projects on local and municipal government, parliamentary elections, civil society, and economic reconstruction. He is currently doing research on Euro-Mediterranean relations, the Arab-Israeli peace process, and public finance. In 1992–93, he was a research associate at the International Institute for Strategic Studies, London. From 1989 to 1991 he was a fellow at the Olin Institute for Strategic Studies at Harvard University.

Index

Afghanistan, 66–67, 75
Ahmad, Aziz, 57
Albania, 146
Algeria, 43, 45, 65, 78, 146
Angola, 120, 123
Arab League, 62, 64, 67
Arap-Moi, Daniel, 123
Armenia, 36, 86, 132, 144, 146
Augsburg, Treaty of (1555), 21, 29
Austro-Hungarian Empire, 29–30, 37–38, 129
Azerbaijan, 132, 144, 146

Badinter Commission, 10, 122, 159, 161–62, 165–66
Bangladesh, 139, 147, 159
Beetham, David, 167
Berlin, Congress of (1878), 36, 38, 41
Bodin, Jean, 17–19, 28, 166
Bosnia-Herzegovina, 3, 10, 15, 75, 143, 151, 161, 163–64, 172, 175–76
Boutros-Ghali, Boutros, 81, 98–99, 106, 128, 131–32, 152
Brazil, 190, 196
Brierly, James L., 114
Britain, 8, 27, 29, 31–32, 36–38, 40, 42–45, 61, 69, 71, 83, 94, 118–19
Bull, Hedley, 43
Burma (Myanmar), 132, 143, 146–47, 190
Bush, George, 77, 81, 92, 198

Caldwell, Lynton, 181
Calvin, John, 30, 34
Cambodia (Kampuchea), 3, 82, 91, 120, 175, 177
Carr, E. H., 25–26, 82, 84, 98
Cateau-Cambrésis, Treaty of (1559), 27, 29
Chechnya, 75
China, 92, 97, 122, 146
Clemenceau, Georges, 41

Clinton, Bill, 107
Cobban, Alfred, 133
Cold War, 44, 47, 92, 126
Conca, Ken, 184, 187
Concert of Europe, 35, 83–86, 88–89, 148
Congo, 138
Council on Security and Cooperation in
    Europe (CSCE). *See* Organization for
    Security and Cooperation in Europe
Crimean War (1853–56), 36, 38
Croatia, 10, 99, 145, 160–61, 164, 176
Czechoslovakia, 132, 153

Djibouti, 143
Durkheim, Émile, 24

East Timor, 132
Egypt, 44, 62, 65–67, 71–72, 78
El Salvador, 120
Eritrea, 132, 143
Ethiopia, 131–32, 146–47
European Bank for Reconstruction and
    Development, 123
European Community, 11, 34, 93–94,
    145–46, 165–66, 172, 174
European Union, 3, 13, 15, 19–20, 22,
    94–97, 100–101, 167, 173, 200

Faisal ibn 'Abd al-'Aziz, 71–73
Figgis, J. N., 50
France, 8, 19, 27–29, 31–32, 36–37, 42–46,
    94, 191

Geneva Conventions (1949), 100, 124
Genocide Convention (1951), 90, 124
Georgia, 132, 147
Germany, 31–32, 40, 43, 84, 93–94, 139–40,
    191
Ghana, 41
al-Ghunaimi, Mohammad Talaat, 54
Gilpin, Robert, 25
Greece, 36, 148
Gross, Leo, 28
Grotius, Hugo, 19, 30
Gulf War (1990–91), 9, 76–78, 91, 95, 103,
    117–18, 170

Haiti, 118, 122, 125, 172
Helsinki Final Act (1975), 140, 162
Hinsley, F. H., 51–52
Hobbes, Thomas, 17–19, 26

Holy Roman Empire, 26, 29–30, 33, 50
Hungary, 174
Huntington, Samuel P., 5
Hurd, Douglas, 133
al-Husaini, Amin, 63–64
Hussein, Saddam, 76–77, 92

India, 9, 42, 56, 61, 63–64, 66, 69, 146–47,
    182, 184, 188–89
Indonesia, 11, 66–67, 184, 190–92, 195, 199
International Court of Justice, 99, 111, 125,
    173
International Covenant on Civil and
    Political Rights (1966), 139–40, 159
International Tropical Timber Agreement
    (ITTA), 199–203
International Tropical Timber
    Organization (ITTO), 11, 13, 191, 197,
    199–201
Iqbal, Muhammad, 57–60
Iran, 51, 62, 66–67, 69, 72, 79, 143, 146
Iran-Iraq War (1980–88), 75–77
Iraq, 3, 15, 62, 66–67, 69, 71–72, 75, 82, 92,
    103, 144, 147
Israel, 65, 72, 74
Italy, 29, 93–94, 191

Jackson, Robert, 44–45, 155, 176–77
Jama'at-i Islami, 57, 60, 68
James, Alan, 154–55
Japan, 11, 43, 84, 191–204
Jinnah, Muhammad 'Ali, 57, 59–60, 63

Kant, Immanuel, 94, 101
Kenya, 123
Keohane, Robert, vii, 187
Khaliq al-Zaman, Chaudhri, 61–63
Khan, Liyaqat 'Ali, 63–64, 69
Khan, Zafrallah, 63, 66–69
Khilafat movement, 56–57
Khomeini, Ruhallah, 75–76
Krasner, Stephen, 4
Kurds, 91, 99, 117–18, 132, 143, 147, 151,
    170–71
Kuwait, 76–78, 92

League of Nations, 36, 40, 42, 81, 84–87, 89,
    100–101, 137
Lebanon, 66–67, 71, 144
Liberia, 119, 121
Libya, 118–19, 151, 171–72

Lippmann, Walter, 4
Lloyd George, David, 40
Luther, Martin, 28, 30–31, 34

Maastricht, Treaty of (1991), 3, 95, 122
Macedonia, 143, 147
Machiavelli, Niccolo, 25–26
Mahathir Bin Mohamad, 182
Malaysia, 11, 182, 184–85, 188–90, 192–204
Marxism, 24
Mawdudi, Abu al-A'la, 57, 60
Mayall, James, 166
Middleton, K. W. B., 110
Mitterrand, François, 123
Moldova, 132
Morgenthau, Hans, 25
Morocco, 46, 65, 72, 146
Mozambique, 120
Mu'tamar al-'Alam al-Islami, 63–64, 70
Muhammad, Ghulam, 63
Muhammad, the Prophet, 53
Muslim League, 57, 59–62, 65

Namibia, 120
Nasser, Gamal Abdel, 71
Nazim al-Din, Khwaja, 66, 68–69
Netherlands, 29, 31–32, 34
Nicaragua, 120
Nigeria, 131, 138
North Atlantic Treaty Organization
    (NATO), 93, 95–97, 103

Organization for Security and Cooperation
    in Europe (OSCE), 108, 140–41, 153,
    172–73
Organization of African Unity (OAU), 158
Organization of American States (OAS),
    122, 125
Organization of the Islamic Conference
    (OIC), 7–8, 13, 73–80
Ottoman Empire, 6, 36–37, 52, 56, 61, 83,
    129, 148

Pakistan, 7, 51, 57, 59–70, 72, 78–79
Palestine, 61, 64–65, 68, 72, 74–75
pan-Arabism, 52, 57, 65, 70–71
pan-Islamism, 7, 51, 57, 70–71
Papua New Guinea, 190, 195
Paris, Treaty of (1856), 36
Pérez de Cuéllar, Javier, 116
Philippines, 191, 195

Poland, 38–40
Portugal, 191

Qur'an, 51, 53–55, 75

Rabitat al-'Alam al-Islami, 71
Reformation, Protestant, 5, 7, 16, 27–34, 47
Rhodesia, 117, 122, 171
Rosecrance, Richard, 102
Rosenau, James, 4, 185
Rousseau, Jean-Jacques, 18
Ruggie, John G., 135
Rumania, 143
Russia, 36, 83, 92, 132, 143, 146–47
Russo-Turkish War (1878), 37–38
Rwanda, 15, 172

Saint-Pierre, Bernardin de, 94, 101
Saudi Arabia, 7, 51, 62, 66, 71–73, 78
Serbia, 10, 36, 146, 160, 164
Slovakia, 174
Slovenia, 145, 160
Smith, Anthony D., 157
Somalia, 15, 82, 91, 97, 105–8, 118–19, 146,
    151, 171–72
South Africa, 117, 120, 122, 126, 131, 171,
    177
sovereignty
    definitions of, vii, 4–5, 17–22, 108–15,
        134–35, 154–56, 159, 187
    and human rights, 8–9, 86–87, 90–92,
        97–100, 105–8, 115–30, 161, 170–77
    in Islamic theory, 7–8, 51–56
    and liberalism, viii–ix, 4, 16, 37–41, 47,
        108, 126–30, 176
    and realism, 5, 16, 22–26, 32–33, 37–38,
        43–44, 82, 84, 88, 109–13, 116
    and self-determination, 9–11, 34–46, 86,
        129–34, 135–49, 153–54, 156–63, 165,
        174
    and the Third World, 1–2, 13, 52, 101,
        103, 177, 182–85, 188–90
    Westphalian model of, 1, 5, 9–10, 28–34,
        135, 156
Soviet Union, 2, 44–45, 92–93, 132, 139,
    153, 173, 191
Spain, 29–30, 34, 131, 191
Sri Lanka, 132, 147
Strang, David, 46
Sudan, 132, 147
Sweden, 31–32, 34, 36

Syria, 56, 62–63, 66–67, 71–72, 143

Thailand, 144, 146
Thant, U, 138–39
Thirty Years' War (1618–48), 26–27, 29, 32, 34, 47
Thucydides, 25
Tibet, 97
Tilly, Charles, 33
Tolba, Mostafa, 186
Tunisia, 65
Turabi, Hasan, 78–79
Turkey, 56, 66–67, 69, 72, 118, 132, 144, 146–47

Uganda, 143
Ukraine, 146, 168
United Nations, 3–6, 8–9, 13–15, 41–43, 52, 61, 69, 81, 87–93, 96–104, 121–22, 144, 148, 153
    charter, 6, 20, 82, 88, 98, 100, 114, 119–20, 129, 138, 157–58, 162, 169–70, 175–76
    Conference on Environment and Development (UNCED), 181–82, 187–88
    Conference on the Human Environment, 184, 186–87
    General Assembly, 2, 68, 122, 125, 128, 139
    Security Council, 8, 77, 82, 84, 88–89, 91–92, 95–97, 99, 101–6, 111, 117–20, 124, 139, 147, 158, 169, 170–72, 175

United States, 8, 38, 40, 44–45, 69, 71, 92, 112, 118–19, 123, 188, 195
Universal Declaration of Human Rights (1948), 128
'Uthman, Adam 'Abdallah, 70
Utrecht, Treaty of (1713), 34

Versailles, Treaty of (1919), 6, 41, 138
Vienna, Congress of (1815), 37, 39, 83
Vietnam, 123

Waltz, Kenneth, 25
Westphalia, Peace of (1648), 6, 16, 20–22, 26, 28, 30, 33–34, 47, 135, 156
Wilson, Woodrow, 6, 36, 39–40, 45, 86, 137
World Bank, 123, 198
World War I, 16, 27, 36, 38, 42, 47
World War II, 27, 42, 45–47

Yugoslav War-Crimes Tribunal, 124–25, 172
Yugoslavia, 2, 9–10, 15, 36, 64, 92, 95, 101, 119, 122–23, 132, 145–46, 153, 160–63, 168, 171, 173

Zia al-Haq, Muhammad, 75
Zubaida, Sami, 79